Marxist Historiography in Transformation

East German Social History in the 1980s

Edited by
GEORG IGGERS

Translated by
BRUCE LITTLE

BERG
New York / Oxford
**Distributed exclusively in the U.S. and Canada by
St. Martin's Press, New York**

Published in 1991 by
Berg Publishers, Inc.
Editorial offices:
165 Taber Avenue, Providence, RI 02906, U.S.A.
150 Cowley Road, Oxford OX4 1JJ, UK

© Georg Iggers

British Library Cataloguing in Publication Data
Marxist historiography in transformation : East German
 social history in the 1980s.
 1. Germany. Social conditions, history
 I. Iggers, Georg G.
 943
 ISBN 0–85496–228–X

Library of Congress Cataloging-in-Publication Data
Marxist historiography in transformation : East German social history
 in the 1980s / edited by Georg Iggers ; translated by Bruce Little.
     p.   cm.
 Articles translated from German.
 ISBN 0–85496–228–X
   1. Germany (East)—Social conditions. 2. Marxian historiography-
- Germany (East) I. Iggers, Georg G.
 HN460.5.A8M36   1991
 306'.09431—dc20   90–20251
                                                          CIP

Printed and bound in Great Britain by
Billing and Sons Ltd, Worcester

Contents

List of Tables

Acknowledgments

I am very grateful for the extensive help that I received from friends, colleagues, and students in both parts of Germany and in North America during the preparation of this volume. I have been in close contact with historians in the GDR since my first visit there in 1966. Since 1967 I have been invited repeatedly to lecture there. My intensive occupation with historical studies in the GDR, however, dates from the fall of 1985 when I accompanied my wife, who held an IREX grant, to Leipzig. Prof. Wolfgang Küttler of the Zentralinstitut für Geschichte at the Academy of Sciences of the GDR was generous enough to permit me to present my theses on the development of recent GDR historiography in his section on the theory and methodology of history at the Zentralinstitut in March 1986. My theses, which later in slightly revised form were published in German in the Federal Republic and in English in the United States, were in many ways critical of what was being done in the GDR, particularly in the area of political history, although more positive of certain new directions in the writing of social history.

In preparing this volume I very consciously intended to present not typical examples of historical studies in the GDR but work that I believed deserved attention internationally. The Introduction to this volume has gone through several versions. The first version was written in the summer of 1989 and read by all the contributors as well as by other colleagues, including Wolfgang Küttler, Hans Schleier, Werner Berthold, and Rüdiger Horn in the GDR, Rudolf Vierhaus, Alf Lüdtke, and Hans Medick in the Federal Republic, and Konrad Jarausch, Volker Berghahn, and Geoff Eley in the United States. During the fall and winter of 1989 to 1990, all the contributions were translated. The events that occurred during that time led me to rewrite the Introduction during the spring and summer of 1990. In April I discussed the theses at length with students and faculty in Gerald Diesener's historiography seminar at the Karl-Marx-Universität in Leipzig. I found this open discussion very useful. Once more I discussed the theses in June at the Stiftung für Gesellschaftsanalyse in East Berlin, the former Akademie für Gesellschaftswissenschaften, a forum that because of its past association with the SED, could have been expected to be critical of my presentation; in fact this proved to be a frank discussion. Again all the contributors read and commented on the Introduction in its revised form as did those persons who read the earlier version whom I could reach and involve on short notice, including Werner Berthold, Wolfgang Küttler, Rüdiger Horn, Ralf Possekel, Wolfgang Wächter, Ulrich Hess, and Thomas Kuczynski in the GDR, Hans Medick, Rudolf Vierhaus, Jürgen Schlumbohm, and Rüdiger Scholz in the Federal Republic, and Konrad Jarausch and Volker Berghahn in the U.S. I am particularly thankful for the extensive and penetrating comments by Fritz Klein and Harald Dehne from the Academy of Sciences as well as by two students from the Karl-Marx-Universität, Stefan Hoffmann and Beate Hartlieb. All but two of the contributions were translated by Bruce Little of Toronto; Sigrid Jacobeit's essay was translated by Alan Nothnagle of Buffalo. My wife Wilma carefully corrected the English of Helga Schultz's essay. I would like to thank my good friend and former student Peter Walther from the Akademie der Wissenschaften zu Berlin in West Berlin for carefully checking the factual accuracy of the Introduction and my wife once more for reading the various stages of the Introduction. The Max-Planck-Institut für Geschichte in Göttingen, where I wrote both versions of the Introduction, as always proved to be an excellent place for the exchange of ideas. Finally I wish to thank the Akademie Verlag for not only having given me permission to publish the various articles by Jürgen Kuczynski, Wolfgang Jacobeit, Hartmut Zwahr (both articles), Hartmut Harnisch, Hans-Heinrich Müller, Jan Peters, and Helga Schultz, but for generously waiving a fee, as did also the Dietz Verlag for Dietrich Mühlberg's article.

GEORG G. IGGERS
Göttingen
August 4, 1990

Introduction

1. Why a Volume on East German Historiography Today

This project to present recent writings in social history from the German Democratic Republic to the English-reading public was begun three years ago. Very little had been known in the English-reading world about historians and historical studies in the GDR. Virtually nothing had been translated into English.[1] There exists no comprehensive study except Andreas Dorpalen's *German History In Marxist Perspective: The East German Approach*,[2] published posthumously in 1985, which deals primarily with interpretations by historians in the GDR of aspects of the political history of Germany since the Middle Ages, but which unavoidably, since it was completed around 1980, fails to consider some of the most interesting reorientations in historical writing in the GDR that have occurred since then.

There were good and not so good reasons for this neglect. Historians in the GDR themselves had avoided contacts with their Western colleagues until the 1970s, although contacts never broke off fully, and Western historians had viewed the work of their colleagues in the socialist countries with a great deal of skepticism. Some of the roots of this skepticism lay in cold war ideologies, but

---

1. Among the few translations are Hartmut Harnisch, Christel Heinrich, and Hainer Plaul in Richard J. Evans and W.R. Lee, *The German Peasantry: Conflict and Community in Rural Society from the Eighteenth to the Twentieth Centuries* (London, 1986); Adolf Laube, Ernst Engelberg, and Günter Vogler, very short contributions to Janos Bak, ed., "The German Peasant War of 1525," special issue of *Journal of Peasant Studies* 3 (1975–76); iii, iv, 1–144; also as a book (London, 1976); Jürgen Kuczynski, *The Rise of the Working Class* (New York, 1968).

2. (Detroit, 1985), foreword by Georg G. Iggers.

others were well founded in the close political supervision under which historians worked in the GDR.[3] When the articles for this volume had been translated at the end of the fall of 1989, the political situation there had changed completely. The volume rests on the assumption that since the mid-1970s historical studies in the GDR covered a broader spectrum, particularly in certain areas of social history. This opening – away from narrow political and ideological restrictions of the 1950s and 1960s – was to a historiography that still proceeded from Marxist-Leninist conceptions of history, yet sought to answer the questions it posed honestly on the basis of a critical examination of the historical evidence. The question that arises after November 9, 1989, is whether this historiography can still make a contribution to the international discussions among historians, and particularly social historians, or whether it is now merely of antiquarian interest.[4]

Yet even before November 9, 1989, the question had to be raised whether these articles indeed had a contribution to make to modern social history or whether they were merely of interest as a reflection of the ideological changes in socialist societies. It was an easy temptation to measure East German writings in social history by the standards of the new trends in social and cultural history in the West. From this perspective GDR historiography at its best merely illustrated what was possible within the limits of the then-existing political restrictions and of Marxist-Leninist ideology. Once these constraints would disappear, as they did after November 9, it could be expected that historical writing in what was once the GDR would become indistinguishable from historical writing in the remainder of Germany. To an extent it undoubtedly will. Nevertheless, I never approached the volume in these terms. I believed that these selections could stand on their own, that they had value for historians beyond the GDR that was independent of the political and ideological setting in which they were written. All of the selections in this volume are either Marxist in their assumptions or

3. See Günther Heydemann, *Geschichtswissenschaft im geteilten Deutschland* (Frankfurt a.M., 1980).
4. For an extensive examination of the situation in historical writing in the last days of the GDR, see the multivolume work by Alexander Fischer and Günther Heydemann, eds., *Geschichtswissenschaft in der DDR* (Munich, 1988–). Vol. 2 appeared in the late spring of 1990. Except for the Dorpalen volume (above, n. 2), there is no extensive historical treatment of historical studies in the GDR. For a GDR collection of brief biographies of deceased historians still published before the events of November 1989, see *Wegbereiter der DDR-Geschichtswissenschaft. Biographien* (Berlin/GDR, 1989).

at least very much indebted to the intellectual heritage of historical materialism. The question, of course, arises whether after the events of the fall of 1989 in Eastern Europe and in the USSR, Marxism does not best belong to the dustbin of history as an ideology deeply rooted in the nineteenth century and refuted by a historical development that was not foreseen in the Marxist tradition. However, I believed then, as I believe now, that because of its Marxist perspective the historiography represented in this volume has a unique contribution to make to social history as it is practiced internationally today.

2. The Place of History in the Political System of the GDR

Any study of historiography in the GDR must, of course, take into consideration the very different conditions under which historical studies were conducted there – and in other socialist countries – from those that prevailed in the West. Western historians have contrasted the pluralism of interpretative approaches in the West with the limits that an official interpretation of history placed on the work of the historian in the socialist countries. As it has been crudely put, historians in the West derived their findings from the evidence; those in the socialist countries fitted their evidence into their preconceived conclusions. This, of course, is a vast oversimplification on two counts. No historical study is free of prior assumptions that guide the research. Nor has research been as free in the West or as directed in the East as this juxtaposition suggests. As Winfried Schulze has documented in a recent study of the West German historical profession from 1945 to 1960[5] and others have shown for the period before,[6] a conservative nationalistic orientation dominated the universities in Germany since the mid-nineteenth century and fairly effectively barred dissenting historians from university positions. While historians who

---

5. *Geschichtswissenschaft in Deutschland nach 1945* (Munich, 1989); also Ernst Schulin, ed., *Deutsche Geschichtswissenschaft nach dem 2. Weltkrieg, 1945–1965* (Munich, 1989).
    6. See Wolfgang Weber, *Priester der Klio: Historisch-sozialwissenschaftliche Studien zur Herkunft und Karriere deutscher Historiker und zur Geschichte der Geschichtswissenschaft, 1800–1970* (Frankfurt, a.M., 1985); also G. Iggers, *The German Conception of History: The National Tradition of Historical Thought from Herder to the Present*, 2d ed. (Middletown, Conn., 1983); Bernd Faulenbach, *Ideologie des*

had served the Nazi regime were quickly reintegrated into the West German historical profession after 1945, Walter Markov, who had spent ten years in Nazi prisons as a Communist, in 1946 was denied the opportunity of submitting the second dissertation (*Habilitation*), required for university teaching, at the University of Bonn[7] and left for what became a distinguished career at the Karl-Marx-Universität in Leipzig. Only in the 1960s did a younger generation introduce a more critical perspective on the German past and more diverse methodological and conceptual approaches into the West German universities.[8]

Nevertheless, even before the emergence of critical voices and alternative methodological approaches in the 1960s the pressures for conformity in West Germany were by no means comparable with those in East Germany, where very soon after 1945 party and state assumed direct political control over research, teaching, publication, and recruitment. After a brief period of transition until about the mid-1950s, when so-called bourgeois, i.e., non-Marxist, historians coexisted with historians who represented the viewpoint of the Socialist Unity Party (SED), the latter, once cadres of professionally trained historians were available, assumed a monopoly in the universities, research institutions, and schools. Very early after 1945 the guidelines were laid for historical research and writing.[9] The resolutions promulgated by the SED at its party congresses in the early 1950s and reiterated by Walter Ulbricht demanded that historical research, writings, and teaching were to be partisan (*parteilich*), i.e., function in the service of the party. A major task of the historian was to be the polemical confrontation with historical

deutschen Weges: Die deutsche Geschichte in der Historiographie zwischen Kaiserreich und Nationalsozialismus (Munich, 1980); Hans Schleier, *Die bürgerliche deutsche Geschichtsschreibung der Weimarer Republik* (Berlin/GDR, 1975); on the social and intellectual context of the German professoriate, see Fritz Ringer, *The Decline of the German Mandarins: The German Academic Community, 1890–1933* (Cambridge, Mass., 1969).

7. Letter from Walter Markov to Georg G. Iggers, Leipzig, June 25, 1990.

8. See Georg G. Iggers, *The Social History of Politics: Critical Perspectives in West German Historical Writing since 1945* (Leamington Spa, 1985), especially the introduction. See also Hans-Ulrich Wehler, "Geschichtswissenschaft heute," in Jürgen Habermas, ed., *Stichworte zur "Geistigen Situation" der Zeit* (Frankfurt, a.M., 1979), 2:709–53.

9. For a good discussion, see Heydemann, *Geschichtswissenschaft im geteilten Deutschland* (above, n. 3); more extensively in Fischer and Heydemann, eds., *Geschichtswissenschaft in der DDR* (above, n. 4), the introduction by the editors, 1:3–30 and the articles by various contributors in the section "Zur Entwicklung der Geschichtswissenschaft in der SBZ/DDR," 1:33–175.

interpretations in the capitalist countries. Marxism-Leninism was to serve as the sole comprehensive theoretical framework for the study and writing of history. The ideological guidelines were closely integrated into a system of political control and discipline of the historical profession. The recruitment process enforced ideological and political conformity. Admission to the university required an *Abitur* from the *Erweiterte Oberschule*, which followed the basic eight, more recently ten, grades. Admission for study rested not only on academic performance but very heavily on nonacademic factors such as involvement in the youth organizations of the party, in the earlier years of the GDR also on class background, whereby membership in the working class was interpreted broadly enough to favor the children of loyal party functionaries.[10] Active church membership or refusal to belong to the party youth organization, the Free German Youth (FDJ), eliminated many. Similar criteria were involved in admission to university. Not always in the natural sciences, but generally in the social and cultural sciences, including history, party membership played an important role as did, in the case of male students, the willingness to serve an extra year and a half in the armed forces in addition to the compulsory eighteen months of military service. By the 1960s virtually all full professors of modern history[11] were members of the Socialist Unity Party or, occasionally, one of the parties associated with it in the National Unity Front. The disciplining of Walter Markov[12] and Jürgen Kuczynski in the 1950s as well as that of young historians in 1988 who protested the ban in the GDR of the Soviet magazine *Sputnik*[13] demonstrated how even limited dissent among loyal party members was not brooked. Among church historians at the theological faculties of the univer-

10. This rests in part on my interviews with persons in the GDR.
11. In the early years after 1945 "bourgeois" historians, like Otto Hoetzsch, Heinrich Stroemberg, Fritz Rörig, Fritz Hartung, Eduard Winter, Hellmut Kretzschmar, Kurt Griewank, Friedrich Schneider, Hans Haussherr, and Martin Lintzel occupied professorships in the Soviet zone of occupation and the GDR. See Harm Klueting, "Parteilichkeit war wichtiger als Objektivität," *Frankfurter Allgemeine Zeitung*, May 8, 1990, pp. 13–14. Walter Markov was excluded from the SED in 1951 because of political deviation but ultimately retained his chair. After polling colleagues in the GDR, I was able to find only Wolfgang Töpfer, a medievalist at the Humboldt University in Berlin, as a historian with a chair who was not a member of the SED or one of the parties associated with it.
12. Markov mentions this very guardedly in *Zwiegespräche mit dem Jahrhundert* (Berlin/GDR and Weimar, 1989), pp. 197–98.
13. Based on my interview with Rüdiger Horn, one of the historians disciplined; see also the *Stern* interview with him in no. 22, May 23, 1990, pp. 25–27.

sities, there were as expected a number of scholars who were neither Marxists nor members of the Socialist Unity Party, but who were nevertheless committed to interpreting the Christian experience in a socialist society. A non-Marxist social historian of international reputation, Karlheinz Blaschke, was unable to obtain a university post; after losing his position at the Saxon State Archives in Dresden, he was able to find poorly paid employment as a historian only at the church-operated theological seminary in Leipzig, not a part of the university. Similarly the major publishing houses, among which the Akademie Verlag and the Verlag der Wissenschaften were the most important, published exclusively works written from a Marxist-Leninist viewpoint, as did the state-financed scholarly periodicals. Religiously oriented publishers such as the Union Verlag provided limited opportunities for the publication of other viewpoints, but the Union Verlag, as the publishing house of the Christian Democratic Union in the GDR, had only restricted leeway for dissent and divergence. Occasionally publication in the West was approved or tolerated. Thus little room was left for dissent and nonconformity.

History occupied a very important role second only to Marxism-Leninism in the hierarchy of academic disciplines because of the special function it served in legitimizing the regime. Hence the subordination of historical research and writing to the party. The mechanisms of enforcing conformity were thus much more evident and direct than in the Western democracies. The key institution that coordinated research and teaching was the Council for the Historical Sciences, directly attached to the Central Committee of the Socialist Unity Party.[14] This committee supervised the "Central Plan for the Sciences of Society," in which the overall plan for the entire profession of historians in institutions of higher education and research in the GDR formed an important part. The Institute for Marxism and Leninism, in addition to preparing in cooperation with its parallel institution in the Soviet Union the critical edition of the works of Marx and Engels, concerned itself with ideological conformity, as did the Academy of Societal Sciences, which until the fall of 1989 was attached to the Central Committee of the Party.[15] Research was highly centralized in the

14. See Heydemann, *Geschichtswissenschaft im geteilten Deutschland* (above, n. 3), pp. 177–78. The Council for the Historical Sciences has been disbanded since November 1989.

15. Both institutions, now named the Institute for the History of the Working

mammoth Academy of Sciences of the GDR, with its very large number of researchers, patterned closely on the Soviet Academy of Sciences. The six universities, the teachers' colleges, and the technical universities were conceived primarily as teaching institutions (although professors and assistants, like their counterparts in the West, were expected to do research). As German unification approached in the course of 1990, the great diversity between the organizational framework of research and higher education in the two parts of Germany became very apparent. West Germany, where research was conducted largely at the universities, had no institution comparable to the Academy of Sciences in the GDR. At the universities in the GDR, moreover, the areas of teaching and study not dealing directly with the political aspects of the modern period were badly underrepresented, as were medieval and ancient history. Marxism-Leninism, as the official and only ideology of studies in the sciences of society and thus of history, further limited the possibilities of research and expression. The ideology, moreover, led to the ritualization of language in the form of a terminological code that prevented intellectually honest communication.

Within this highly centralized system of control with its prescribed conceptions of history and society, there nevertheless existed at all times a degree of diversity and broad areas in which independent work was possible, although more so in the past two decades than in the previous twenty years after the consolidation of power by the GDR in the 1950s. Georgi Verbeeck, a Belgian observer who has studied the historical profession in the GDR in depth, has recently described the GDR of the post-Stalin era as an authoritarian rather than a totalitarian society.[16] In practice under no modern regime, neither of the Soviet nor the Fascist model, has the state or the party ever succeeded in attaining complete control over historical research or writing.[17] Subtle forms of conformity and of dissent often reinforced or weakened central control. The Communist regime in the GDR, despite its control of mass media

Class and the Foundation for Societal Analysis respectively, underwent significant changes and reduction in personnel after the events of the fall of 1989. The Foundation for Societal Analysis was dissolved in December 1990.

16. Georgi Verbeeck, "Kontinuität und Wandel im DDR-Geschichtsbild," *Aus Politik und Zeitgeschichte*, March 9, 1990, pp. 30–42, which contains an excellent discussion of the interrelationship of scholarship, ideology, and institutions in the GDR since its beginnings.

17. On Nazi attempts to control the German historical profession, see Helmut Heiber, *Walter Frank und sein Reichsinstitut für die Geschichte des Neuen Deutschland* (Munich, 1966).

and of police power, was never able to generate the degree of consensus among historians that, alas, the Nazi regime was able to solicit; in part this was because the latter succeeded for a long period where the former failed in establishing its claim to national legitimacy among the historians it sought to control. There developed a very large gulf between the published work of the historians and their official pronouncements on the one hand and what they really thought on the other. Again the ritualization of language to which we referred imposed a conformity that to the reader who could not read between the lines and note the silences appeared total.

One of the reasons for my decision to edit this volume was my belief that beginning in the 1970s an opening occurred in historical studies away from narrow dogmatism to international standards of scholarship[18] that was accompanied by a more active participation of historians in the GDR in the international community of scholars. At all times there were limits to how far one could go. The least freedom existed in sensitive areas of political history after 1917, although even here there was some movement. The further removed historical study was from the twentieth century or from the role of the party in this period, the greater were the possibilities of free expressions. Yet although historians increasingly moved away from the standard interpretations of the German past by the party and the dogmatic analysis of social and cultural life inherent in official Marxist-Leninist ideology, they at no time began publicly to question the basic political and ideological assumptions upon which the regime rested and which almost all had come to doubt. History did not fulfill the critical function that literature often had done in the GDR since the 1960s, nor did the historians have the courage of their Czech colleagues who after 1968 worked in menial jobs or went to jail. Until the last minute the historians, many of whom enjoyed special privileges such as travel to the West, obediently wrote what state and party expected them to write. Yet despite the stubborn refusal of the regime to institute structural reforms in the face of a deepening crisis of the social, economic, and political system, in practice the 1970s and 1980s saw an increasing move away from older dogmatic positions of scholarship as this volume demonstrates.

One of the sad aspects of the historical profession in the forty years of the existence of the GDR was the failure of historians to

18. This is also Verbeeck's assessment; see above, n. 15.

take advantage of the possibilities for free expression that existed. Historians in the GDR with whom I have spoken are not convinced that the reluctance to explore new directions in social history and even in sensitive areas like the study of fascism was fully the result of regimentation. The restrictions that governed the work of the historians do not by themselves explain why new methods and subject matters, for example, in the study of everyday life and culture and of mentalities, which were well established not only in the West but also in Poland and Hungary and were not entirely absent in the Soviet Union, were not pursued in the GDR. Moreover, research was not as closely monitored as the existence of the Council for Historical Science and the master plan for the profession seemed to suggest. The historians at the universities and at other research and teaching institutions were consulted but seldom provided input into new imaginative directions. Nor did the plan prevent them from following their research interests and, provided it remained within the general guidelines of Marxist doctrine, to find a publisher.

In part the opening in historical scholarship also resulted from the desperate desire of the GDR government to gain international acceptance and respectability. Very early GDR historians began to participate in international conferences.[19] The requirements of scholarship that would be taken seriously by the international community of scholars thus came into conflict with ideology. Notwithstanding the ritual citations of Marx, Lenin, Brezhnev, and Honecker, in earlier years of Stalin and Ulbricht, and the invocation of simplistic class analysis, GDR historians, as Andreas Dorpalen demonstrated,[20] often made very substantial contributions to international scholarship, especially in less sensitive areas of study such as agrarian history and the history of the Middle Ages. The normalization of international relations through the treaties of the early 1970s, with which not only the Western powers but also West Germany recognized the existence of the German Democratic Republic as a member of the international community of nations, made international scholarly dialogue easier, although the GDR continued to maintain barriers to the free exchange of scholars between the two Germanies, and particularly with West Berlin. The

---

19. See Karl-Dietrich Erdmann, *Die Ökumene der Historiker. Die Internationalen Historiker-Kongresse und das Comité Internationale des Sciences Historiques* (Göttingen, 1987).
20. See Dorpalen, *German History in Marxist Perspective* (above, n. 2).

1980s saw an increasing amount of international exchanges involving senior but also in some cases junior scholars and doctoral candidates, which in the second half of the 1980s more frequently included the Federal Republic of Germany. The growing opening and sophistication of scholarship in the GDR made these exchanges meaningful. Exchanges and cooperative projects dealt with a broad variety of topics, from the meaning and character of the Protestant Reformation to comparative studies of the bourgeoisie in nineteenth-century Europe, from the historical and theoretical significance of Max Weber to, most recently, the Nazi regime.

The opening in historical studies in the past twenty years was accompanied by changing assessment of the German past. We may perhaps distinguish three phases since 1945 in the official interpretation of this past. Immediately after the war, the party pursued a critical line toward the German past that in some ways resembled the *Sonderwegthese* of democratically oriented historians later in West Germany. Since the decision of the Comintern in 1935 to call for a popular front with bourgeois democratic parties, the German Communist Party had located the source of Germany's problems in its failure to follow the path of democratic development in the West.[21] The reactionary character of Prussia from Frederick the Great via Bismarck to Hitler was stressed in a line which went back to Luther's subservience to the princes. This thesis was most forcefully put forward in the book by Alexander Abusch, written in Mexican exile, *Der Irrweg einer Nation*[22] (*A Nation Goes Astray*), and aimed directly at freeing Germany from the political and ideological heritage that had fed into Nazism. The political function of history was reaffirmed in a speech by Walter Ulbricht in July 1952 and elaborated by Leo Stern in the same year in a long article that proposed guidelines for the historical profession in the GDR.[23] Henceforth German history was not to be seen as one long "misery" (*Misere*); rather the "progressive" elements in the German past were to be separated from the "reactionary" and were to be cultivated. The historians in the GDR were to trace the "traditions of

---

21. See Werner Berthold, *Marxistisches Geschichtsbild – Volksfront und antifaschistisch–demokratische Revolution: Zur Vorgeschichte der Geschichtswissenschaft der DDR* (Berlin/GDR, 1970). See also Klaus Kinner, *Marxistische deutsche Geschichtswissenschaft, 1917 bis 1933. Geschichte und Politik im Kampf der KPD* (Berlin/GDR, 1982).
22. Berlin, 1946.
23. See Verbeeck (above, n. 15), p. 32, n. 12; also Heydemann, (above, n. 3), pp. 147–48.

freedom and struggle of the German people back into the High Middle Ages" and establish a link between the great German achievements in the cultural and scientific spheres and the GDR as a "progressive" society. German history was thus seen as split into two traditions, one with its roots in the authoritarian aspects of Prussian history, which led to 1933 and according to GDR theorists has still not been repudiated by many historians in the Federal Republic, the other built on the memories of the Peasant Wars, the "Wars of Liberation," the 1848 revolution, the Social Democratic working-class movement in Imperial Germany, and the Communist party in the Weimar Republic and in the anti-Fascist resistance, which identified almost solely with the Communist party and provided an historical orientation for the new GDR and for the "progressive" forces elsewhere in Germany. This conception presupposed an irreconcilable confrontation between the two German states.

Beginning with Erich Honecker's succession to Walter Ulbricht as First Secretary of the Socialist Unity party, which coincided approximately with the treaties of the early 1970s granting the GDR international recognition, a reorientation took place in the assessment of the German past. On the one hand the Socialist Unity party now rejected the older hope of a united socialist Germany as well as the West German conception of "two states but one nation" and stressed that not language or ethnicity but class and social system were the basis of nationhood, in other words that the GDR represented a socialist German nation; on the other hand the party claimed the entire German past as the "heritage" (*Erbe*) of the socialist nation. To be certain the "heritage" that constituted the whole of the past, good and bad, was distinguished from the positive "tradition" (*Tradition*) on which the GDR could build its sense of national identity.[24] The basis on which the new socialist nation, the GDR, sought to establish its legitimacy was thus much broader than the "progressive" tradition that it formerly had claimed, although it continued to identify itself with these "progressive" traditions. Historians were, however, called upon now to do justice to the past and to avoid the former schematism that had distinguished sharply between "progressive" and "reactionary" personalities and forces. The concept of "tradition" in its traditional

24. There is an extensive literature on "Erbe und Tradition." For a collection of main statements see Helmut Meier and Walter Schmidt, eds., *Erbe und Tradition in der DDR. Die Diskussion der Historiker* (Berlin/GDR, 1988).

sense was now understood more broadly to comprehend not only the heroic line from Thomas Münzer through Karl Marx and August Bebel to Karl Liebknecht and Ernst Thälmann and finally the leaders of the GDR – and perhaps as a second thought the unnamed working poor who in Brecht's words had built Thebes – but also those who in paving the way for German nationhood had created the possibility of a socialist Germany. The five-hundredth anniversary of Luther's birth in 1983, which overshadowed that of the hundredth recurrence of the date of Marx's death, was an occasion of reassessing the role of Luther as initiator of a broad revolutionary movement including all oppositional classes and strata.[25] Biographies of great men, particularly those of Luther by Gerhard Brendler,[26] of Frederick II by Ingrid Mittenzwei,[27] and of Otto von Bismarck by the dean of GDR historians, Ernst Engelberg,[28] played a crucial role in the reassessment of the German past.

Generally, this reevaluation of the course of German history produced a greater openness and a commitment to understanding historical phenomena in the context of their time. What is striking about this new approach to German history is its identification with political and methodological conceptions that in crucial ways resemble much more those of historians who have been identified with conservative nationalistic traditions of historiography in Germany than with the democratic critics of the past. Part of the return to traditional methodologies is also the revived interest in the biographies of great men,[29] such as Engelberg's biography of Bismarck. Although in 1982 the general introduction to the new twelve volume *Deutsche Geschichte* emphasized "the decisive role of the popular masses in history,"[30] these are now being played down. One positive aspect of the new approach is the call, not always realized in practice, to see the past as it was, free from ideological projections.

From the perspective of an observer like myself, who was forced

25. See "Thesen über Martin Luther. Zum 500. Geburtstag," *Zeitschrift für Geschichtswissenschaft* 29 (1981): 879–93; also Hartmut Lehmann, "Die 15 Thesen der SED über Martin Luther," in Fischer und Heydemann (above, n. 4), 2:215–34.

26. *Martin Luther, Theologie und Revolution* (Berlin/GDR, 1983).

27. *Friedrich II von Preussen. Eine Biographie* (Berlin/GDR, 1979).

28. *Bismarck. 2 vols. (Berlin/GDR and West Berlin, 1985–1990).*

29. See Ernst Engelberg and Hans Schleier, "Zur Geschichte und Theorie der historischen Biographie," *Zeitschrift für Geschichtswissenschaft* 38 (1990): 195–217.

30. (Berlin/GDR, 1982–), 1:5.

to flee the Nazi regime, the attempts by the official GDR historio-graphy to lay claim to the German national tradition as part of the positive heritage of the GDR – i.e., essentially the Prussian tradition – have been disquietingly oblivious of the antidemocratic aspects of this tradition. Luther is thus modernized with little willingness to recognize the premodern aspects of his thought[31] – and incidentally his anti-Semitism. As a symbolic expression of the concern with the national "heritage and tradition," the statue of Frederick the Great could now be restored to its former place on Unter den Linden. The shrill chauvinistic and racist tones (*Deutschtümelei*) of Jahn, Arndt, and Fichte and later of the *Burschenschaften* are recognized but seen as a marginal aspect of a basically progressive movement. The Prussian war against Napoleon in 1813 and 1814 is idealized as a "war of national independence" forced upon the reluctant Prussian monarchy by the "spontaneous movement of the popular masses [*Volksmassen*]."[32] Even the Franco-Prussian War of 1870 is referred to as a "national war of defense," although actually, as the *Deutsche Geschichte* and Ernst Engelberg admit, Bismarck "provoked" the war and the "leading Prussian military men and the representatives of the haute bourgeoisie pursued expansionist aims from the beginning." The war, it is argued, was nevertheless jus-tified, because "a German victory was in the interest of historical progress."[33] This was, of course, also the view of Marx and Engels in the summer of 1870 in contrast to Wilhelm Liebknecht and August Bebel,[34] who on the spot assessed the effects of unification under the auspices of the Prussian monarchy much more realisti-cally. Considering the nature of the GDR regime prior to Novem-ber 1989 it is not surprising that it should have utilized autocratic traditions of the military and of state authority to legitimate its own autocracy.

Yet this call for a new openness had only limited bearing on those topics that bore directly on the legitimacy of the GDR regime and its relationship to the Soviet Union, although here too there was gradual movement before 1989 towards greater honesty. The role of the Communist party in the last months of the Weimar Republic, the fate of German Communists who had fled to the Soviet Union,

31. This is also true of Brendler (above, n. 24), although he does frankly discuss Luther's anti-Semitism, ibid., pp. 435–38.

32. *Deutsche Geschichte*, 4:110.

33. Ibid., 4:502. A very similar formulation is found in Engelberg, *Bismarck*, vol. 1, p. 726.

34. See August Bebel, *Aus meinem Leben*, pt. 2 (Stuttgart, 1911), pp. 176–81.

and, of course, the Hitler-Stalin pact continued to be taboos.[35] In part GDR historians were able to adapt the Prussian interpretation of history to their needs because they had made no attempt to deal adequately with the problem of the rise of Nazism to power and the character of the Nazi regime. Ironically the very insistence on the part of GDR historians that politics must be seen in terms of social forces prevented them from examining Nazism in its social context because of the limits their doctrine placed on their social analysis. Their proclaimed "antifacism" served as a shield behind which they could hide from a serious examination of the social origins of the Nazi movement and of the uses of power that in uncomfortable ways paralleled those of the later GDR. This parallelism was not fundamentally negated by the invocation of a "humanism," devoid of clear definition, to legitimate the political order erected after 1945 on the territory of what became the GDR.

In a strange way, Communists shared with conservative apologists of the German past, such as Gerhard Ritter and Hans Rothfels, the conviction that Nazism had no specifically German but generally Western roots[36] and that therefore a critical reexamination of German national traditions was not needed. As late as 1977 the volume *Unbewältigte Vergangenheit. Kritik der bürgerlichen Geschichtsschreibung der BRD (The Unmastered Past: A Critique of Bourgeois Historiography in the German Federal Republic)* reiterated the position adopted at the VIIth Congress of the Communist International in 1935 that "fascism," under which German National Socialism was subsumed, is "the open terrorist dictatorship of the most reactionary, most chauvinist, and most imperialist elements of finance capital"[37] and rejected the thesis found in Western interpretations that fascism had a broad basis in the population. Moreover such a definition, by using fascism as a generic term, prevented any attempt at analyzing the specific character of the Nazi regime with its genocidal policies. In itself the attempt to search for sources of Nazism in the economic structure of Germany was fully justified

35. See Hermann Weber, "'Weisse Flecken' in der DDR-Geschichtsschreibung," *Aus Politik und Zeitgeschehen*, March 9, 1990, pp. 3–15.
36. See Gerhard Ritter, *Europa und die deutsche Frage* (Munich, 1948); also Hans Rothfels, *The German Opposition to Hitler: An Assessment* (Chicago, 1947).
37. (Berlin/GDR, 1977), p. 334. On later treatments of fascism that modify this interpretation without questioning the above definition, see Dietrich Eichholz and Kurt Gossweiler, *Faschismus-Forschung* (Berlin/GDR, 1980); Joachim Petzold, *Die Demagogie des Hitler-Faschismus* (Berlin/GDR, 1983), Kurt Gossweiler, *Aufsätze zum Faschismus*, 2 vols. (Berlin/GDR, 1988).

as was the serious commitment in 1945 to prevent the restoration of forces and traditions that had led to dictatorship, war, and genocide. But GDR scholarship went beyond this to impose preconceived answers rooted in dogma on past reality and to instrumentalize historical studies to bolster a dictatorial political party that in its manners of organization and control, even if not in its basic aims, in many points paralleled those of the Nazis. Nor did it explain why Germany alone among industrialized nations turned fascist. Finally it was unable to come to terms with the broad basis that the regime had in the population. The identification of workers as victims and resistance fighters did not address the actual complexities by which workers, including Communist workers, accepted the national legitimacy of the regime and did their duty in the work place or on the front, so that in many ways the workers as the supposed victims of the regime became accomplices in its crimes.

Still in 1977 the authors of *Unbewältigte Vergangenheit* accused Western writers of "exaggerating" (*Überhöhung*) the role of anti-Semitism in Germany.[38] Jürgen Kuczynski in the 1960s spelled out the persecution of the Jews, the bestiality, and the mass murders, as did occasional other publications, without touching on the question of popular support or involvement in these actions.[39] The prime focus on the victims of Nazi persecution remained on the "antifascist resistance" identified as the Communist resistance. Nevertheless in all these areas of study, there was perceptible movement toward greater openness in the 1980s. This was least true of the literature on the Communist party in the 1930s and on the Hitler-Stalin pact, although even here Soviet policy leading to the war was scrutinized by the late 1980s with greater candor.[40] Questions that before had been shunned were now approached cautiously. Thus Joachim Petzold began in 1975 to recognize the limitations of the monopoly capitalism thesis, to which he still adhered, to explain the broad basis of popular support for the Nazis. Kurt Gossweiler called for a comparative study of fascism to understand more clearly the specific context within which National Socialism arose in Germany.[41] Finally Kurt Pätzold began a serious investigation of

38. Ibid., p. 335.
39. See, e.g., Jürgen Kuczynski, *Die Geschichte der Lage der Arbeiter unter dem Kapitalismus*, 6:137–38.
40. See Dietrich Eichholtz and Kurt Pätzold, eds., *Der Weg in den Krieg. Studien zur Geschichte der Vorkriegsjahre, 1935–36 bis 1939* (Berlin/GDR, 1989).
41. See n. 37.

anti-Semitism and Jewish persecution,[42] themes that had been dealt with much earlier in some novels in the GDR.[43]

By 1989 GDR scholarship on Nazism and the Holocaust had reached the point where it could finally make its contribution to international scholarship. Two events in 1989 reflect how far GDR scholarship had gone and how far it still had to go. In May 1989 American and GDR historians held a conference on terror and resistance under the Nazis in which there was a very open exchange of research findings and interpretations.[44] In time for the fiftieth anniversary of the outbreak of the Second World War, GDR historians published a volume on the road to war that still began with an article on the central role of finance capital in determining German policy and ended with a discussion of the attitude of German Communists in 1939 toward the Hitler-Stalin pact, seen by them generally as a defensive move on the part of the Soviet Union, with no mention of the secret protocols on the division of Eastern Europe.[45]

What November 1989 meant for GDR historiography was that at last the remaining ideological restraints on honest scholarship and on honest confrontation could be dismantled. It is striking that immediately on its convocation in April 1990, the first democratically elected parliament of the GDR acknowledged that the GDR too must assume its responsibility for the German past. Although Marxism also had a critical perspective on society that should have provided the starting point for a critical reexamination of the past

42. See his *Faschismus, Rassenwahn, Judenverfolgung. Eine Studie zur politischen Strategie und Taktik des faschistischen deutschen Imperialismus* (Berlin/GDR, 1975); *Verfolgung, Vertreibung, Vernichtung, Dokumente des faschistischen Antisemitismus, 1933–1942* (Berlin/GDR, 1984); *Kristallnacht. Zum Pogrom 1938* (Berlin/ GDR, 1988); see also Rudolf Hirsch and Rosemarie Schuder, *Der gelbe Fleck, Wurzeln und Wirkungen des Judenhasses in der deutschen Geschichte* (Berlin/GDR, 1988).

43. A number of literary works, beginning with Bruno Apitz, *Nackt unter Wölfen* and including works by Johannes Brobowski, Franz Fühmann, Jurek Becker, Peter Edel, Helmut Eschwege, Heinz Knobloch, and Christa Wolf, dealt with the Holocaust as did the DEFA film *Ehe im Schatten* (1946).

44. For the GDR contributions, see "Deutscher Faschismus – Terror und Widerstand", published by the Akademie für Gesellschaftswissenschaften beim ZK der SED (Berlin/GDR, 1989); several of the American contributions will be published in a forthcoming issue of *Central European History*.

45. Dietrich Eichholtz and Kurt Pätzold, eds., *Der Weg in den Krieg* (Berlin/ GDR, 1989). See the opening article by Eichholtz, "Das Expansionsprogramm des deutschen Finanzkapitals am Vorabend des 2. Weltkrieges," pp. 1–39, and the concluding article by Heinz Rührich, "Der deutsch-sowjetische Nichtangriffsvertrag vom 23. 8. 1939 aus der zeitgenössischen Sicht der KPD," pp. 517–51.

guided by the archival or oral evidence rather than by ready-made dogmatic formulae, GDR scholarship did not succeed before November 1989 in coming up with an alternative Marxist, or non-Marxist, analysis of Nazism. The best it could offer, and this was important, was an expansion of archival findings. There thus did not develop in the GDR a social history of politics, which in West Germany since the 1960s had made important contributions to a critical examination of the German past, including the Nazi Period.

3. The Role of Social History

The term *social history*[46] was spurned until very recently as a bourgeois concept. Like the term *sociology*,[47] it seemed to imply the existence of a civil society at least partly autonomous from the economic basis upon which, according to Marxist theory, the superstructure of social and political institutions, culture, and ideology rests. Historical materialism as a general sociological theory of historical development made sociology – and thereby also social history – unnecessary as separate disciplines or fields. As late as 1982, the introduction to the new *Deutsche Geschichte* reiterated "the lawful succession of economic social formations that replace each other;" the view of this "historical development as an objective process determined by social interests;" and finally "the decisive role of popular masses in history"[48] as the foundation on which this history was to be written, ideas that were repeated almost ritually until the collapse of the regime in November 1989. Yet a distinction can be made between historical materialism as a philosophy of history and as a

46. Horst Handtke, "Zur sozialgeschichtlichen Forschung in der DDR," *Zeitschrift für Geschichtswissenschaft* 34 (1986): 291–302; see also his article, "Sozialgeschichte – Stand und Entwicklung in der DDR," in Jürgen Kocka, ed., *Sozialgeschichte im internationalen Überblick* (Göttingen, 1989), pp. 89–108. An earlier position was represented in Konrad Irmschler and Gerhard Lozek, "Historismus und Sozialgeschichte in der gegenwärtigen bürgerlichen Geschichtsschreibung," *Zeitschrift für Geschichtswissenschaft* 27 (1979): 193–208. Jürgen Kuczynski used the term *social history* already in his *Wirtschafts- und Sozialgeschichte Englands, 1832–1900* (Berlin/GDR, 1965).
47. For considerations of a Marxist sociology, see the discussion begun already by Peter Bollhagen, *Soziologie und Geschichte* (Berlin/GDR, 1966) and the more recent *Jahrbuch für Soziologie und Sozialpolitik*, published since 1980.
48. (Berlin/GDR, 1982), 1:5.

methodology. As a philosophy of history and society, historical materialism presages the course of history and to an extent prejudges empirical inquiry; yet historical materialism can provide impulses for a methodological approach that examines the conditions of life as they are defined by economic and social factors within which politics, social relations, and culture can be viewed. In the past twenty years there has been an increasing movement in GDR scholarship away from grand theory to the empirical study of society and culture and with it increasingly the adoption of the terms "social history" and "cultural history." At the same time, as in the West and in other socialist countries, aspects of culture and consciousness that were once considered to be parts of the "superstructure" received increasing attention.

In practice, although never in theory, there has always been a distinction in the GDR between political and social history. It is striking that the close relationship between the two that developed in West Germany in the 1960s, as historians critically examined the German past, never had its counterpart in the GDR. In the GDR historians of politics postulated a relation between economic forces and politics, e.g., in their conception of fascism as a function of monopoly capitalism, and buttressed their theory with facts gathered from the archives but never empirically examined the economic and social foundations of power. Social history in the GDR, on the other hand, moved increasingly away from politics as it emancipated itself from the more dogmatic aspects of historical materialism. It nevertheless preserved the concern with work and culture with a focus on the working classes, i.e., peasants and manual workers. Paradoxically in a historiography that labeled itself as Marxist, social history was given a subordinate role to political history. It was marginalized. And yet because it was marginalized, it also enjoyed a degree of freedom. Social history may thus have offered its practitioners a partial way out of their dilemma between their own understanding of Marxism, which called for a history of below, and Marxist-Leninist doctrine, which imposed the primacy of party and state.

The authors in this volume derived a great deal of their inspiration from fields at the margins of the discipline of history proper, folkloristics (*Volkskunde*), economic history (*Wirtschaftsgeschichte*), and regional history (*Regionalgeschichte*). Common to all three was the classical Marxist conception of the class struggle and the concentration of what they saw as the irresistible transition from a feudal to a capitalist and to a socialist social order.

Volkskunde, as it constituted itself as a discipline in the 1950s, differentiated itself from the classical tradition of *Volkskunde* and *Kulturgeschichte*, which from Wilhelm Heinrich Riehl in the mid-nineteenth to Gunther Ipsen[49] in the twentieth century propagated a romantic notion of a preindustrial national community (*Volksgemeinschaft*), defined in folkish terms. These ideas fitted in well with the ideology of the Nazis and contributed to its formation.[50] In the place of a unified, organic racial community, the new Institut für deutsche Volkskunde, founded in 1952 under the directorship of Wolfgang Steinitz at the Academy of Sciences at East Berlin, focused on what it conceived to be the conflict between two cultures in the countryside, one reflecting the dominating, the other the popular exploited classes. Envisaging a continuity of a plebeian culture in the countryside since the Peasants' War, Steinitz and his associates edited an immense collection of folk songs that gave voice to protest and class conflict.[51] Undoubtedly and avowedly the new *Volkskunde* was ideological, as was its predecessor, in reading the concerns of the present into the past. It succeeded in laying the foundations for an extensive study of what it called *Kultur und Lebensweise*, that is, culture conceived in a very broad sense as encompassing the material conditions of life, work, housing, food, clothing, but also sociability and attitudes. The stress was still on the countryside, but less on the premodern than on the modern period of transition to a capitalist economic order with all its social and cultural concomitants.

Economic history in the GDR as a discipline in the 1950s and 1960s moved in very different directions from the West in those years. Working with the concepts of classical economics, economic history in the West increasingly conceived itself as a rigorous science employing highly quantified growth models. Both politics and culture were excluded as extraneous from this history. While Marxist historians such as Juhan Kahk in Estonia and somewhat

---

49. By discipline Ipsen, who had an immense influence on the development of a folkish historiography in the Weimar Republic and the Nazis, was actually a sociologist and not a folklorist.

50. Cf. Schultz, *Deutsche Geschichtswissenschaft nach 1945* (above, n. 5).

51. Wolfgang Steinitz, ed., *Deutsche Volkslieder demokratischen Charakters aus 6 Jahrhunderten* (Berlin/GDR, 1955–1962). On the history of *Volkskunde* in the GDR, see Hermann Strobach et al., "Volkskundliche Forschungen in der Deutschen Demokratischen Republik," *Jahrbuch für Volkskunde und Kultur* 17 (1974): 9–39 and Wolfgang Jacobeit, "Wege und Ziele der Volkskunde in der DDR," *Blätter für Heimatsgeschichte* 1 (1985): 37–58.

later Thomas Kuzcynski[52] in East Berlin brought modern mathematical methods into economic history, the main thrust went in a different direction into a broad history of society and culture. Between 1961 and 1972 Jürgen Kuczynski published the thirty-eight volume *Geschichte der Lage der Arbeiter unter dem Kapitalismus*[53] (*History of the Condition of the Workers under Capitalism*), which as the title indicates, dealt with conditions of working-class life. Although the work was criticized in the West as schematic in its use of Marxist categories and superficial as a work of synthesis, assessing the secondary literature rather than presenting findings of its own, it nevertheless, as the West German critic Jürgen Kocka observed, constituted the first attempt by any historian, East or West, to undertake a comprehensive history of the working class and despite its weaknesses should be seen as a pioneering work.[54] In fact, the volumes amassed a wealth of data not only on material conditions of work but also on social aspects, including three volumes dealing specifically with laboring women and children.[55] This broad social and later increasingly also cultural scope also extended to the *Jahrbuch für Wirtschaftsgeschichte* (*Yearbook for Economic History*) under Jürgen Kuczynski's editorship and is reflected in the three selections by members of the institute, Hartmut Harnisch, Hans-Heinrich Müller, and Jan Peters, in this volume.

A great deal of the recent work in social history has involved the close cooperation beyond disciplinary lines of folklorists and economic historians, almost never political historians. Three major research projects were initiated in the 1970s with the cooperation of ethnologists and economic historians: the studies of the impact of capitalism on the transformation of three regions from the late eighteenth to the twentieth century, namely, the Magdeburg *Börde*, the Oberlausitz region in Saxony, and the Mecklenburg countryside. The most extensive studies, however, have been on the Magde-

52. See, e.g., Thomas Kuczynski, ed., *Wirtschaftsgeschichte und Mathematik. Beiträge zur Anwendung mathematischer, insbesonders statistischer Methoden in der wirtschafts- und sozialhistorischen Forschung* (Berlin/GDR, 1985).

53. 38 vols. (Berlin/GDR, 1961–1972).

54. For reviews of each volume, see *Archiv für Sozialgeschichte* 14 (1974): 471–542; see Kocka's comment on p. 471.

55. Vol. 18 on working women, vols. 19 and 20 on working children. Vol. 20, which consists of documents, was edited by Ruth Hoppe. An earlier version of the last two vols. was published already in 1958.

burg *Börde*.[56] The Magdeburg region was selected intentionally because here the transition to modern forms of production took place relatively early. Starting from the material basis of a culture, the means of production, and the relationship between ownership and demographic development, the authors proceeded to a comprehensive study of the region that included working conditions, social structure, but also culture in a broad sense including not only food, housing, and fashion, but also language, schooling, clubs, and festivals.

These studies, not surprisingly in view of the Marxist assumptions from which they proceed, stress much more strongly the economic and social context of popular culture than studies of popular culture in the West generally do, but they do not ignore modes of life and consciousness. What is also interesting is the very positive attitude towards modernization, and that essentially also means capitalism, in contrast to many non-Marxist studies in the West. There is no nostalgia for the precapitalist past. The losses that the triumph of capitalism in the countryside entails are recognized: a degree of impoverishment for the lower strata; the growing gap between the culture of the upper strata, who in language and life patterns become increasingly urban, and the rest who remained excluded from this bourgeois culture. Yet even for the rest, capitalism meant progress and liberation, even if limited, from drudgery and from what Marx had called rural idiocy.

These works have all dealt with rural areas, although ones affected

---

56. On the Magdeburg Börde, see Hans-Jürgen Rach, *Bauernhaus, Landarbeiterkaten und Schnitterkasernen: Zur Geschichte von Bauen und Wohnen in der Magdeburger Börde des 19. Jahrhunderts* (Berlin/GDR, 1974); Rach and Bernhard Weissel, *Landwirtschaft und Kapitalismus: Zur Entwicklung der ökonomischen und sozialen Verhältnisse in der Magdeburger Börde vom Ausgang des 18. Jahrhunderts bis zum Ende des 1. Weltkrieges* (Berlin/GDR, 1978–79); Hainer Plaul, *Landarbeiterleben im 19. Jahrhundert* (Berlin/GDR, 1979); Rach und Weissel, eds., *Bauern und Landarbeiter im Kapitalismus in der Magdeburger Börde* (Berlin/GDR, 1982). Rach, Weissel, and Plaul, eds., *Die werktätige Bevölkerung in der Magdeburger Börde. Studien zum dörflichen Alltag vom Beginn des 20. Jahrhunderts bis zum Anfang der 60er Jahre* (Berlin/GDR, 1986) and from the same editors, *Das Leben der Werktätigen in der Magdeburger Börde. Studien zum dörflichen Alltag vom Beginn des 20. Jahrhunderts bis zum Anfang der 60er Jahre* (Berlin/GDR, 1987). See the sections on social clubs (*Vereinswesen*) and language in Hans-Jürgen Rach and Bernhard Weissel, eds., *Bauern und Landarbeiter im Kapitalismus in der Magdeburger Börde. Zur Geschichte des dörflichen Alltags vom Ausgang des 18. bis zum Beginn des 19. Jahrhunderts* (Berlin/GDR, 1982). On Electoral Saxony, see B. Schöne, *Kultur und Lebensweise Lausitzer Bandweber* (Berlin/GDR, 1977); R. Weinhold, ed., *Volksleben zwischen Zunft und Fabrik* (Berlin/GDR, 1982).

by nearby industrializing urban centers. Greater attention was paid to urban studies in the new field of *Regionalgeschichte*,[57] which, as the name suggests, centered on local history. The use of the term was intentional, to suggest a break with the more conservative established tradition of *Landesgeschichte*. Again much of the work in local history in the early years of the GDR closely reflected official ideology in dealing with the history of the organized working-class movement and of strikes with a focus on the Communist party. Yet the regional histories of the past two decades have also built on a tradition of regional histories initiated by Karl Lamprecht in the 1880s in his famous study of material culture in the Moselle valley in the Middle Ages,[58] in which he attempted to write what the French later called an *histoire totale* of a region, proceeding from the base of economics and human geography to social structures and culture. It is no accident that Hartmut Zwahr, about whom we shall say more later in this introduction, was trained in the late 1950s by Heinrich Sproemberg, Gerhard Heitz, and Carl Czok, who continued the tradition of an interdisciplinary history of a region associated with the Institute of Cultural and Universal History founded by Karl Lamprecht in 1909.[59] Helga Schultz in her social history of Berlin from 1650 to 1800, which was published in 1987[60] and is one of the few books to identify itself in the title as a social history, approaches Berlin as such a totality for the first time and applies the methods of Western demographic historians as a basis of a broader history of society.

It is to be expected that Marxism would focus on the life of the common people and thus create the basis of a history of everyday life, an *Alltagsgeschichte* as it has been called in West Germany since the 1970s[61] and more recently in the GDR.[62] This, however, was

57. An important journal for these studies is the *Jahrbuch für Regionalgeschichte*.
58. *Deutsche Wirtschaftsgeschichte im Mittelalter. Untersuchungen über die Entwicklung der materiellen Kultur auf dem platten Land auf Grund der Quellen zunächst des Mosellandes*, 3 vols. in 4. (Leipzig, 1885–86).
59. The institute itself was closed in 1951 with the reorganization of historical studies along Marxist-Leninist lines. Cf. Walter Markov, *Zwiegespräche* (above, n. 12), p. 191. Within the history department at the Karl-Marx-Universität in Leipzig a section for Landes- und Siedlungsgeschichte was established in the 1950s that in many ways continued the tradition of the earlier institute.
60. *Berlin, 1650–1800. Sozialgeschichte einer Residenz* (Berlin/GDR, 1987).
61. See Alf Lüdtke, ed., *Alltagsgeschichte. Zur Rekonstruktion historischer Erfahrungen und Lebensweisen* (Frankfurt, a.M., 1989).
62. See Harald Dehne, "Dem Alltag ein Stück näher?" in Alf Lüdtke, ed., *Alltagsgeschichte* (above, n. 61), pp. 137–68; also Dehne, "Aller Tage Leben. Zu

only partly the case. The party, notwithstanding its proclamations, was an autocratic institution willing to mobilize the general population yet always maintaining control from the top. This perspective on the history of the working class becomes evident in the preface to the eight-volume history of the German labor movement published by the party in 1968, which proudly identifies its sources as the Marxist classics and the "resolutions of the party of the working class and the addresses and essays of the functionaries of the German working-class movement."[63] More recently books have been dedicated to proletarian life and culture such as those coming from Dietrich Mühlberg's Chair for the Study of Culture (which in this sense means popular culture) and Aesthetics at the Humboldt University in East Berlin. The aim of the authors is not to write scholarly monographs based on extensive archival research and empirical study, but to make the world of the Berlin working class come alive to a broad public through readable paperbacks and even more so by visual means, through exhibits of photographs and artifacts.[64] In purpose and approach this history from below has many similarities with the history workshop (*Geschichtswerkstätten*) movement in West Germany, with which there were even exchanges of exhibits in very recent years, namely between Mühlberg's circle and the West Berlin history workshop.[65] In fact in the last dozen years, during which the contributions included in this volume were written or published, an intensive dialogue has begun between social historians in the GDR and historians and social scientists in nonsocialist countries on methods and approaches in social history but particularly the history of everyday life. This exchange was made possible not only because of an opening in the writing of history, especially social history, in the GDR, but also because the way in which history was viewed and written changed generally in the world. The old political history

neuen Forschungsansätzen im Beziehungsreich von Alltag, Lebensweise und Kultur der Arbeiterklasse," *Jahrbuch für Volkskunde und Kulturgeschichte* 28 (1985): 9–48.

63. *Geschichte der deutschen Arbeiterbewegung* (Berlin/GDR, 1966), 1:7.

64. Important publications by the circle include Dietrich Mühlberg and Horst Groschopp, *Arbeiterleben um 1900* (Berlin/GDR, 1983); Horst Groschopp, *Zwischen Bierabend und Bildungswesen* (Berlin/GDR, 1985); Dietrich Mühlberg, *Proletarier, Kultur und Lebensweise im 19. Jahrhundert* (Berlin/GDR, 1986).

65. See above, n. 64. There also exists a cooperative project on working-class culture and leisure time in the Weimar Republic between Mühlberg's circle and a circle at the University of Hannover headed by Adelheid von Saldern involving colloquia and exhibits.

focusing on events and great personalities had generally given way
in the West by the mid-1960s to a history of social structures, often
using the methods of the quantifying social sciences, and then,
especially in the 1970s and 1980s, to a history that increasingly
sought to recreate life as it was experienced by concrete common
people. Jürgen Kuczynski's *Geschichte des Alltags des Deutschen
Volkes*[66] (1980–81), by the dean of GDR economic historians,
although still very much in its phraseology and its categories in the
orthodox Marxist vein, was a call finally to address the life of the
common people, which paradoxically had become a matter of
concern for historians in the capitalist countries well before it had in
the GDR. Several of the essays in this volume explore this new
concern. Jan Peters, who is represented in this volume, and Harald
Dehne, who is not, have in recent years pointed to new conceptual
and methodological approaches in the West–Jan Peters to the
Annales's[67] in-depth studies of consciousness placed into the concrete social setting of a region, and Harald Dehne,[68] in his study of
the changing character of mealtimes in an industrializing world, to
new anthropological approaches that, like those of Pierre Bourdieu,
have sought to explore the symbolic manifestations of collective
behavior.

4. The Authors of this Volume

The selections in this volume indicate the direction in
which social history has gone in the GDR in the past fifteen years.
In all of them consciousness and culture, understood in the broadest
sense as the way in which human beings think and act, occupy a
central role. Yet at the same time the authors continue to be
indebted to historical materialism in the way they locate consciousness and culture in a social framework where relations of production and class play an important role. They also inherited from

66. 5 vols. (Berlin/GDR, 1980–81); a sixth vol. was published in 1985 in response
to his critics.
67. Jan Peters, "Das Angebot der 'Annales' und das Beispiel Le Roy Ladurie.
Nachdenkenswerte über französische Sozialgeschichtsforschung," *Jahrbuch für
Wirtschaftsgeschichte* 1 (1989): 139–59.
68. Harald Dehne, "Aller Tage Leben. Zu neuen Forschungsansätzen im Bezie-
hungsfeld von Alltag, Lebensweise und Kultur der Arbeiterklasse," *Jahrbuch für
Volkskunde und Kulturgeschichte*, 28 (1985): 9–48; see also Jan Peters, "Alltag im
Aufbau. Überlegungen zum Artikel von Harald Dehne, 'Aller Tage Leben'," ibid. 30
(1987): 185–88.

historical materialism the focus on the transformation of modern society from a precapitalist, feudal economy to a capitalist market economy oriented toward production and profit. At the same time subjective factors of culture assumed an ever greater importance in their writings.

All of the selections represent attempts to write social history; only the first selection from the prefatory remarks to Jürgen Kuczynski's *Geschichte des Alltags des Deutschen Volkes* of 1980 is programmatic. It is an open call to Marxist historians to turn away from a history of the labor movement from above to a concern with the everyday life of laboring people. As we saw above, Kuczynski himself pointed the way to a history of the social conditions under which men, women, and children live and labor. Now his concern is with the existential conditions of everyday life, not only wages and working conditions, but how this life with all its anxieties is experienced. Kuczynski stressed how ironically Marxist historiography in the GDR, in its avowed concern with the lot of the workers, had neglected these aspects of working-class existence and instead had devoted itself to the movement and the spectacular confrontations that marked it. Marxist historians in the GDR thus had much to learn from non-Marxist historians in the West. Born in 1904, the son of the famous labor statistician and left democrat Robert Kuczynski, Jürgen Kuczynski represents an older generation of committed Communists who in 1950 moved from West to East Berlin after two extensive stays abroad, one at the Brookings Institution in Washington, D.C. as a young man and the other in exile in Great Britain from 1936 to 1945.[69] His broad acquaintance with international intellectual and scholarly currents contributed to his success in gaining a respect in the international community of scholars for the Institute of Economic History at the Academy of Sciences and the *Jahrbücher für Wirtschaftsgeschichte*, which he founded, despite its Marxist orientation, a respect that no other group of historians in the GDR was able to obtain.

The second selection, by Wolfgang Jacobeit, born in 1921, is taken from the Magdeburg *Börde* project discussed above. Jacobeit himself was a folklorist by training who in 1948 in Göttingen, West Germany, completed a doctoral dissertation on the yoke in the history of Central Europe and who in 1956 transferred to East

---

69. See his autobiography, which ends before his return to the GDR, *Memoiren: Die Erziehung des J.K. zum Kommunisten und Wissenschaftler* (Berlin/GDR, 1973).

Berlin to direct the inventory of agricultural tools in all museums in the GDR. From tools he turned to conditions of life in the country-side, beginning with a book in 1962 on sheep raising and shepherds.[70] Since then he has been a folklorist in the history depart-ment of the Humboldt University in East Berlin. The selection, first published in 1982, reflects the attempt to proceed from a relatively traditional Marxist conception of the primary role of the material conditions of life, e.g., means of production, demography, housing, and nutrition, to a broader concern with the patterns of life, consumption, education, mores, and customs, from the family meal to festivals and funerals. All this is placed within the context of the transition in the countryside from feudalism to capitalism with its increasing social differentiation.

Hartmut Zwahr, born in 1936 of partially Sorbian ancestry, was trained at the Karl Marx University in Leipzig by historians who, as we already mentioned, although Marxists, continued a tradition begun by Karl Lamprecht in Leipzig early in the century that was committed to the in-depth study of a region and that combined economic, social, cultural, and political history. For the first time in the GDR Zwahr placed labor history on a solid empirical basis. His book on the formation of the Leipzig proletariat,[71] which was completed as an *Habilitation* in 1974 but published only in 1978 after his work had attained international renown, is traditionally Marxist in proceeding from the economic aspects of the transform-ation of Leipzig into an industrial center with the accompanying emergence of an industrial working force to an analysis of the social conditions under which this working force became a social class and finally achieved consciousness of itself as a proletariat, a conscious-ness that is defined in terms of its identification with the organized Social Democratic party conceived as a revolutionary movement. What is new in the book is the effort to place Marxist conceptions of class on the basis of mass data, in this case the utilization of hundreds of records in the Leipzig city archives for the years 1827 to 1867 that cast light on the lives of thousands of Leipzig workers who moved to the city, and the empirical analysis of family and friendship patterns that throw light on the social character of the working class. We have selected the introduction to the book, in

70. Wolfgang Jacobeit, *Schaftshaltung und Schäfer in Zentraleuropa bis zum Beginn des 20. Jahrhunderts* (Berlin/GDR, 1962).
71. *Zur Konstituierung des Proletariats als Klasse. Strukturuntersuchung über das Leipziger Proletariat während der industriellen Revolution* (Berlin/GDR, 1978).

which Zwahr explains his methodology, and the sections in the second part of the book on the social formation of the proletariat, in which he examines the choice of godparents by Leipzig workers on the basis of his mass data. In the years since the publication of the book, Zwahr organized a working circle[72] devoted to empirical studies of not only the working class but also the middle classes in the nineteenth century and coordinating the efforts of folklorists, economists, and regional historians. The fourth selection by Susanne Schötz, born in 1958, who recently completed her doctoral dissertation, deals with the recruitment of the middle classes from the working classes in nineteenth-century Leipzig, a process that ran counter to the established Marxist concern with the recruitment of the proletariat from a middle class destroyed by capitalism. The article, written in 1989, works with the conceptions of class generally associated with classical Marxism. Yet at the heart of the article is the examination of the values of workers aspiring to become tavern keepers or in other ways ascend on the social scale and the effects this work ethic has on the way they conduct their lives.

The next three selections are all by members of the Institute of Economic History at the Academy of Sciences and reflect the broad sense in which economic history was conceived by the members of the institute. All three are agricultural historians. They share a concern not only with objective historical processes but with mentalities; and with all of the contributors to this volume they share an insistence that mentalities must always be understood in the framework of a comprehensive social order in which the transition from feudalism to capitalism takes place. In this sense they differ emphatically both from the *Annales*, with their frequent neglect of political factors and of historical change, and from those alternative historians of the *Alltag*, some of whom in their enthusiasm for microhistory, tend to neglect the larger contexts in which this history takes place. Until the events of October and November 1989, all the contributors to this volume affirmed their belief, as Jan Peters worded it in 1987, that "the historical research into ways of life [*Lebensweiseforschung*], as it is beginning to develop in the GDR, has grown directly out of the theory of historical

---

72. The circle was originally called Arbeitskreis Klassenentwicklung und bürgerliche Umwälzung (Working Circle: The Development of Classes and the Radical Transformation of the Bourgeoisie) to avoid the term *social history* but was then actually increasingly referred to as the Arbeitskreis für Sozialgeschichte (Working Circle for Social History).

materialism."[73] This assertion must, I believe, not be seen as an act of political conformity even if in the theses he presented in Hartmut Zwahr's Working Circle for Social History in Leipzig on November 1, 1989,[74] a week before the opening of the Berlin Wall, he no longer used the term historical materialism. He continued to warn against one-sided microhistorical research into the *Alltag* that neglected the link with the "'great' social and societal processes," but at the same time warned against the proclivity of GDR historians to submerge the subjective in empty generalizations.[75]

It is significant that Hartmut Harnisch, born in 1934, came to economic history after completing degrees in geography and archival sciences. From 1959 to 1973 he was attached to the Central Archives in Potsdam before joining the Institute of Economic History. Like his colleague Hans-Heinrich Müller, he concerned himself with the role of the Prussian bureaucratic state in facilitating the emergence of a modern capitalistic agriculture under aristocratic auspices.[76] The old Marxist stereotype of an unqualifiedly feudal Junker class gave way in his work to a much more qualified picture of a Prussian monarchy which through its bureaucracy carried out a revolution from above which left the aristocracy intact but created a modern economic order. The selection in this volume portrays the outlook of peasants in a period of transition in the late eighteenth-century period when on the one hand they still remained subordinated in an older feudal pattern that required submission and obedience, while on the other hand they developed attitudes and aspirations in accordance with the new situation created by an emerging market economy.

Hans-Heinrich Müller, born in 1926, brought similar concerns to the study of mentalities in a Prussian countryside moving toward capitalism within an aristocratic and bureaucratic context. Müller has dealt at depth with changing technologies in the countryside and has been centrally involved in the edition of a three-volume *History of Productive Forces in Germany*.[77] His colleague Jan Peters criti-

---

73. "Alltag im Aufbau," (above, n. 68), p. 185.
74. Mimeographed paper.
75. Ibid.
76. Hartmut Harnisch, *Kapitalistische Agrarreform und industrielle Revolution. Agrarhistorische Untersuchung über das ostelbische Preußen zwischen Spätfeudalismus und bürgerlich-demokratischer Revolution 1848/49 unter besonderer Berücksichtigung der Provinz Brandenburg* (Berlin/GDR, 1984).
77. Rudolf Berthold et al., *Geschichte der Produktivkräfte in Deutschland von 1800–1918*, 3 vols. (Berlin/GDR, 1985). Müller shared responsibility for the second

cized the work for failing to consider the "subjectivity of the 'productive force' man."[78] While the criticism may be justified for this volume, it hardly applies to Müller's overall work. Müller's conception of productive forces at all times went beyond the instruments of production to see in science itself a major force in revolutionizing production, and science in turn was rooted in culture. Müller thus in 1975 published a study on essays submitted to the Prussian Academy of Sciences in the eighteenth century in competition for its prizes on agricultural economics.[79] The background of the essay in this volume is the emergence of a capitalist market economy in the countryside with the accompanying advances in agricultural technology. Yet the focus of the essay is not the impersonal objective processes but what the owners of the crown estates, who here appear increasingly as modern farmers rather than as traditional Junker, make of the new opportunities. At the same time Müller looks at their life style, their family relationships, the education they receive and give their children, their circle of friends, and the social and professional associations to which they belong, as these could be reconstructed from the sources.

Jan Peters's work is even more clearly focused on what since the early 1980s he has called *Alltag* and *Mentalitäten*. Born in 1932, he emigrated with his parents to Sweden during the Nazi period, returned to Berlin in 1946, and studied and then taught history before joining the Institute for History at the Academy in 1964. Several of his studies have dealt with individuals, such as the edition of testimonals by dairy farmers in Mark Brandenburg on which he cooperated with Hartmut Harnisch. His own theoretical position as it relates to the history of mentalities is well stated in his examination of *Annales* methods, which he published in early 1989.[80] Like Jürgen Kuczynski's "Prefatory Remarks" to his *Alltagsgeschichte*, but with a much clearer formulation of what these methods mean for the historian of mentalities, he points here to the need of historian in the GDR finally to take cognizance of what social and cultural historians are doing in the West and thus overcome the

---

vol., which, covered the period 1870 to 1917–18 and appeared in 1985. Vol. 1 had not yet appeared in the summer of 1990.
78. See Peters, "Alltag im Aufbau" (above, n. 68), p. 186.
79. *Akademien und Wissenschaft im 18. Jahrhundert. Agrarökonomische Preisaufgaben und Preisschriften der Preußischen Akademie der Wissenschaften* (Berlin/GDR, 1975).
80. See Jan Peters, "Das Angebot der 'Annales'," (above, n. 67).

Introduction

poverty of their own history. Peters does not repudiate historical materialism but rather recognizes what historical materialism and the *Annales* have in common: an affirmation of the interrelatedness of consciousness and culture with economic and social structures. This perspective also characterizes the selection in this volume on church seating as well as a related essay on Sunday law infractions in the seventeenth- and eighteenth-century countryside.[81] Religion is seen here less as an attitude toward life than as a reflection of internalized conceptions of social status and social control. At the same time, Peters, as becomes clear in his *Annales* article, is aware of the extreme complexities that accompany the interaction of economic and political substrata and of mentalities. Peters calls for a more critical approach to the sources than that practiced by both historians trained in Rankean methods of source criticism and the majority of Marxist historians who too easily take the document at its word. He agrees with Lucien Febvre that "the manifestations of life in past epochs always appear in a hidden [*verschlüsselt*] form so that not the source but its symbolic significance must be grasped." This for him requires a much more subtle methodology, akin to that of the anthropologist, which recognizes the radical otherness of epochs and past experiences.[82]

Helga Schultz's research and publication career similarly reflects the very profound transformation that social history has undergone in the GDR in the last fifteen years. Born in 1942, she was trained and later taught at the University of Rostock, next to the Institute for Economic History in Berlin the most important center for the study of rural history. Her doctoral dissertation investigated the transformation of artisan crafts in the Mecklenburg countryside under the impact of emerging capitalism.[83] In 1987 she published a social history of Berlin from 1650 to 1800 based on mass data drawn from church registers in two parishes in Berlin in that period, including 150,000 entries that were processed by computers in the first such major project in the GDR.[84] Schultz is very much aware of the Western literature, particularly in historical demography, which constitutes the starting point of her study. She wanted to write

81. "Sonntagsverbrecher in Schwedisch-Pommern. Zur bäuerlichen Belastbarkeit durch Arbeitsrente," *Jahrbuch für Wirtschaftsgeschichte* 4 (1982): 89–113.
82. See Jan Peters, "Das Angebot der 'Annales'" (above, n. 67).
83. *Landhandwerk im Übergang vom Feudalismus zum Kapitalismus. Vergleichender Überblick und Fallstudie Mecklenburg-Schwerin* (Berlin/GDR, 1978).
84. *Berlin, 1650–1800. Sozialgeschichte einer Residenz* (Berlin/GDR, 1987).

a comprehensive history of a defined locality from a Marxist perspective, an *histoire totale* in the *Annales* sense, giving weight to long-standing demographic structures and to the political and social processes that led to their transformation. She thus touches on population and disease but also on the consolidation of absolutism in Brandenburg-Prussia, the effect thereof on the transformation of Berlin from an artisan to a manufacturing economy, and the subsequent changes in social stratification. She then deals with various aspects of life, clothing, food, marriage, households, children, sexuality, infanticide, forms of punishment, entertainment, changes in life styles, all in relation to social structure. Finally the Enlightenment is given its due with a discussion of intellectuals and of the emancipation of Jews and women. In her subsequent book, published in the following year, an annotated edition of the chronicle of a Berlin master baker in the eighteenth century, *Der Roggenpreis und die Kriege des großen Königs*[85] (The Price of Rye and the Wars of the Great King), she proceeds from macro- to microhistory to place the baker into the concrete setting of Berlin in this period of transformation under Frederick II. Here the broad categories that define Schultz's larger book on Berlin yield to an account in which the life of Master Baker Johann Friedrich Heyde, his family, his place in guild and society as a respected craftsman and burgher occupy a central place and offer a key to the understanding of eighteenth-century Berlin. The article included in this collection was a lecture delivered in 1987 at the State University of New York at Buffalo before the publication of the book.

Dietrich Mühlberg's selection on leisure time among Berlin workers around 1900 reflects an approach to the history of working-class life akin to that of recent writings on the history of common people in the West as practiced in the history workshops already mentioned. Not archival documents, but oral and written testimonies of common people and tangible artifacts such as furniture, clothing, mementos, and photographs reflecting tenements, garden colonies, and leisure activities constitute the key sources. Mühlberg, born in 1936, studied philosophy, German literature, and art history and was called to the Humboldt University in the mid-1960s to develop the field of *Kulturwissenschaften* with a specific focus on the German working class. In a sense all of the selections we have presented so far have been professional in a

---

85. (Berlin/GDR, 1988).

narrow sense, written by historians for historians. Mühlberg's work is aimed directly, as is the work of the history workshops in the West, to creating a sense of identity and heritage among a broad public. It is surprising how few scholars in the GDR, which viewed itself officially as a workers' state, in fact did this. Despite its identification with the classical German working class, the publications by members of Mühlberg's circle carefully avoid fitting the history of the workers into the Marxist theory of immiseration. In fact what distinguishes the history of everyday life by all of the writers included in this volume from many of the historians of the *Alltag* in the West is the total lack of any longing for a precapitalistic, preindustrial past, although there is perhaps a romantic nostalgia for an urban working-class culture that has disappeared. Indeed the picture drawn of working-class life in the transition from countryside to metropolis, from small workshop to factory, is one in which working people were liberated in many ways from the narrow confines of a premodern world. It will be interesting to see to what extent this optimism will survive the integration of the GDR into a capitalist society.

The work of Sigrid Jacobeit, born in 1942, similarly reflects the transition away from a history using the historical and social categories and also the political language common in GDR writings fifteen years ago to a much more open and many-sided approach. Sigrid Jacobeit has been one of the few historical folklorists who has devoted attention to the everyday experiences of women. She also began relatively early to deal with the condition of women in the Third Reich. Her dissertation dealt with the life and work of women servants on farms during World War II and examined Nazi attitudes toward women and class. A subsequent study dealt with the fate of women in the Nazi concentration camp Ravensbrück.[86] Her oral history work, like the Ravensbrück book, concentrated largely on women who fitted the GDR conception of working-class and Communist party resistance. The captions she wrote for the photographs to be included in the three-volume illustrated history of the everyday life of the German people, based on Jürgen Kuczyinski's history of the German *Alltag*,[87] which she

---

86. Sigrid Jacobeit et al., *Kreuzweg Ravensbrück. Lebensbilder antifaschistischer Widerstandkämpferinnen* (Berlin/GDR, 1987)
87. *Illustrierte Alltagsgeschichte des deutschen Volkes*. Vol. 1, 1550–1810, appeared in Berlin/GDR, 1986; vol. 2, 1810–1900, in 1987; the concluding volume, 1900–1945, has not yet appeared.

is writir with her husband, Wolfgang, still reflect little break with orthodox GDR perspectives on society and politics. In contrast, the article in this volume, completed in 1989 before the events of the fall, represents a remarkable liberation from the older conceptions and language without surrendering her concerns for everyday life and forms of social and political oppression. She combines a chapter in the history of the life of women, largely neglected in the GDR until now except in a narrow political context, with an examination of anti-Semitism as it manifested itself in the everyday life of clothing and fashion.

The final selection goes the furthest in freeing itself from traditional Marxist patterns of thought, as they were understood in the GDR, without losing the sense of the concrete social and even material conditions within which intellectuals live. Here Zwahr deals with individual fates, the hopes, worries, and suffering, personal and professional, of two early nineteenth-century scientists, Carl Friedrich Gauß and Moritz Wilhelm Drobisch. The personal testimonies of these men, as reflected primarily in their correspondence, are the sources for this study. But this is not intellectual history in the traditional sense of a history of ideas of great men. Rather it is an attempt to recreate the concrete world in which these two scholars lived, not only their thought processes and scholarly aspirations but also the tangible world of communication and transportation regulating interchange between scholars and the biological factors of disease and childhood deaths that set the limits within which the scholars could pursue their work and careers.

Zwahr's essay on the young academics points in a direction very different from the older, empirical social history he had introduced into the GDR a decade earlier in his book on the formation of the Leipzig working class. As these lines are being written, a new work by Hartmut Zwahr, *Herr und Knecht*, which has been in preparation since 1982, is about to appear.[88] The book had been accepted for publication in 1988 and was in press at the time of the revolutionary events in the fall of 1989. It is an indication of what could be written and published in the GDR in the 1980s despite the restrictions that were in force. It also reflects new interests and directions in historical thought in the GDR that well preceded the collapse of the regime. The title, approximately translated as *Master and Servant*, is taken from Hegel's examination of the dialectical

88. Urania Verlag, Leipzig.

relationship between master and servant that results in the master himself being transformed and misformed by the power he exerts and the obedience he expects. Beginning in the period of the formation of feudal patterns of personal dependence in the ninth century and continuing to the consolidation of a market economy in the sixteenth, Zwahr examines various forms of the master-servant relationship in their historical context. The book is richly illustrated, not only to fulfill an aim, sadly neglected by professional historians in both German states, to write scholarly history, as the French and Italians have done in our days, so that it can be read by a broad public, but also because these illustrations constitute for Zwahr, as they did for Marc Bloch, a major source for the study of past attitudes and behavior.

5. After the Fall of the GDR

At the time of writing in July 1990, the situation in historical studies in the GDR is very much in flux. The central institutions of control were either abolished, like the Council for Historical Studies, or lost their controlling function, as did the Institute for Marxism-Leninism and the Academy for Societal Sciences, which, as we mentioned above, were reorganized. Elsewhere the old institutions at the Academy of Sciences and the universities remain intact, although the future organization of both, and in the case of the academy its very existence, are in doubt. Remarkably few changes in personnel have occurred yet, although plans for massive dismissals have already been announced. The Historians' Association of the GDR reconstituted itself in February, repudiated the past instrumentalization of scholarship, without fully freeing itself from the traditional phraseology, and continued for the most part to be directed by the persons who until then had occupied key roles in the profession. Younger historians early in 1990 formed the Independent Historians' Association with a scathing attack on the political and intellectual integrity of the historical profession in the GDR.[89]

89. See "Aufruf zur Bildung einer Arbeitsgruppe unabhängiger Historiker in der DDR," January 10, 1990. The group constituted itself as the Independent Historians Association in the GDR on April 21, 1990. The Historians' Association of the GDR dissolved itself in December 1990.

The question naturally arises what will remain of forty years of historical scholarship in the GDR. It is important to stress once more that an important opening in historical studies had occurred well before the fall of 1989. The events in the Soviet Union and elsewhere in Eastern Europe since 1985 could not be ignored. The gulf between what was written and said officially and what was discussed privately and among colleagues and students, which predated perestroika, grew immensely. As we saw, in the last fifteen years, and particularly in the last five years, such issues as that of the popular support of National Socialism and of the complexities of the anti-Nazi resistance,[90] which went beyond the older doctrinal explanations, were cautiously approached.

Historical studies in the GDR thus were by no means a "desert," the term West German critics recently used to describe the scholarly and scientific scene in the GDR.[91] This, as we have noted, was even less true of the writing of social history than of political history, and even there, once the ritualistic obeisance to the Marxist-Leninist phraseology was discounted, there remained, as Andreas Dorpalen already noted, much solid scholarship. That the old taboos, particularly in the sensitive areas of history since 1917, could not be maintained was now recognized as even historians who had always supported the positions of the SED called for "a radical renewal of the historiography on the GDR"[92] and an honest confrontation with the past. Even the attempts of the last fifteen years to come to terms with the "whole heritage and tradition" of the German past now seemed outdated as the state that had sought unsuccessfully to build on this past to gain legitimacy in the eyes of its population passed out of existence.

In contrast, the social and cultural historians whom we have singled out in this volume took up the themes and problems that had become concerns of scholarship internationally much sooner.

90. See, e.g., Werner Bramke, "Der unbekannte Widerstand in Westsachsen, 1933–1945. Zum Problem des Widerstandsbegriffs," *Jahrbuch für Regionalgeschichte* 13 (1986): 220–53.
91. See the article "Im Mittelmaß Weltspitze" in *Der Spiegel*, July 23, 1990, pp. 136–41. See, however, the much more balanced assessment of historical studies in the GDR in the "Declaration of the Association of the Historians of Germany [the West German association] on the Present Situation of Historical Studies in the GDR," June 30, 1990, and the article by its chairperson, Wolfgang Mommsen, "Hilfe statt Beckmesserei. Die deutschen Historiker zur Lage der Geschichtswissenschaft in der DDR," *Frankfurter Allgemeine Zeitung*, July 13, 1990.
92. See Heinz Heitzer, "Für eine radikale Erneuerung der Geschichtsschreibung über die DDR," *Zeitschrift für Geschichtswissenschaft* 38, no. 6 (1990): 498–509.

Admittedly, until November 1989 they occupied a relatively marginal role in the historical establishment of the GDR because their
work did not serve the aims of the state and party as directly as did
the history of politics. From Jürgen Kuczynski to Jan Peters and
Harald Dehne,[93] they were painfully aware of how social and
cultural history in the GDR lagged behind international scholarship. Ironically Marxism, at least in its dogmatic Leninist form, had
delayed or even prevented the development of an empirical historical study of society and culture or of the everyday life of the broad
population that should have been part of a Marxist history. In the
West at least since the 1960s, the borderline between a Marxist
historiography renewed by critical theory and a critical non-Marxist
history of society and culture became increasingly fluid as historians
turned away from a preoccupation with anonymous structures to an
increasing concern with the elements of culture and conflict that
shaped the everyday experiences of common people.[94] These were
also the concerns of the small number of historians in the GDR who
began to approach the problems of the *Alltag*.

The events since November 1989 intensified discussions that had
already been underway, as were projects of inter-German and
international cooperation.[95] But at least until 1987, and largely even
after that, the majority of historians in the GDR, who did not

93. For Kuczynski, see selection 1, "Prefatory Remarks," in this volume; Jan
Peters, "Das Angebot der 'Annales'," (above, n. 67) and Harald Dehne, "Aller Tage
Leben," (above, n. 68).
94. On discussions on social history and *Alltagsgeschichte*, see Harald Dehne's as
yet unpublished report, "Sozialgeschichte/Alltagsgeschichte – woher, wohin?" – an
exchange of opinions at the Institute for Economic History at the Academy of
Sciences of the GDR on January 10, 1990. Harald Dehne also played a key role in the
formation of a history workshop in East Berlin in December 1989.
95. Such projects included the participation of GDR scholars in the comparative
project on the European *Bürgertum* in the nineteenth century at the Center for
Interdisciplinary Research at the University of Bielefeld in 1976–77 and the invita-
tions by the Max-Planck-Institut für Geschichte to social historians from the
Academy of Sciences of the GDR, particularly the Institute for Economic History,
and to social historians from the Karl-Marx-Universität in Leipzig. Since 1982
historians from the GDR regularly participated on panels with West German and
American historians at meetings of the German Studies Association in the United
States. Western scholars were increasingly invited in the 1980s to lecture at the
Academy of Sciences in East Berlin or at GDR universities. An exchange of visiting
professors for a whole semester between the Universities of Bielefeld and Leipzig
was initiated in 1989 before the events of November. However, participation was
generally restricted to established scholars with regular permission to travel (*Reise-
kader*). Only recently were younger scholars permitted to participate as they were in
exchange initiated in 1987 between the Department of History at the State University
of New York at Buffalo and two of the historical institutes at the Academy.

belong to the privileged group who could travel, and particularly the younger scholars, were excluded from such contacts and indeed had only very inadequate access to foreign literature, which was often absent in libraries not granted hard currency for acquisitions. It is to be expected that this isolation will now be overcome as historical writing in what has been the GDR will become part of the international scholarly community.

The question arises of what will remain of historiography on the old territory of the GDR that reflects the character of historical studies in that area until now. With the collapse of the SED regime, the ideology of Marxism-Leninism with its specific linguistic code will come to an end, although this will not necessarily mean the end of Marxism as an intellectual tradition. This residue of Marxism may also characterize the historians whom we have presented in this volume. Like historians elsewhere they have increasingly turned from social structures to culture and experience; but beginning originally from a perspective derived from a historical materialism, they have maintained a greater awareness of the links binding culture and society than many contemporary historians in the West. November 9, 1989, did not mean the end of the history they have been writing. Particularly the historians we have selected, but others too, moved away in the last decade and a half from the dogmatism imposed on them. They also became increasingly aware of scholarship elsewhere and began to participate in a discourse extending beyond the borders of the GDR. The demise of the regime will, however, mean a liberation from the restraints on free research and communication that marked the GDR throughout its history.

JÜRGEN KUCZYNSKI

The History of the Everyday Life of the German People

Prefatory Remarks to Volume 1

We Marxists still have great strides to make even in our historical descriptions of class struggles.* If we look at the way in which Karl Marx depicted these struggles, especially those in France around the middle of the nineteenth century, it is apparent how carefully he analyzed the tactics and strategy of all the relevant classes and social strata. However, in our own depictions of class struggles, we still often focus our entire attention just on the oppressed. As a result, there appears to be only one class that is doing all the struggling. But how can its tactics and strategy possibly be accurately assessed when those of its adversaries are only roughly outlined, if not omitted altogether?

Most importantly, the class struggles are not seen to rouse any creative responses in the ruling classes. The manifold defeats suffered by the oppressed go down in our histories simply as unfortunate occurrences, although the victorious ruling classes often analyzed their victories and drew conclusions that played a key role in the future progress of society. When the ruling classes failed to do this, or drew the wrong conclusions, then their victories – for instance that in the German Peasant Wars of 1525 – could have disastrous consequences, not only for those who lost the class struggle but for the society as a whole.

We pay too little heed as well to the fact that there were two kinds

* from Jürgen Kuczynski, *Geschichte des Alltags des Deutschen Volkes* (Berlin, 1981), vol. 1, *1600–1650*, pp. 12–15.

of class struggle, so to speak: the momentous battles and the quiet, everyday struggle. Marxist historiography tends to concentrate on the momentous battles, of which it then even takes a one-sided view as noted above. Very little has been written about the everyday struggle, whether the reluctant toil of slaves and their small acts of sabotage or the diminished productivity of peasants carrying out their feudal obligations as compared with their efforts on their "own" fields. All we hear about, by and large, are the momentous battles waged by the oppressed, their transcendent victories and stunning defeats. Too little is said about the everyday life of those who carried on the class struggle.

Thus we return to our central theme. We still lack a history of the German people, of the laboring classes, just as all other countries lack a coherent history of their peoples. The disregard for routine class conflict is evident in the manner in which we Marxist historians depict the struggle – while bourgeois historians now do their best not to mention it at all! Not only is the everyday class struggle not portrayed, but the everyday life in general of the common people is overlooked. This is especially true of the peasantry, whose fate of a life of grinding rural poverty was shared by the vast majority of the German people until late in the last century.

A discussion in *The Times Literary Supplement* (February 3, 1978) of the fourth volume of *Histoire de la France rurale* by Michel Gervais, Marcel Jollivet, and Yves Tavernier begins in the following way:

Like literacy, history is an urban art. It is not surprising that it has largely ignored folk and activities beyond its ken. The country could serve as backdrop, its inhabitants faceless, sunk in savagery and routine. Civilization was urban, like citizenship and civility; so were politics, the affairs of the polis, which history was about. The record of men acting in time ignored the vast majority of mankind. La Bruyère's surprise was only part-feigned, to see the dark wild animals who tore the earth open reveal a human face. Noble savages overseas could provide inspiration; real savages nearer to home evoked disgust, or fear, or pity.

This took a long time to change. Romantic historians treated "the people" in terms of city folk. Even Michelet, who tried to look beyond it, confessed that country people remained closed to him. The city poor imitated their betters, wore their cast-off clothes, spoke (or tried to speak) their language. The peasants lived in other cultures with other ways, it seemed. Their speech was different – in the late nineteenth century a traveller near Limoges, not 300 miles from Paris, could not

make himself understood. And they did not write. Records of peasant
life and ways, when they exist, are second-hand: officials, publicists,
priests, explorers, tourists and exiles from the city speak of and sometimes for them. The literate peasant himself ceased to be a pea˙ ˙ ˙t, spoke
a different language, handled a different culture with a convert's zeal,
despised or forgot his own. The documents on which traditional historians fed were absent. In France, while most of its inhabitants lived on
the land or very close to it, few cared what they were about.

What is said here about France holds more or less true for all the
countries of Western Europe at least. So far as Germany is concerned, there has always been ever since the end of the eighteenth
century the occasional person (though not historians!) who has
taken an interest in everyday peasant life, from Justus Möser to
Immermann and Wilhelm Riehl, from Jeremias Gotthelf and Karl
Lamprecht to Wolfgang Steinitz in our own time. However, very
little systematic research has been done, even in the period following the Second World War, apart from specialized studies of such
topics as proverbs and sayings or customs that today strike us as
rather quaint.

However, a school of French historians, presently led by Fernand
Braudel, has been researching for decades the everyday life of the
people in the more remote past, including both comprehensive
studies and thematically or geographically limited studies. Some of
their works, such as Braudel's *Civilisation matérielle et capitalisme,
XVe–XVIIIe siècle* (1967), require vast interdisciplinary knowledge
and a flair for imagining and depicting concrete details. Others
require years of detailed study of documents and tales, parish
registers, and physical remains (whether household utensils,
clothes, or buildings) of a village or a quarter of a city. Their
objective always remains to circumscribe the everyday life of the
people or of particular classes or social strata: what they ate, how
they dressed, how they lived, what generally concerned them, what
their working lives were like, how they rested and slept, what
happened to them when they fell ill, in what social circles they
married, whether they moved from one place to another or stayed
put, what the relationship between children and parents was, what
happened to old people, etc. In other words, what concerns these
historians most is truly just the daily lives of these people. In this
they are taking up ideas of French historians and historical philos-
ophers of the second half of the eighteenth century (even la

Bruyères in part) and of Scots of the same period. To some extent they are the successors of those who wrote the international travel literature of the last five centuries that has portrayed the everyday life of the people in "faraway" lands, superficially in some cases but also quite thoughtfully in others. Historians of everyday life have yet to thoroughly analyze and consider this travel literature.

It is curious that educated travelers to faraway countries have tended to take a deeper and more progressive interest in the local population than historians have in their own people.

We Marxist historians will of course see some things differently than the Braudel school, but not very many. The salient fact for us is that these historians study the everyday life of the people (though "of course" not in the present).

So long as we fail to take up this same kind of approach, we will never write a real history of the German people. It will certainly be years before we have sufficient information. If we visit our museums in order to gather material, we find festive outfits belonging to wealthy peasants of the feudal era, but no everyday clothes; we find equipment from the homes of wealthy peasants, but none of the straw on which so many had to sleep. When we read the documents that have been preserved, we can discover what the peasants had to turn over to their feudal lords in kind (either in money or direct labor), but not what they themselves ate and how they prepared it. What goes through the minds of people who go to church to hear mass in a language they cannot understand?

In so far as these matters are concerned, we know far more about the everyday life of workers in the nineteenth century and later in the capitalist era, though much more could still be uncovered if our historians oriented their research more in this direction. However, our history books take scarcely any notice of the fair amount of knowledge that we already have accumulated. Some specialized studies do exist of course (more in the FRG than in the GDR). There it is, the bulk of the history of the German people – the everyday life of the working class – tucked away in a few specialized papers! What a curious state of affairs in a country that calls itself socialist!

Even today a veteran researcher would still only be able to write another specialized study based on archival research, whether of a certain area, perhaps a village or a town, or of a particular aspect, for instance the average marrying age of apprentices and the social strata from which their wives came. But this is not what I hope to achieve. Such specialized studies are of course necessary and represent an essential prerequisite for a really thorough history of the everyday life of the German people. Can a veteran researcher not perhaps offer something a little more useful? At a time when a history of everyday life is so acutely needed and when we cannot wait another thirty years for hundreds of young scholars to generate sufficient information – at least about the period since the Peasant Wars, the first phase of the bourgeois revolution – can a researcher not offer a survey of at least some aspects of everyday life on the basis of the specialized studies that are currently available? Perhaps he may point out particularly striking gaps in the research, employ his long experience to draw attention to certain situations, and make use of certain materials that are now available but insufficiently well known in order to help lay the foundations for a history of the everyday life of the German people. In so doing, he shall exclude of course the everyday life of that tiny minority of the ruling classes about whom so very much is known, including even the digestive habits and sexual proclivities of the most celebrated of its offspring.

The following volumes are dedicated to this goal.

WOLFGANG JACOBEIT

The Lifestyle and Culture of the Village Population on the Magdeburg Plain during the Emergence of Capitalist Agriculture from the Late Eighteenth Century to the 1830s and 1840s

The Magdeburg plain was one of the agricultural areas in which capitalism developed most quickly and extensively in all areas of life.* This was not an isolated phenomenon, however, but part of the regular pattern by which feudalism was displaced by capitalism. This process took on a particular significance during the first few decades of the nineteenth century in that the capitalist forces of production now became powerful enough (though with some geographical distinctions) to seriously undermine and destroy the feudal forces of production. This occurred in many different ways that became elements in the transition from one great type of antagonistic class society to another.

1. Socioeconomic Conditions

The capitalist forces of production developed more quickly and encountered fewer impediments on the Magdeburg

* taken from Hans-Jürgen Rach and Bernhard Weissel, (eds.), *Bauer und Landarbeiter im Kapitalismus in der Magdeburger Börde. Zur Geschichte des dörflichen Alltags vom Ausgang des 18. Jahrhunderts bis zum Beginn des 20. Jahrhunderts* (Berlin/GDR, 1982), pp. 1–41.

plain than in other agricultural areas of Germany for several reasons: the proximity of the commercial center of Magdeburg as a principle market and reshipment center and the absence of serfdom and demesne dependency of the kind that long continued east of the Elbe. Of course, the "need to provide various fees and services to the estate owners and legal authorities (local princes, aristocratic and non-aristocratic lords of the manor, cities, churches, foundations, etc.)" remained until the agricultural reforms were finally fully implemented. These requirements affected even elements of the rural population who were not peasants. Only the owners of freehold estates were free of both feudal services and fees.[1] However, "farm production for market purposes" was especially well developed on the Magdeburg plain and it provided "a source for the accumulation of money."[2] As a result, feudal services were increasingly replaced by monetary payments, and economic activities became relatively independent of the feudal authorities. At the same time, the replacement of feudal services by monetary rents made it possible to employ more laborers on each farm – "an additional inducement if not a compulsion . . . to market a high percentage of goods."[3] Increased profits also made it possible to purchase additional land, which led to "mounting distinctions in the amount of land owned by the peasant class."[4] If one considers that whole communities of farmers, but also individual large farmers or small landholders who pooled their resources were able to buy out feudal estates or take them over in the form of hereditary tenancies,[5] lease out their own parcels of land, etc., this means that under the specific

---

1. Hainer Plaul, "Grundzüge der Entwicklung der sozialökonomischen Verhältnisse in der Magdeburger Börde unter den Bedingungen der Durchsetzung und vollen Entfaltung des Kapitalismus der freien Konkurrenz in der Landwirtschaft, 1830 bis 1880," in Hans-Jürgen Rach and Bernhard Weissel, eds., *Landwirtschaft und Kapitalismus. Zur Entwicklung der ökonomischen und sozialen Verhältnisse in der Magdeburger Börde vom Ausgang des 18. Jahrhunderts bis zum Ende des ersten Weltkrieges,* vol. 1, pt. 1 of *Untersuchungen zur Lebensweise und Kultur der werktätigen Dorfbevölkerung in der Magdeburger Börde,* (Berlin/GDR, 1978), p. 175.
2. Hartmut Harnisch, "Produktivkräfte und Produktionsverhältnisse in der Landwirtschaft der Magdeburger Börde von der Mitte des 18. Jahrhunderts bis zum Beginn des Zuckerrübenanbaus in der Mitte der dreißiger Jahre des 19. Jahrhunderts," in Rach and Weissel (above, n. 1), p. 123.
3. Ibid, p. 124.
4. Ibid, p. 123.
5. Harnisch says, "There is no doubt that leases for a certain period of time on agricultural land were a typical element of capitalist production and number among many features in the socioeconomic structure of this area that were at odds with feudalism." (Ibid, p. 145).

conditions prevailing on the Magdeburg plain, farmers were largely able to buy out piece by piece the feudal conditions of production to which they had long been subject.

These and similar transformations occurring ever more rapidly on the plain beginning in the second half of the eighteenth century were accompanied by another phenomenon, which Karl Marx described as follows:

The passage from rents paid in kind to monetary rents was not only accompanied by but even anticipated by the emergence of a class of dispossessed day laborers who proffered their services in exchange for money. As this class emerged, more prosperous leasehold farmers became accustomed to hiring and exploiting rural laborers on their own behalf. . . . Gradually these farmers accumulated a certain wealth and transformed themselves into the capitalists of the future.[6]

Marx indicates here – in a point fully confirmed by developments on the Magdeburg plain – that capitalism began to evolve within the feudal order and indeed to such an extent that signs of the dissolution of feudal society were inescapable, even though feudalism continued to set the tone in many spheres of life until the agrarian reforms. As a result, the culture and lifestyle of the rural population were also increasingly marked by transitional forms, though this did not occur of course in absolutely lockstep fashion. The rural population was therefore generally progressive, and the following comment is particularly true of the Magdeburg plain:

To the extent that the peasants participated in the development of the forces of production, they had a revolutionary effect as the most important element in these forces and as the basis of historical progress. They therefore helped to drive history, even though their revolutionary potential was forcibly repressed to a great extent by the reactionary forces of feudalism. The peasants nonetheless made an objective contribution to the emergence of the capitalist method of production.[7]

One of the prime features of this transition process was the mounting social differentiation between village inhabitants and within the

6. Karl Marx and Friedrich Engels, *Werke* (Berlin/GDR, 1957–68), 25:807.
7. Hans-Heinrich Müller, "Zur Geschichte und Bedeutung der Rübenzuckerindustrie in der Provinz Sachsen im 19. Jahrhundert unter besonderer Berücksichtigung der Magdeburger Börde," in Rach and Weissel (above, n. 1), p. 166.

peasant class itself.[8] As has already been demonstrated at length
elsewhere, the "distribution of the means of production in a primarily agrarian society, that is, one that lived largely off the land,
was diametrically opposed to the social structure"[9] on the Magdeburg plain in the period between 1750 and 1800. This disproportion
continued to develop, so that shortly after 1840 farmers accounted
for only 15.9 percent of the village population while the rural poor
(small landholders, cottagers) accounted for 84.1 percent.[10] This
signifies that the class structure that had begun to appear in the
eighteenth century was now fully developed:

> A numerically small but economically powerful stratum of large capital-
> ist farmers who exploited others' labor on a large scale was now fully
> formed. . . . Alongside them was a stratum of medium-sized farmers who
> occupied a middle position between individual producers and small-scale
> exploiters. At the same time, the peasant class also included a broad
> stratum of small farmers extending from small, independent producers
> living off their land to the many types of tiny producers who worked
> primarily as artisans and earned a pittance on the side through farming or
> who earned wages as rural laborers while farming a tiny plot of their
> own. The vast majority of the rural population was composed however
> of landless laborers who lived solely from the sale of their labor.[11]

As capitalism progressed, market conditions caused shifts in these
social strata, especially among the farmers, so that a *Vollspänner* (a
farmer who possessed a full team of horses) with at least four hides
of land could fall to the level of a *Halbspänner* (who possessed only
half a team) with only two hides of land, and the latter could
become a cottager with only one hide of land or less. Upward

---

8. In conscious distinction to the reactionary, romantic views that have appeared
among bourgeois historians, we intentionally avoid here the term *village community*
(*Dorfgemeinschaft*), which falsely implies that a real community still existed during
the period under study. In actual fact, the villages were increasingly divided into
social classes and strata, which had existed throughout the feudal era and which
struggled against one another to defend and establish various rights. What bourgeois
anthropologists called the village community was primarily the community of
peasants that constituted a feudal class both legally and in terms of lifestyle. The very
different communities of the rural poor (as classified by Jan Peters, 1967) were
ignored, as were their mounting exploitation by large- and middle-sized farmers and
the ensuing class warfare.
9. Harnisch (above, n. 2), p. 114.
10. Plaul (above, n. 1), p. 186.
11. Harnisch (above, n. 2), p. 172.

mobility was also possible, though it was very difficult for rural laborers to work their way into the farming class. The comment of one of their fellows in 1806 continued to apply: "The small landholders, cottagers, and tenants live from their labor and depend for their existence on the prosperity of the larger landowners."[12]

The culture and lifestyle in the countryside and within individual classes and social strata can only be understood in the context of the particular socioeconomic situation on the Magdeburg plain. Before we proceed to a more detailed investigation of these matters, it should first be noted that the socioeconomic developments described above resulted from the measures taken in this area after the mid-eighteenth century to release crop and animal husbandry from the straightjacket of feudal conditions. This frequently occurred at the initiative of the farmers themselves (fallow fields planted in summer with fodder and commercial crops, separation of fields, elimination of the pasture rights of great landholders, introduction of new crops and methods of cultivation, elimination of statute labor, etc.), over the objections of the feudal lords. On the other hand, progressive bourgeois leaseholders and even some noble landlords sought to improve and rationalize production in the ways mentioned above and to influence the peasants in this direction. This shows a similarity to the development of capitalist agriculture in western Europe. Even before the actual agrarian reforms began, there was already a widespread tendency to buy oneself free of the feudal services that hindered production and to increase yields on one's own farm by hiring and exploiting outside labor. The result was an accumulation of surplus value that finally led to a substantial change in lifestyles, especially in areas highly influenced by the market forces of capitalist production, as the farming class became increasingly differentiated and the conflict between farmers who owned land and impoverished rural laborers grew more intense.[13]

The French Revolution and its aftermath[14] had a substantial effect on the socioeconomic development of the Magdeburg plain. The introduction of freedom of occupation led to a mounting number of small manufactures, restaurants, breweries, and distilleries in the villages, thus breaking the monopoly of those who previously had held exclusive rights to a particular profession or type of

12. Cited in Harnisch (above, n. 2), p. 113.
13. See first and foremost Harnisch (above, n. 2).
14. Constitution of the Kingdom of Westphalia of November 15, 1807, Article 13.

production.[15] Danneil reports that the quartering of French troops contributed to more general shifts in lifestyle. The customs of saying grace at table and family singsongs gradually disappeared. Since the ringing of bells was forbidden for military reasons, "quiet" funerals became the standard practice. Even "honorable" girls started going to public dances in inns and supposedly even started chasing after men contrary to all traditions.[16] Contacts with billeted French troops must have been intensive even in wealthier circles, as shown by the large numbers of French words that were taken over into the local German dialect, for instance, *Kuntant* (*content*), *kunteröhr* (*au contraire*), *awangk* (*avant*), *orgenär* (*originaire*), *Kujoon* (*cochon*), *Grant malhör* (*grand malheur*).[17] The fact that previously unknown "clear soups" began to appear on the tables of farmers in the Magdeburg plain after the Westphalian period indicates that French influence was considerable. There were probably French cultural influences among the upper social strata already in the eighteenth century, but the French occupation considerably strengthened these influences and extended them to all levels of the population.

Prussian legislation after 1815 sought to reverse much of the social progress that had been made as a result of the French Revolution and its aftermath. The dissolution of feudalism continued, but in tune with the gradual "Prussian way." However, the transition from feudalism to capitalism was unstoppable, a process for which the changes in the socioeconomic structure were largely responsible.

2. Production

The emergence of capitalist forces of production lapping at the socioeconomic basis of the feudal order began to become apparent after the mid-eighteenth century. Work methods, however, were hardly mechanized or even improved at all until the mid-nine-

15. Wilhelm Schulze, *Schönebeck und seine Nachbarorte während der Franzosenzeit* (Schönebeck, 1938), pp. 78f.

16. Johann Friedrich Danneil, *Geschichte des evangelischen Dorfschulwesens im Herzogtum Magdeburg* (Halle, 1876), p. 231.

17. Seeländer, "Vom Bördeplatt," *Montagsblatt der Magdeburgischen Zeitung*, no. 6, 79 (1927): 48; Danneil reports that the field hands liked to play "Ventin" in the pub on Saturday nights, i.e., the French card game "Vingt-un." See Danneil (above, n. 16), p. 433.

teenth century. The traditional "old German" plow with its relatively flat, asymmetrical plowshare, moldboard, colter, and forward wheel support remained the basic implement used in the cultivation of such primary crops as wheat and barley, which were valuable commercial products shipped out of Magdeburg in large quantities. Agricultural tools hardly changed at all before 1800.

One can basically concur in Harnisch's assessment that the predominant agricultural practice was the "improved three-field system" with ever less recourse to fallow fields and stabling and with increased fertilization. This system, still based on feudalism but with some emerging capitalist elements, typifies the transitional nature of the first few decades of the nineteenth century, especially as the planting of fallow fields in the summer facilitated not only the production of animal fodder but also of some commercial crops that were a source of handsome profits, given the proximity to the marketing center of Magdeburg.[18]

The takeoff in agricultural techniques was sparked by chicory root, which was grown in large quantities around 1800 in the Magdeburg area as a fallow-filed commercial crop before being processed in the city into a coffee substitute. The cultivation of chicory root required deep working of the soil, resulting in the first real intensification of tillage. There were no deep ploughs, at first, but large numbers of landless laborers were available to turn up the soil of the feudal lords and of the large- and medium-sized farmers three spades deep. This extensive exploitation of the reserve army of landless and already proletarianized laborers reflected the increasingly capitalistic nature of agriculture on the Magdeburg plain.

These various developments, which had been gathering momentum since at least the mid-1700s and which had been furthered by the French-Westphalian reform legislation, now culminated in a terrific surge in sugar beet production. The impact of this boom during the period under discussion can scarcely be imagined, and it prompted changes in lifestyle that typified the transition to the new, capitalist environment.

The development of the forces of production, especially of deep

18. Heinz Nowak, *Über Erscheinungen der materiellen Volkskunst im dörflichen Bereich der Magdeburger Börde in der Klassengesellschaft* (ms., 1968), p. 25. The agricultural association in Alach near Erfurt discussed the question after 1845: "What is the reason why spade cultivation produces higher yield than ploughs, even though the latter dig just as deep?" *Zeitschrift des landwirthschaftlichen Central-Vereins der Provinz Sachsen* (1847), p. 118.

working of the soil, requires some further discussion, even though this leads us well beyond the 1830s. As early as 1803, Achard had noted the excellent sugar beet harvests on the Magdeburg plain because the farmers here plowed more deeply than in any other province. The development of this approach would only be possible, under the conditions of the time, through the introduction of plows drawn by draft animals with blades set at an optimal depth. Beginning in the 1830s, there were many attempts by artisans as well as some farmers and bourgeois leaseholders to develop such plows. The plow that was finally generally adopted by the 1860s was a steep-bladed plow according to the Ruchaldo principle developed by Behrendt, a master smith from Wanzleben. Thanks to the so-called Wanzleben plow, sugar beet production was free to expand.

It should be noted that it was artisans and farmers who experimented with various deep-cutting plows for some thirty years before the Wanzleben plow was finally developed. It represented a decisive improvement in the means of production, and sugar beet output soared in response to the new, capitalist conditions. This is not the place to examine in detail the history of sugar beet cultivation and the production of sugar,[19] but it should be pointed out that the role played by farmers, landless laborers, and artisans was not limited to improved and intensified farming. Numerous sugar factories were established by farmers (largely wealthier operators but also some smaller people), even though the major role was played by "capitalist proprietors of estates, crown leaseholders, and industrialists, who at least assumed the leading positions in the companies, boards of directors, management boards, etc., and exercised a decisive influence on production and the way in which it evolved."[20] Nevertheless in the 1830s and 1840s, the capital share of farmers and other workers in the relevant joint-stock companies is calculated at up to 80 percent in the areas around Braunschweig and Hannover and in the province of Saxony, where capitalist agriculture through sugar beets was introduced early.[21]

By the 1840s, some farmers and other village inhabitants (though

19. See in this regard, among others, Baxa an Bruhns (with a list of further reading) as well as Müller,
20. Gerhard B. Hagelberg and Hans-Heinrich Müller, "Kapitalgesellschaften für Anbau und Verarbeitung von Zuckerrüben in Deutschland im 19. Jahrhundert," in *Jahrbuch für Wirtschaftsgeschichte*, pt. 4 (Berlin/GDR, 1974), p. 140.
21. Ibid, p. 133.

primarily the commercial middle classes) had become shareholders in the sugar factories concentrated at first around Magdeburg. As such, they were required to deliver their harvest of sugar beets to "their" factory. They also began to lease their land to the sugar beet factories for extended periods and to go over to the monoculture of sugar beets. Others leased sugar beet fields to the factories just for the season and took over the fields again after the harvest. Toward the end of the period under study, the type of capitalist sugar beet farmer began to emerge, increasingly distant from the remainder of the rural population.[22]

The sugar factories in and around Magdeburg employed respectively some two hundred to four hundred people and contributed greatly to the development of a local proletariat.[23] However, ever since 1767 "the bulk of what could be termed an early form of proletariat could be found in Altenweddingen, where War Councillor Gansauge had been granted the privilege of operating a coal mine,"[24] which in 1798 employed forty-five workers and produced 34,440 bushels of coal. Although these coal miners were still listed in the historical records as cottagers, they doubtless belonged, as well as their fellows working in stone quarries, limekilns, and brickworks around 1800, to an early proletariat. They, together with others working in the emerging glassworks,[25] the machine shops founded by Nathusius around 1817,[26] and the pottery and

22. Already by 1840, there was not sufficient space on the fields close to Magdeburg for the mounting number of sugar factories. "In order to meet the demand, the factories rented almost all the farms in the villages of Westerhusen, Fermersleben, Salbke, Dodendorf, Lemsdorf, Klein-Ottersleben, Ebendorf, Olvenstedt, and Barleben. The peasants therefore lived like great lords off their annual revenues of from 2,000 to 5,000 *Taler*. Many sugar factories rented 1,200 acres of land and paid annual fees of 15,000 *Taler*." ("Der Ackerbau in den Landgebleten der Städte," in *Annalen der Landwirtschaft in den Könislich Preußischen Staaten*, ed. Alexander von Lengerke, vol. 7, supplemental issue, pp. 148f.)

23. Cf. among others C.A. Schmidt, *Chronik der Stadt Buckau* (Magdeburg, 1887), p. 106; C. Peicke, *Zur Geschichte der Dörfer Groß Ottersleben, Klein Ottersleben und Benneckenbeck* (Groß Ottersleben, 1902), pp. 103 and 198.

24. Harnisch (above, n. 2), p. 136; Gerhard Wunderling, *Chronik der Bördedorfes Welsleben* pt. 2 of *Unter brandenburg-preußischer Herrschaft. Die Welsleber Feldmark* (Schönebeck, 1935), p. 25.

25. Hermann Kratzenstein, *Chronik des Dorfes Altenweddingen* (ms., n.d.), p. 71.

26. Harnisch (above, n. 2), p. 168. One of the best-known agricultural entrepreneurs in the province of Saxony was Gottlob Nathusius, the son of a small merchant from Baruth. He served an apprenticeship in Magdeburg and later managed a large firm here (manufacturing especially tobacco products). When this firm declined in the early nineteenth century as a result of all the military campaigns, he purchased the cloister of Althaldensleben and the estate of Hundisburg. "Here he gradually

stoneware works founded in Magdeburg[27] around 1780, participated in the rise of capitalism on the Magdeburg plain and thereby
helped to change the lives of those who lived here. The pottery and
stoneware works produced numerous articles for regular home use
that were always on display[28] in order to encourage the population
to purchase them.

3. Social Classes and Strata

a) Farmers

Above the entrance to farm number twenty seven in
Klein Rodensleben was an inscription dated 1817: "May the Economy Flourish." This text could be taken as the byword of socioeconomic development throughout the Magdeburg plain. The
peasant class, though more and more differentiated, played a major
role in this development. This was especially true of freeholders and
large farmers whose annual sales of wheat alone amounted to some
900 *Reichstaler* around the turn of the century, as has been shown
for instance in the case of a freeholder named Wellmann in
Domersleben.[29] When Wellmann died, he left cash savings of over
3,200 *Reichstaler* in gold and of 1,163 *Reichstaler* in silver. He had
also lent substantial amounts to the royal bank and had provided
mortgages to farmers and artisans in his home town and surrounding villages.[30]

---

combined his large agricultural operation with all sorts of industrial facilities for
processing raw materials, such as a sugar factory, a distillery, a brickworks, a
brewery, a mill for grain, oils, and barley, and a porcelain and pottery works. He
thus developed the estates into an exemplary large business." (Karl Bielefeldt, *Das
Eindringen des Kapitalismus in die Landwirtschaft unter besonderer Berücksichtigung der Provinz Sachsen und der angrenzenden Gebiete*[Ph. D, 1910].)

27. Johann Christian Friedrich Berghauer, *Magdeburg und die umliegende
Gegend*, pt. 2 (Magdeburg, 1801), pp. 110f.

28. Ibid, pp. 110f.

29. According to Harnisch (above, n. 2), p. 148, "Krieg reports in relation to
Dreileben, for instance, that many farmers annually sold two hundred *Taler*'s worth
of cabbage in Magdeburg (probably in the second half of the eighteenth century). A
travel report published anonymously in 1791 relates that farmers on the Magdeburg
plain would sell grain, cabbage, carrots, potatoes, and flax in the city every week and
that their wives would sell eight to twelve pounds of butter and one or two shocks of
cheese and eggs. The receipts from this must have been quite substantial."

30. Ibid, p. 150.

Other strata of the peasant class were also quite prosperous on their own levels. In 1808, thirty-four people in Diesdorf had loaned out a total of 29,745 *Taler* to banks, private individuals, and in the form of mortgages. This sum was reached "even though the people naturally concealed quite a lot (from the authorities). . . . Twenty-two of the forty-nine cottagers admit to a total capital accumulation of 10,745 *Taler*.[31] Though only a few examples have been provided, they are all the more instructive if one considers that the peasant law of inheritance in the Magdeburg plain "was intended to preserve farms and land under the unity principle,"[32] meaning that only one child inherited the farm while all the others were owed substantial sums of money that had to be paid off often over decades. It is therefore understandable "that peasant families attempted to reduce the number of their children in order to preserve their wealth. Large farmers [even before 1800] usually limited possible marriage partners for their children to those families able to provide a sizeable dowry."[33] A well-known saying on the Magdeburg plain ran: "Man kann in einen Dâe mêr frîen as sîn lêwe dag verdeinen"[34] (You can woo more in a day than you can earn in a lifetime). In 1836 the writer Marie Nathusius commented in a similar vein: "A real peasant girl marries not primarily the man but the farm."[35]

Farmers in the Magdeburg plain consequently appeared very vain and proud, a characteristic that was often mentioned by contemporary observers and that Harnisch ascribes to their economic independence. Once they had accumulated the slightest wealth, they left all the farm work to their fieldhands and outside laborers. They preferred to spend their time in the local pub rather than on the farm and adopted a luxurious lifestyle.[36]

31. Franz Huschenbett, *Geschichte der Landgemeinde Diesdorf* (Magdeburg, 1934), pp. 44f.

32. Plaul (above, n. 1), p. 176.

33. Harnisch (above, n. 2), p. 148. According to Wunderling (above, n. 24), p. 10, "Marriages between children from different social strata were generally not acceptable. As a result, relatives frequently married one another, primarily in order to preserve adjoining farms and to enlarge holdings. This marrying of relatives spelled the demise of many old peasant families in the village. Many families were completely eradicated in Welsleben, and elsewhere, after first degenerating physically and mentally.

34. Wilhelm Garke, *Geburt und Taufe, Hochzeit und Tod im Volksbrauch und Volksglauben des Magdeburger Landes*, no. 3 of *Veröff. der Gesellschaft für Vorgeschichte und Heimatkunde des Kreises Calbe* (Schönebeck, 1930), p. 56.

35. Ibid.

36. Cf. Harnisch (above, n. 2), p. 152.

b) Village Artisans

Conditions on the Magdeburg plain were rather bountiful in comparison with other agrarian regions in Germany – especially for many peasants during the transition period from feudalism to capitalism – and this necessarily had an effect on a stratum of the rural population that has hitherto been mentioned only in passing but that had a substantial influence on the rural lifestyle and culture: village artisans.

The gradual erosion and destruction of the guild system, especially after the mid-eighteenth century, was an important indication of the developing forces of production in the area of trades and handicrafts. This evolution was especially rapid in areas like the Magdeburg plain where there were greater opportunities for profit than in the cities where the artisans were tightly regulated by guild laws. The lure of increased profits combined with the elimination of many feudal regulations in the Kingdom of Westphalia, and the declaration of freedom of occupation produced a rapid increase in the number of village artisans. The almost stereotypical types of village tradesmen under feudalism – smiths, wheelwrights, carpenters, tailors, and weavers – gave way to a much more variegated system as the number of trades mushroomed in response to the demands of the prosperous farmers and leaseholders on the Magdeburg plain as well as those of the rural proletariat and the poor. According to Harnisch, artisans already accounted for some 20 percent of the total population of the Magdeburg plain around 1800,[37] even though the rural population certainly purchased no small proportion of its manufactured goods from artisans in Magdeburg and other towns.

The foremost new trades that emerged alongside the traditional occupations enumerated above were those of bakers, bricklayers, and cobblers. The building trades also enjoyed spectacular growth between 1778 and 1804 as a result of the construction boom in the villages of the Magdeburg plain. The proclamation of freedom of occupation also prompted a rapid increase in the number of traveling tradesmen such as musicians, organ grinders, harpers, wild animal tamers, marionette and puppet players, tightrope walkers, potion and medicine dealers, and peddlers of printed materials and boot polish, furniture polish, etc. The impact of these traveling

---

37. Harnisch (above, n. 2), p. 124.

tradesmen on village life must have been considerable, not only in respect to the products they made available but also the vast opportunity for political and social influence through printed materials, pictorial broadsheets, etc.

c) The Rural Proletariat and the Poor

The culture and lifestyle of the many landless or virtually landless people living in the villages of the Magdeburg plain also deserve special consideration, which they have already received in extensive research into the socioeconomic development of this area.[38] These strata increased rapidly in numbers due to changes in agricultural conditions, developing industry in the nearby city of Magdeburg, and the incipient mining of coal and salts. The mounting numbers of proletarians and rural poor are a clear indication of the transition to capitalist production. These social strata, though all exploited by prosperous farmers, bourgeois leaseholders, and entrepreneurs, cannot simply be lumped together as a homogeneous group, for they were as highly differentiated and diverse in their behaviors as the strata discussed above.

The most important stratum in so far as agriculture was concerned was the farm laborers working both for wealthy farmers and on the great estates. Following the proclamation of the Farm Laborer Ordinance in the Duchy of Magdeburg after 1789, this stratum became dependent on its employers and worked for them in exchange for cash payment as well as farm produce to a certain extent.

Farm laborers grew increasingly mobile as outside opportunities to increase their wages improved with the surge in chicory root and later sugar beet production and, even more importantly, with the elimination of feudal statute labor thanks to the French-Westphalian edicts. As a result, the Farm Laborer Ordinance of 1789, conceived in accordance with feudal conditions, was increasingly undermined, despite the best efforts of large farmers and estate owners.

In accordance with the capitalist methods of production, monetary compensation was at the economic and juridical core of the new

---

38. Cf. above all Harnisch (above, n. 2), Plaul (above, n. 1), and Rudolf Berthold, "Bevölkerungsentwicklung und Sozialstruktur im Regierungsbezirk Magdeburg und in den vier Börde-Kreisen von 1816 bis 1910," in Rach and Weissel (above, n. 1) (1979).

style of employment, which already predominated in the early nineteenth century. However, wages were so low that a day laborer's entire family had to work in order to survive. These people frequently augmented their incomes by working on the side as artisans or peddlars or by cultivating a piece of land that they owned or leased. Day laborers and similar strata usually aspired most of all to purchase or at least to rent some land. When they could not succeed in this as individuals, they often pooled their resources.

The stratum of the rural poor and proletariat comprised not only people living in local villages but also the seasonal workers who had been moving onto the Magdeburg plain since well before the mid-nineteenth century, when they came to cultivate and harvest sugar beets. The sources contain little information about the number of these seasonal workers who remained in the Magdeburg area and how they influenced the local population. However, by 1750 there was apparently not a single village on the plain in which some "foreign" workers had not settled. Hans Hermann Merbt reported in his *Chronicle of Domersleber*[39] that twelve settlers' villages had arisen on the plain. It is therefore clear that settlers played a significant role in the development of the forces of production on the Magdeburg plain – whether they were farmers, threshers, reapers, or wage earners attracted by their improved legal position.

4. Lifestyle and Culture

The transition on the plain from feudal to capitalist forms of exploitation after about 1750 was apparent in the increasing differentiation of the peasant class and, to an even larger extent, of the village population. The development of the sugar beet industry increased the pace of this differentiation and intensified class antagonisms.

In what follows, we shall investigate how the "traditional" lifestyle and culture of the various classes and strata changed during the transition to capitalism, how new structures emerged, some old structures were preserved, and how lifestyles and culture reflected and responded to the socioeconomic processes at work.[40]

39. Hans Hermann Merbt, *Die Geschichte des Bördedorfes Domersleben* (Ms., Domerslebem, 1956), p. 158.
40. This is not the place to discuss the theoretical question of whether and to what

a) Buildings and Homes

The developments discussed above are visible to this day in the structure of the settlements in the central area of the Magdeburg plain, for instance in the street names of Altenweddingen, which are strongly influenced by the local dialect. The name "Gold and Silver Street," which can be traced back to the late feudal period, indicates that the large farmers lived here, while cottagers and small farmers lived in faraway Little Street. Quite separate from these two neighborhoods was Sow Street, where the poor and the shepherds had their homes.[41] These examples taken from the village of Altenweddingen could be found in other settlements in the area as well. The separation of the various social classes and strata into different quarters of the villages was becoming ever more apparent. This is especially visible in the types of houses they constructed, which was a key element in a style of living based on class.[42] It was also apparent in behaviors, attitudes to events, activities, and disputes over changing the socioeconomic situation.

Whereas large, wealthy farmers felt ever more inclined to build massive homes, half-timbered houses remained popular among medium and small farmers, while pisé-work houses (with walls of rammed earth) dominated in poor areas.[43] The differentiated social structure of the village can be seen most clearly in the size of the

extent elements of culture and lifestyle reflected, in whole or in part, socioeconomic conditions or political events. Before any generalizations can be made, this question must first be studied in several different geographical areas with differing social, economic, and cultural structures.

41. See among others Heinz Nowak, *Bauern und andere dörfliche Schichten in der Magdeburger Börde vom Ausgang des 18. Jahrhunderts bis zum 1. Weltkrieg – Demographischer Aufriß der Bevölkerungsstruktur in einem Agrargebiet, Teil I: 1785 bis 1860* (diss., Humboldt-Universitat, Berlin, 1970); for Altweddingen in particular, see n. 140.

42. Hans-Jürgen Rach, *Bauernhaus, Landarbeiterkaten und Schnitterkaserne. Zur Geschichte von Bauen und Wohnen der ländlichen Agrarproduzenten in der Magdeburger Börde des 19. Jahrhunderts* (Berlin, 1974), p. 29, understands living or style of living as "the sum of all activities carried out at home in order to satisfy needs that are gratified here." Ute Mohrmann, "Untersuchungen zur Entwicklung der Wohnweise und Wohnkultur in den Dörfern der DDR," in Wolfgang Jacobeit and Paul Nedo, eds., *Probleme und Methoden volkskundlicher Gegenwartsforschung. Vorträge und Diskussionen einer internationalen Arbeitstagung in Bad Saarow 1967* (Berlin, 1969), p. 145, describes living conditions, alongside working conditions, as the most important aspect of lifestyle. They provide the sphere in which life is physically restored and reproduced. Although living conditions cannot be exhaustively portrayed by a description of buildings, they did play a major role.

43. Rach (above, n. 42), p. 46.

homes and in the building materials used.[44] In the houses of large
farmers, the rooms began to be rearranged so as to separate the
family from the servants. For instance, the kitchen was moved from
the center of the house to one side so that a long central hallway
could be added.[45] The strengthening social differentiation can also
be seen in the interior fittings of large farmers' houses (doors,
windows, flooring), which, by 1815, were built by skilled joiners
and cabinetmakers, while the lower classes made do with the
services of a simple carpenter or used gypsum, clay brick, or tile
floors instead of "farmer's flooring."[46]

The houses of the large farmers were largely built around 1815
and they are distinguished by a certain solidness. Thereafter, economic developments made it necessary to construct additional farm
buildings, and the housing of large farmers did not begin to catch up
to the evolving styles of the urban middle class until the very end of
the period under study. However, even the homes built in the first
decades of the nineteenth century reveal an increasing need to
appear distinguished and elegant in order to set the occupants off
from the lower social orders in the village.

Since there was usually plenty of room for the family and all its
various needs, the rooms are clearly distinguishable as bedrooms,
children's rooms, and living rooms, as well as the working areas of
the kitchen and the cellar. Open hearth fires were replaced by
stoves. Open chimneys disappeared and full ceilings became standard. An additional warm room, a kind of kitchen-living room, was
consequently added for the farm laborers. Farmers added to the
amenities in their living quarters by installing tiled stoves, rape-oil
lamps to provide a good source of light, tables, chairs, at least one
large cabinet, benches around the stove, chests, and wallpaper.[47]
New types of chimneys made it possible to heat the bedrooms and
children's rooms in the upper story. However, sanitary facilities still
remained primitive.[48]

---

44. Ibid., pp. 27 and 102ff.
45. Ibid., pp. 58f.
46. Ibid., p. 26.
47. According to ibid., p. 62, there were already two carpet factories in Halberstadt around 1840. According to J. Mertz, *Handbuch für die Polizei-Verwaltung im
Regierungs-Bezirk Magdeburg. Nach amtlichen Quellen*, ed. J. Mertz (1860), p. 459,
an edict of the year 1859 warned against the harmful effects of some rugs, drapes, and
blinds colored with a green paint containing arsenic as well as some other furnishings
colored with the same green paint.
48. Rach (above, n. 42), p. 62.

New houses were also relatively rare among the medium-sized farmers.[49] Like large farmers, they initially spent most of their accumulated capital on the expansion of farm buildings. It was not until the middle of the century that medium-sized farmers began to renovate their homes and to employ new construction materials in an attempt to emulate their wealthier counterparts.

After about 1815, there was a rapid increase in the number of houses constructed by the rural poor. Often whole clusters of poor housing arose on open areas in the village, or else their housing was scattered. The housing constructed by the *Neuanbauer* (proletarians and artisans) in the first half of the nineteenth century meant that "the numerical predominance of this social stratum now became quite visible in the housing stock [of the villages]. Since the villages were already quite compact, whole clusters of these small houses were frequently erected on what was the edge of the village, forming virtually a little quarter of their own."[50] The royal building inspector, Hedemann, described this housing as follows in 1850: "The usual plan of these houses is very simple. They consist of a room fifteen or sixteen feet in length and width, a hallway eight or nine feet wide with the heating at the back, and beside this hallway another little chamber some eight feet wide."[51]

The housing of the early agricultural workers, the day laborers, etc., was hardly any different. All this housing was very cramped, and the zone in which the family lived and reproduced itself was not nearly as extensive as it had become among farmers. All domestic life was crammed into the hallway, kitchen, living room, chamber, and the lean-to. Since chimneys were open, the kitchen could not be heated any more than the small chambers. The latter in any case often served as storage areas because the houses lacked cellars. Living conditions were especially miserable in the winter when most life was concentrated in the single heated room, even though much of the space was occupied by beds[52] and possibly by a weaving loom as well.

---

49. According to ibid., p. 15, "the quarters of the 'same farmers' (prior to 1815) can no longer be accurately determined, since this portion of the peasant class" very often collapsed into rural proletariat.

50. Ibid., p. 53.

51. Ibid., p. 60, n. 103.

52. According to ibid., p. 32, "The most important function of this housing for day laborers was to provide sufficient room for sleeping, because more time was spent on sleeping than on any other home activity. Beds therefore occupied most space."

The rural poor also included lodgers who, as capitalism developed in the countryside, were evicted from the houses of farmers and were forced to seek shelter in the already overcrowded housing of other strata of the rural poor. Field hands also counted among the rural poor, though they together with the lodgers differed from the rest in that they had no shelter of their own. Until about 1815, field hands on farms and aristocratic estates slept in the animal stalls; thereafter, they were occasionally assigned sleeping quarters of their own, often over the fodder stall, which also served as a dayroom. Little changed among female servants, who in the late feudal period already lived and slept in their own rooms in the farmer's house.[53]

b) Clothing and Peasant Costumes

"Peasant costumes on the Magdeburg plain reached their apogee early in the nineteenth century: beautiful, sensuous, highly local, delighting in strong colors and yet harmonious, exuding character and a strong feeling for the atmosphere of the plain. The clothing of our forebears had genuine flair."[54] In this passage as elsewhere, the so-called *Heimatliteratur* of the early twentieth century provides extensive descriptions of the peasant costumes in the Magdeburg plain. Very few authors mention, however, that this clothing reflected the socioeconomic developments and the resulting strong class divisions that emerged during the first third of the nineteenth century.

A key factor in the evolution of peasant clothing on the plain was the relative proximity of Magdeburg and its strong commercial ties to the surrounding villages. City fashions therefore exercised a strong influence, whether through direct purchases or indirectly through their sway over local artisans. The accoutrements on wedding dresses and the clothing of wealthy farmers' wives (ostentatious amber chains, silver filigree work, silver buttons, and spangles of all sorts) bore a striking resemblance to those in other areas where capitalism was also progressing rapidly (e.g., Dithmarschen, Danzig Marshes (Danziger Werder), etc.). These pieces of jewelry, intended primarily to convey the wealth of the wearer, therefore have little to do with the folk art with which they were often associated. They were pieces of jewelry manufactured in factories or

53. Ibid., pp. 21 and 56.
54. Richard Hecht, "Über die Volkstracht in den Magdeburgischen Dörfern," *Geschichtsblätter für Stadt und Land Magdeburg*, 42 (1907): 242.

produced by artisans, sometimes in response to specific orders,[55] which soon also served the desires of the less prosperous in town and country for adornment and status symbols.

Although peasant costumes apparently reached their apogee in the first third of the nineteenth century, the following description of the Atzendorf costume shows that it was already highly developed and influential around the middle of the eighteenth century:

> The men's outfit consisted of a long, lined, blue shirt (a type of vest) without pockets or cuffs. Below this was worn a colorful plastron or jabot. On Sundays, a long, black coat with cuffs and lined in red was worn under the blue shirt. This costume was completed by leather pants, grey or white stockings, and buckle shoes. A cocked hat was worn to church, the broad side to the front so that the clasp could be seen. When traveling, a roqueleur was worn, that is, the type of overcoat worn by city folk in the eighteenth century.... The female costume was especially lavish. On workdays, (allegedly) even servant girls wore a red skirt with an ornamental band, a bodice, a blue apron, and a black cap. On Sundays, especially splendid clothing was worn: silk or velvet caps, fine linen mufflers oversewn on the sleeves, silk bodices, half-silk skirts, fine, plain-weave cotton aprons, velvet muffs with gold stitching (a kind of a wristlet), red, woven stockings and cordovan shoes.[56]

Subsequent changes arose primarily from the use of even finer, more expensive materials and from additional adornments and stylish designs from the city. It should be emphasized that these

55. According to ibid., p. 253: "The jewelry worn in the rural areas around Magdeburg bear comparison with the best products of German goldsmiths. The various necklaces, rings, pendants, bracelets, clasps, buckles, jacket buttons, pieces of filigree, etc., demonstrate the loveliest of forms and delightful detail. They harmonize beautifully with the taste and mores of the area. The connoisseur can find real delight in the study of old, peasant jewelry. The most popular and best known pieces were the heavy amber necklaces. Some of the pieces of amber weighed up to 600 or 700 g and represented a considerable amount of capital. Polishers came to the villages at certain intervals and restored clarity to the clouded jewels. Also very popular were necklaces made of "moon-beam pearls."

56. Kratzenstein (above, n. 25), p. 111; see as well Samuel Benedikt Carsted, *Atzendorfer Chronik (1761)*, ed. Historische Kommission für die Provinz Sachsen und Anhalt (Magdeburg, 1928), pp. 98–100. The readiness with which outdated fashions were laid aside and new styles were adopted can be seen in the replacement around 1815 of the tricorn hat by the cylindrical, rough-haired *Timpenhut* with a bent brim. In the Neuhaldensleve area at about the same time, a hat with a visor known as a Russian cap became popular. Its origins went back to a uniform cap from the time of the Wars of Liberation (see Eduard Stegmann, *Aus dem Volks- und Brauchtum Magdeburgs und der Börde*, no. 4 of *Magdeburger Kultur- und Wirtschaftsleben* (Magdeburg, 1936), p. 85 and Merbt (above, n. 39), p. 202).

additional refinements, adornments, etc., were largely confined to the holiday outfits of large farmers: the small and medium farmers could not keep pace. They attempted to satisfy their need for status by renting the necessary accoutrements, for wedding costumes, for example, or by making glass or tin copies of the genuine jewelry displayed by the wives of large farmers.[57] When peasant costumes went into decline between 1840 and 1870, the rural poor and even the proletariat were little affected. They had never worn peasant costumes, and if they did wear more festive clothing at all, they preferred the urban suits and styles of the petty bourgeoisie.[58]

An attractive part of female peasant clothing at this time was the hats and head wear, which have been described time and again as "wonders of peasant art"[59] – though they were usually made by milliners residing in most villages. "If she was good at her art, she could attract a circle of customers from miles around."[60]

We know very little about the clothing of the rural poor and proletariat on the Magdeburg plain. Peasant costumes originated among the farming class and remained their sole preserve until the final triumph of capitalism. Proletarians and the rural poor were denied entry into the farming class and were increasingly even segregated from its housing. They therefore had little incentive, let alone financial means, to purchase peasant costumes to wear on special occasions. The rural poor and proletarians were therefore the first people in the villages to wear city clothing.[61]

In regard to the quotation at the beginning of this segment on clothes and peasant costumes, little evidence can be found of the "values" that this clothing allegedly embodied. The main motivation behind peasant costumes was the desire to enhance one's status. The newly wealthy farmers on the Magdeburg plain were no longer actively engaged producing this so-called folk art and influenced it only as consumers who purchased the handiwork of

57. One's social position also determined the materials used. According to Paul Hollop, *Trachten im Allertal. Heimatjahrbuch für den Reg.-Bez.* (Magdeburg, 1924), p. 47, poorer women wore cotton clothes, the wives of medium-sized farmers wore three–quarter silk, and the wives of wealthy farmers wore velvet and heavy materials.

58. Hecht (above, n. 54), p. 243; Stegmann (above, n. 56), p. 77.

59. Cf. Merbt (above, n. 39), p. 204.

60. Merbt (above, n. 39), p. 204.

61. Seen in this way, the fact that only farmers wore peasant costumes was due not only to financial resources but more importantly to class considerations, and it must be understood in this way.

local artisans. The clothing these wealthy consumers preferred was actually increasingly influenced by the urban styles of the upper classes. Artisans and factory owners, on the other hand, strongly encouraged farmers to buy the colorful and expensive accessories for peasant costumes that they produced and thus contributed to the great renaissance in this clothing. Even though peasant costumes reached their zenith on the Magdeburg plain during the period under study, socioeconomic developments had already made them an anachronism.[62] The final flowering of peasant costumes was accordingly driven by prosperous farmers eager to show off their wealth, encouraged by the artisans and merchants who dealt in these articles. In fact, the sugar beet industry was about to deliver the coup de grace to this remnant of the feudal order as well. The abrupt shift in the contemporary perception of peasant costumes – so glorified in the opening quotation – is indicated by the fact that by the end of the century very little of the jewelry and accessories associated with these costumes during the 1830s was still in use on the Magdeburg plain, with the exception of amber necklaces. "The rest of the jewelry met its end at the goldsmith's, who melted it down and turned it into modern items."[63]

c) *Food and Cuisine*

Alongside housing and clothes, food and cuisine are further key factors that help to illuminate material conditions and lifestyles. Food on the Magdeburg plain was generally solid, if not exactly sumptuous. An exception to this rule must be made for the weddings and baptisms of large farmers, primarily for reasons of social status. These occasions have been depicted almost universally as orgies of gluttony and extravagance. With this exception, the food customarily consumed on the Magdeburg plain during the first third of the nineteenth century hardly differed from that in other rural areas. Even the urban influence does not seem to have been especially pronounced, for the farmers still led quite autonomous lives in the early nineteenth century. The few shops and dry goods stores catered primarily to the rural poor, who came from far and wide.

However, wealthier farmers did take advantage of their connections with the city in order to purchase wholesale in the markets and

62. The problems related to folk art have been analyzed in detail in Nowak.
63. Hecht (above, n. 54), p. 254.

shops all those goods that they did not produce themselves but that they considered an essential part of their lifestyle at any given time. These tended to be luxury goods such as spirits, fine *lasijana* tobacco (i.e., from Louisiana), and so forth. Farmers' wives also journeyed to market towns where they sold their wares (while considerably brightening the street scene with their picturesque costumes[64]) and made some purchases of their own, even including bread on occasion. However, during the period under study the villagers on the Magdeburg plain largely retained the old custom of eating a breakfast of porridge or milk soup thickened with flour while sitting at common tables. Coffee was drunk at most on Sunday afternoons, and the Sunday meal was so standardized that the same foods were served in every home in the village, especially stew and dumplings, sauerkraut and dumplings, and in the winter, kale and dumplings.[65] This selection of foods, especially the dumplings, which long remained typical of the plain, would have been impossible without the coke-breeze stove. What was so special about stew and dumplings? Pears, plums, and raisins (= the stew) were stewed with fat, smoked ribs, etc. In the same pot, a kind of yeast cake was then cooked over the stew and the fat in such a way that the pot was surrounded with hot ashes, in accordance with the principle behind the coke-breeze stove, until the contents were cooked. "Dumplings played a major role in households [at the time]. In many villages, they were eaten at every meal, whether hot or cold, with soups or stews, at breakfast or afternoon snack."[66] Apart from dumplings, legumes were also frequently eaten, usually as a thick mash. The extent of their use can be seen in a 1798 inventory from the village of Ummendorf, where the Zimmermann farm harvested for its own use 200 pounds of peas, 225 pounds of lentils, and 300 pounds of beans.[67]

So far as drinks are concerned, a beer known as *Kovent* or

---

64. Cf. Karl Baumgarten, "Damshagen – Bauen und Wohnen in einem mecklenburgischen Gutsdorf (von den Anfängen bis 1945)," in *JfVK*, vol. 16 (rev. ed., vol. 1), (Berlin/GDR, 1973), pp. 142–67, and Ulrich Bauche, "Die Kleidung der ländlichen Händler auf dem Hamburger Markt. Materialien und Gedanken zu Funktionen der Tracht im 18. und 19. Jahrhundert," in *Stadt-Land-Beziehungen*, Verhandlungen des 19. Deutschen Volkskunde-Kongresses in Hamburg vom 1. bis 7. Oktober 1973, ed. Gerhard Kaufmann (Göttingen, 1975) pp. 207–19, in relation to the *Vierländer* peasant women in Hamburg.

65. Hecht (above, n. 54), p. 67.
66. Hecht (above, n. 54), p. 70.
67. Hecht (above, n. 54), p. 71.

Bräuhahn was very popular, whether self-brewed, as was usually the case, or produced by breweries, especially in Egeln. Beer was especially ubiquitous at harvest time.[68]

Even at weddings, meals at first remained very monotonous. Chicken soup and roast pork with rice porridge was the traditional "menu," although it was very nourishing. It took many years before farmers no longer "burned" their teeth on vanilla ice from the city or turned up their noses at meringue cakes with the comment: "We can eat soft cheese at home."[69]

d) Schools and Education

A style of life is influenced not least of all by the education of the various classes and strata. Education played a pivotal role on the Magdeburg plain during the first third of the nineteenth century, and many of the phenomena that have been or will be described cannot be properly understood without an appreciation of education levels.

Essential information about the intellectual achievements of the large farmers on the Magdeburg plain around 1800 can be found, for instance, in the report of a "traveling village preacher":

> The farmers here love to read. In the villages around Magdeburg there are even reading societies, to which much energy is devoted. Now and then you meet very solid, clear-minded farmers for whom I have great admiration. When they have an excellent preacher, they write down the main points of his sermon and later discuss them very intelligently. Newspapers and magazines are read in almost every village, and most of the inhabitants are eager to ponder in their own way the latest political developments. In the restaurants can be found maps of the major cities in Europe, especially those that are mentioned in the newspapers. When a locality is unknown to the farmers, they immediately look it up on the map. In school, the children learn history, geography, and natural science in addition to Christianity, writing, and arithmetic. The teachers in this area are often very educated men. . . . Most schools provide adequately for their teacher, so that he does not have to pursue a second occupation on the side.[70] Many farmers' sons went to school in Magdeburg before

---

68. See among others Huschenbett (above, n. 31), p. 43.

69. Philipp Wegener, "Hochzeitsgebräuche des Magdeburger Landes,"*Geschichtsblätter für Stadt und Land Magdeburg* (1878–79), 13: 225–55; 14: 68–100, 184–222.

70. Other sources report the contrary, as we shall see.

assuming their father's farm or marrying into one. You consequently meet many farmers who think logically and clearly and possess a range of knowledge that you would not expect among their social class. They are eager for contact with people from Magdeburg, which certainly contributes substantially to their knowledge. In addition, they are very attentive, and it is a great pleasure to observe their concentration when you tell them something from the realms of history, geography, or ethnology. Most of them are supportive of religion and contemplation. They take the church service very seriously. During holidays, they spend several hours doing religious exercises. They also encourage their field hands to attend church. The general character of the farmers is good, though some are consumed by sensuality and commit all sorts of misdeeds. The field hands are rough, often crude, and prone to many vices.[71]

This contemporary reporter further states that the farmers on the Magdeburg plain who ran sufficiently large farms that they only directed farm operations and often did not do any physical work not only evinced a surprisingly high level of basic education but also knew how to articulate, apply, and extend it. They enjoyed good educational opportunities because of their higher socioeconomic position. This afforded them an advantage over other social strata, and even other members of their own class, which made it possible for them to provide their children with a good education and, most importantly, to operate their farms in accordance with the most recent scientific and economic principles. It could therefore be said that the stratum of wealthy farmers on the Magdeburg plain was very much "enlightened" in its own sphere and its own times. These farmers were powerful production factors in the development of capitalism, even though their greater knowledge and educational opportunities imbued them with class arrogance.

In so far as education is concerned, contemporary reports vary widely. It is likely that wealthy farmers on the Magdeburg plain were already able by the end of the eighteenth century to hire private tutors, to pay the local minister to provide special instruction for their children, or to send them to a nearby city where the educational system was better. This entire realm cries out for additional research since the educational system can provide important insights into the thoughts and worldview of the working classes and since the question of educational opportunity is evi-

---

71. Franz Huschenbett, "Der Bördemensch," in Paul Baensch, ed., *Heimatbuch des Kreises Wanzleben* (Wanzleben, 1928), pp. 157f.

dently much more complicated than the reports about poor, miserable schools would make it seem.

We should not overlook the fact that educational opportunities for the children of the rural poor and proletariat were much worse than for the children of farmers. First of all, the children of the rural poor and proletariat were forced to miss school while helping their parents in the fields, at least during periods of peak activity, or else while working in factories. They were further handicapped by conditions in their schools, poor teachers, totally unsatisfactory curricula, and the baleful influence of the authorities – for instance during the struggle between the reactionary views of Minister Wöllner and the enlightened concepts of Pestalozzi and the rising tide of his disciples. A few examples will suffice. The widespread saying on the plain "By the Sunday before Easter the children put the books away"[72] is indicative of the fact that children in the villages only attended school on a regular basis in the winter months, beginning in the late autumn. Schooling was so curtailed in the summer months that children only appeared for one or two hours a day, if at all, and occasionally no children showed up for days on end, as in Niederndodeleben in 1809. The authorities were of course concerned and they threatened to punish the parents if their children did not appear at school; but the rural poor and proletariat still felt an overriding need to exploit the labor of their children. School attendance declined further when the sugar beet economy was established and entrepreneurs "employed masses of school children to hoe the soil and thin out the crop, not only during the week but on Sundays as well." This applied as well to the cultivation of chicory root and to spreading factory work.[73]

Teachers on the Magdeburg plain supported themselves from school fees, which they usually collected weekly door to door. Around 1800 the Magdeburg consistorium, which was responsible for these matters, set 100 *Taler* as the minimum annual pay which could support a teacher. "However, 175 teaching positions remained beneath this standard, of which 52 were endowed with an income of less than 50 *Taler*."[74] As a result, there was a high turnover rate among rural teachers in the early nineteenth century.

72. Walther Vorbrodt, "Der Zustand der Schulen im Herzogtum Magdeburg um die Wende des 18. Jahrhunderts," GSLM, 55 (1920): 46.
73. Huschenbett (above, n. 31), p. 77.
74. Vorbrodt (above, n. 72), pp. 41f.

Those who remained were compelled to supplement their earnings by singing at baptisms, writing godparent letters, acting as the bride's messenger at weddings, ringing the churchbells, waking up the farmhands, or singing on New Year's eve, a practice which was little more than begging.[75] All this further weakened a school system that was already unsatisfactory. In addition, people who had not been trained at the consistorium were allowed to act as teachers, for instance, tailors to whom Frederick William I had granted certain privileges in return for carrying out the duties of a teacher.[76]

In so far as the curriculum was concerned, the schools were governed by the old Rural Schools Edict of 1763 prior to the French-Westphalian reforms. It provided for considerable instruction in religion and the catechism, but little else beyond basic reading, writing, and arithmetic. (This can be seen in the original syllabi that are still available.)[77] Around the turn of the century, the influence of the French Revolution began to be felt and the enlightened ideas of Pestalozzi proliferated among teachers on the Magdeburg plain. However, none other than Minister of State Wöllner – who proved so open-minded in agricultural questions – sought "to overcome the Enlightenment by exerting state pressure on the divines and the scholars in order to ensure that Christianity conforming to the creed would be maintained or restored." A review commission of religious instruction in Magdeburg high schools was especially established for this purpose. However, "the review commission did not concern itself with lower-level schools because it knew that there was no danger of the Enlightenment encroaching here."[78]

The extent to which the educational system was changed by the inclusion of the Magdeburg plain in the Kingdom of Westphalia has yet to be determined. However, it is likely that the spirit of the Enlightenment spread more rapidly as a result. For this reason, the new Prussian government was impelled to inquire in 1815 whether

75. .Cf. among others Vorbrodt (above, n. 72), p. 36; Julius Laumann, "Erste Spuren von selbständigen Regungen der Volkschullehrer im Herzostum Magdeburg," *Montagsblatt der Magdeburgischen Zeitung*, 1927, no. 5, pp. 33ff.; Garke (above, n. 34), p. 21.

76. Vorbrodt (above, n. 72), p. 36.

77. Franz Bock, *Geschichte des Dorfes Emden im Kreise Neuhaldensleben* (Neuhaldensleben, 1938), pp. 314ff; Fr. Magnus, *Schulchronik. Historische Mitteilungen über die Entwicklung der evangelischen Schule zu Frohse a. E.* (Berlin, 1881), pp. 22ff.

78. Vorbrodt (above, n. 72), p. 28.

there should be limits on popular education. In the king's view, "there should be no limitations on religious and moral education, but there should be some on education for everyday life." Considerable heed was paid to former Court Pastor Sack, who stated that "in the case of rural children in particular, one should be satisfied with a meager education in keeping with their later position in life as farmers, workers, etc."[79] The king rejected any extension of the curriculum along the lines suggested by Pestalozzi with the words: "One does a person and human society no favor by providing instruction beyond the limits of that person's social rank and occupation, by teaching him things he does not need and by awakening in him needs and desires that cannot be satisfied in his position in life."[80]

However, such views rooted in feudalism were increasingly eroded and resistance mounted on all sides to such measures as the institution of "morality courts" to judge the behavior of the youth, "morality tables" to be displayed in schools, etc. The protests against these measures – including the forced catechization of youths who had already undergone confirmation – reached such a magnitude that journeymen (in Hadmersleben for instance) refused to work with the master artisans; rural laborers moved to other areas; and young men reported prematurely for military service in order to escape catechization. Catechization had lost importance during the Westphalian period, and its restoration was understood by the youth as emblematic of the political reaction and resisted as such.[81]

On the whole, however, there was no containing effort to expand and improve education along the lines advocated by Pestalozzi and the Enlightenment, i.e. studies in a greater variety of fields, improved teaching techniques, and the introduction of a certain amount of musical education, at least vocal music. These tendencies grew even stronger after the mid-nineteenth century when artisan education associations and the first working class associations lent their support. Previously, the rural poor and the rural proletariat had had few opportunities for higher education because they were largely dependent on village schools. These, under the supervision of the consistory responsible in turn to the

79. Danneil (above, n. 16), p. 261.
80. Cited in Danneil (above, n. 16), p. 261.
81. Ibid., p. 273.

reactionary state, taught nothing more than the basics. Improved educational opportunities provided the farming class, with its greater resources, even more institutions where it could seek advice and exchange information about more effective methods and equipment, etc. First and foremost among these institutions were the agricultural associations that arose primarily toward the end of the period under study. Institutions such as the Association for Establishing Agricultural Machinery and Equipment in Magdeburg, founded in 1840, played a major part in the development of the capitalist forces of production. They also concerned themselves with the ever more burning issue of the treatment accorded rural laborers[82] and investigated the possibility of establishing agricultural schools for them.

In conclusion, it can be said that educational opportunities improved for social strata beneath the farming class as the emerging capitalist order made greater demands on them, although their schools long remained very poor and could not be compared with the schools attended by farmers' children.

e) Customs and Morals

Socioeconomic developments also prompted an evolution in the area of customs and morals, changes that were often decried at the time as a decline in standards. The authorities attempted to ensure that religious holidays were celebrated in an appropriate manner and did not become "mere frivolities." Regulations were issued placing limits on the celebration of holidays – a clear indication that field hands and day laborers could not and did not share the attachment of the farmers to religious traditions and to the observance of the Sabbath. The following order was issued as early as 1780: "Since it is contrary to the will of the Almighty that our subjects – especially field hands and laborers – spend the third holiday in idle pursuits such as drinking and carousing, it is hereby ordered that all laborers should be kept working in an orderly way at their usual jobs."[83] For similar reasons, the custom of ringing in the high Christian festivals was abolished as early as 1750, "because

---

82. The *Zeitschrift des landwirthschaftlichen Central-Vereins für die Provinz Sachsen, 1845–1893* provides a unique source of information about further education for farmers that has not yet been exhausted.

83. Br. Haselbach, "Bernburgisches Dorfleben in alter Zeit," *Bernburger Kalender* (1927): 82.

in some places songs were sung from church steeples and masses were celebrated at midnight on high holidays, all of which gave rise to many excesses. Such activities are therefore abolished."[84] The attitude of the rural poor and proletariat toward these high festivals was necessarily quite different from that of the farmers. However, the habitual breaking of the Sabbath by rural laborers was clearly due to the profit motive of capitalist entrepreneurs who considered this supposed day of rest to be a normal working day rather than a time for recuperation. The pastor in Diesdorf commented in 1846:"Year after year, people work on Sundays as every other day in the sugar and chicory factories and on the great plains where the sugar and chicory is grown. Our own village provides hundreds of these workers. They are not only enticed to do this by the need to earn a living; they are also threatened with dismissal if they refuse to work on Sundays."[85]

Although the activities associated in the literature with various annual festivals on Magdeburg plain scarcely differ from those in other areas, the numerous references to the door-to-door begging of poor laborers, teachers, and children do stand out. The rural poor who sustained this custom (for instance at New Year's) thus gave vent to their demands, similar to the reapers at harvest time.[86]

The literature is replete on the other hand with descriptions of the family celebrations of large farmers. Only they could afford to stage the kind of lavish weddings, baptisms, etc. that struck the fancy of our informants and were consequently described at length far more often than the more modest ceremonies of small farmers and the rural poor. Baptisms were so informed by the desire to parade and flaunt one's wealth and importance that a regulation was issued in 1750 ordering "that no one may henceforth give or receive christening presents. Every father of a baptized child should instead ensure that he does no damage to his nutrition through unnecessary extravagance and excess eating and drinking."[87] Such edicts, though often repeated, failed to make much of an impression. Travelers continued to report that "baptisms on the Magdeburg plain are splendid affairs often lasting two days with the wildest music" (1790).[88]

84. Ibid., p. 80.
85. Huschenbett (above, n. 31), p. 78.
86. See among others Wegener (above, n. 69), pp. 247, 251, 387; Danneil (above, n. 16), p. 439.
87. Haselbach (above, n. 83), p. 82.
88. Stegmann (above, n. 56), p. 58.

Marriages were no less magnificent, for instance one occurring in 1763 that was described in the following terms:

We all met at 9 o'clock in the morning at Canon Bredow's, then had breakfast and departed. The wedding could only be compared with that of Gamache in *Don Quichote*. More than 300 people were invited. Immediately after my arrival, I inquired into the provisions of food for such a crowd and was told that there were 42 capons for the bouillon, 36 bushels of wheat for cakes, 150 *Taler*'s worth of carp, 2 cows, 14 calves, 150 *Taler*'s worth of spirits, etc. The bride's trousseau of clothes and linens was worth more than 3,000 *Taler* and her dowry was 14,000 *Taler*.[89]

There were many reports of this kind in the ensuing decades, some even more detailed. Those stemming from the 1820s and 1830s make rather more frequent mention of the rural poor, who were often invited to these wedding feasts and for whom money was sometimes collected. Having already consumed their fair share of cakes at the *Polterabend* held on the eve of the wedding, they were seated at special tables during the wedding feast itself and fed in several shifts. They were usually served a plain rice pudding and allowed to eat their fill, though in contrast to the other guests they were not permitted to take any food away for later consumption. The field hands and servants of the farmer's family were also served a special meal on wedding days. In the 1840s they still ate the same food as the wedding guests – even when the farmer "has the meal prepared by a big-city cook from Magdeburg who usually charges three *Taler* a plate."[90]

The bride's clothing was also very lavish, of course, especially as a single dress rarely sufficed and she usually found it necessary to do three or four different outfits during the festivities. The cost of this bridal array was correspondingly high and around 1800 could easily consume half of the entire profit from the harvest.[91] The features in bridal dresses taken from peasant costumes gradually yielded to modern styles from the city, so that by the 1870s black velvet dresses, for instance, had displaced the older, lighter materials.

Peasant weddings were predicated entirely on money and posses-

---

89. G. Müller, "Der königliche Hof in Magdeburg während des Siebenjährigen Krieges," *Montagsblatt der Magdeburgischen Zeitung* 78, no. 6 (1936).
90. Wegener (above, n. 69), p. 193.
91. Garke (above, n. 34), p. 71.

sions. Marriages with middle-class men or women from the city were already quite acceptable in the first few decades of the nineteenth century. Of considerable importance, alongside money, was a rich trousseau of handwoven and knitted materials. Even maids made every effort "to bring at least one big wooden chest of linens and underclothing as well as a complete bed into their marriage."[92] Finally, funerals were also looked upon as occasions for flaunting one's social standing in the village. The type of ostentation frequently encountered at funerals is intimated in the following edict of 1800: "Since it is customary in some places to honor the corpses of youths and maidens with wreaths and crowns that are displayed in church, they should be placed on the sides where they will not hinder anyone's view or disfigure the church."[93] Until the 1820s, the poor in Magdeburg and the surrounding area were often buried in former pastures or areas where flooding occurred, and their corpses were sometimes exposed by floodwaters or by grazing animals. The lower social strata were not laid to rest in Magdeburg's northern cemetery until 1827.[94] The distinctions in the funerals and burials accorded rich and poor people did not originate in the nineteenth century. An edict of 1750 proclaimed that "the notoriously poor should carry out their corpses and bury them quietly in the evening, without laterns or any burial ceremony."[95] The village notables, on the other hand, were buried in the afternoon with all the customary pomp.

The mounting proletarianization of the rural population as the two basic classes of capitalism emerged prompted not only a stricter differentiation between the classes but also greater homogeneity within each. Large- and medium-sized farmers became part of the village bourgeoisie and, for instance, formed associations for people who had large properties and the concomitant right to a say in local government. In Hadmersleben, for example, wealthy farmers formed an exclusive association through which they annually drew lots among themselves for the fallow fields.[96] The old injunction to help one's neighbor, which had formerly applied to all village

92. Ibid, p. 62.
93. Haselbach (above, n. 83), p. 84.
94. Fr. Tilger, "Die Magdeburger Armenfriedhöfe des achtzehnten Jahrhunderts," *Montagsblatt der Magdeburgischen Zeitung* 13 (1927): 104.
95. Haselbach (above, n. 34), p. 85.
96. Hasselmann, "*Hadmersleben*," in Paul Baensch, ed., *Heimatbuch des Kreises Wanzleben* (Wanzleben, 1928), pp. 240ff.

inhabitants relatively equally, was increasingly thought to apply only to people of one's own social class.

The Brotherhoods of Farm Hands (*Ackerknechte*), which apparently arose after the Thirty Years' War after the model of the guilds and spread throughout the Magdeburg plain, took on the form of official organizations. They played a considerable role in the eighteenth and early nineteenth centuries, before dissolving around 1850 or being replaced by proletarian organizations. The farm servants (*Enken*) were similarly organized. Both these organizations helped to impart a certain stability and coherence to the rural youth. Their main function lay however in gathering together the members of certain social strata for mutual aid and assistance.[97]

Class distinctions also sundered more socially oriented youth groups such as spinning-room associations, small social gatherings, and large and small choirs, when they were not officially divided along class lines. The social gatherings of field hands and maid servants – which arose around 1750 probably as a counterpart to the spinning-room associations that catered more to the children of farmers – may well have been conceived as an exclusively working-class organization.[98] Social clubs did not yet play a pivotal role during the first few decades of the nineteenth century. In the period between 1820 and 1840, Stadelmann points to only eight agricultural associations in the entire province of Saxony.[99] Thereafter, however, they became extremely influential and made a substantial contribution to the development of the forces of production on the Magdeburg plain.

Conclusion

The first third of the nineteenth century was a period of transition between declining feudalism and emerging capitalism, both in general and on the Magdeburg plain in particular. A key feature of this era was therefore the increasing social differentiation among peasants and indeed among all social classes and strata in the

97. Richard Hecht, "Die Knechtebrüderschaften und das Hänseln auf den Dörfern der Magdeburger Börde," *Niedersachsen* 13, no. 3 (November 1, 1907); 45–47; Danneil (above n. 16).
98. Garke (above, n. 34), pp. 50ff.; Wegener (above, n. 69), p. 228.
99. R. Stadelmann, *Das landwirtschaftliche Vereinswesen in Preußen. Seine Entwicklung. Wirksamkeit, Erfolge und weiteren Ziele* (Halle, 1874), pp. 7ff.

countryside. The development of the type of class conflict endemic to capitalism is clearly visible.

The reforms undertaken by the Kingdom of Westphalia expedited this process, though socioeconomic conditions on the Magdeburg plain had begun to evolve in the direction of capitalism as early as the mid-eighteenth century. After the reforms, the fundamental feudal conflict between peasants and great landowners was increasingly eclipsed by the central conflict in capitalism between the rural poor or proletariat and large farmers who tended to integrate into the bourgeoisie. This shift was also visible in the culture and the daily life of the various social classes and strata.

The farming class continued to dominate life on the Magdeburg plain during the first third of the nineteenth century. It also dominated the various aspects of culture and daily life, though the specific manifestations of this also proved transitory as the century unfolded.

HARTMUT ZWAHR

The Genesis of the Proletariat as a Distinct Class: A Structural Analysis of the Leipzig Proletariat during the Industrial Revolution

Foreword

Two reviews written by Jürgen Kuczynski in 1965 and 1966 stimulated my interest in the history of the genesis of the German proletariat as a social class during the nineteenth century.* This book is a contribution to the attempt to provide a complete overview of German classes and social strata within the unfolding historical process. It therefore takes its place in a historical tradition that Ernst Engelberg, Jürgen Kuczynski, and Hans Mottek did much to encourage.

My own research began with an attempt to approach the topic through lists of city addresses, which provide considerable information about the social structure. However, reliance on this source would have artificially limited my study to a kind of social topography of the proletariat and the extent of its social mobility. This would not have sufficed for a topic that required penetrating analysis of the evolution of the proletariat as a class, of the simultaneous evolution of the bourgeoisie, and of the dialectical relations between them. It was not until I analyzed the official records,

* Taken from Hartmut Zwahr, *Zur Konstituierung des Proletariats als Klasse. Strukturuntersuchung über das Leipziger Proletariat während der industriellen Revolution* (Berlin/GDR, 1978), pp. 7–8, 164–76.

registers, and deeds for the years 1827 to 1867 in the Leipzig city archives that I succeeded in getting to the heart of the matter. In all, 1,200 deeds and 850 registry entries were evaluated. From the point of view of the type of source material, deeds and registers are personal documents. They arose as city life in the Kingdom of Saxony grew more complex, and in the case of Leipzig they disclose first and foremost the arrival in the city of more than seven thousand workers who were deprived of all civic rights. The present study is based on this mass of biographic material and the valuable details it provides about the lives of an enormously varied lot of individual proletarians.

Thanks to this material, a typology of local proletarian jobs and occupations was developed, and the internal genesis of a social class started to become visible. Descriptive histories of the labor movement and other sources were also consulted. When all this had been done, the manifold connections and relations between the economic, social and politico-ideological constitution of the working class became apparent.

I began my work in the archives in 1968 and started publishing results in 1971. At the present time, the study is being carried on in the form of interregional comparisons.[1] The response these results have received illustrates the extent to which historians studying the genesis and constitution of the bourgeoisie and proletariat seek international comparisons and are developing new sources. Modern data processing, which could not yet be used for this study, is vastly expanding our ability to evaluate sources and ferret out the facts.

This study is based on thorough statistical analysis. When it seemed appropriate, I included tables summarizing the information gathered from registries, deeds, and various other sources. The position in which working people found themselves was considered only from the point of view of structural history. Biographical details are included in order better to illuminate general or individual aspects of the progression of working people from a so-called workers' estate to a self-confident working class, of the evolution in their thinking from a world of unchanging social estates to modern proletarian class consciousness.

1. Hartmut Zwahr, "Die Struktur des sich als Klasse konstituierenden deutschen Proletariats als Gegenstand der historischen Forschung," in *Probleme der Geschichtsmethodologie*, ed. Ernst Engelberg (Berlin/GDR, 1972), pp. 235–69; idem, "Zur Herausbildung der deutschen Arbeiterklasse. Ein stadial-regionaler Vergleich," Historiker-Gesellschaft der DDR. Wissenschaftliche Beiträge Nr. 13 (Berlin/GDR, 1977).

The proletariat's economic, social, and politico-ideological development constitutes an indivisible whole. Each of these three aspects is studied in a separate chapter, but only because the voluminous source material and the breadth of our inquiry necessitated that focal points be established.

My study of this topic drew to a conclusion in the autumn of 1973. A manuscript ready for printing and derived from a dissertation (B) with the same title was sent to the publisher in 1975. Publications that appeared later could therefore only be noted in passing in both the text and the notes.

Hartmut Zwahr
Leipzig
March, 1978

The Choice of Godparents

The Leipzig proletariat was highly diverse, even in its earliest days. The proximity and mingling of various working-class groups doubtless played an important role in the emergence of the labor movement. However, it is extremely difficult to discover sources that cast light on their vanished structures, and the following analysis is meant only as a first step in this direction. It is based primarily on an examination of the baptismal registers of the Schönefeld parish, which encompassed eleven villages to the east of Leipzig[2] where the city's proletariat came to be concentrated as a result of their proximity to the city and the laying of the Leipzig-Dresden railroad. This study analyzes the choice of godparents in several occupational groups typical of the Leipzig proletariat throughout the Industrial Revolution. No other sources of similar relevance to this study could be found.

This analysis is predicated on the assumption that the choice of godparents in working-class families was no more a matter of chance than in others and that the choices these families ultimately made reveal a great deal about their social origins and surroundings. The short life expectancy of working-class children made the godparents particularly important. Like other classes, the proletariat selected godparents in order to increase the social security of their children and to provide them with additional adult models and

2. Abtnaundorf, Anger, Crottendorf, Neusellerhausen, Reudnitz, Schönefeld, Sellerhausen, Stüntz, Volksmarsdorf, and houses on the road to Volksmarsdorf.

sponsors who enjoyed the confidence of the parents and had an affinity for them for a variety of reasons. These conclusions are supported by the choice of godparents among well-known leaders of the working-class movement in Leipzig.

Let us take, for instance, four members of the Leipzig section of the International Workingmen's Association and cofounders of the Eisenach party: Wilhelm Liebknecht (b. 1826),[3] the cigar worker Friedrich Wilhelm Fritzsche (b. 1825), the joiner and instrument-maker Karl Ernst Seifert (b. 1826), and the bookbinder Wilhelm Taute (b. 1836).

In February 1866 Fritzsche included August Otto (-Walster)[4] among the godparents of his eighth child. In May 1866 Taute along with Fritzsche and Julius Vahlteich became godparents to the eighth child of the Leipzig cigar worker Johann Gotthold Louis Dörfel (b. 1823). In October 1862 Vahlteich numbered among the founders of Vorwärts, a politically oriented workingmen's association, and in May 1863 among the founders of the General Association of German Workers.[5] In April 1868 Taute and Dörfel became the godparents of Seifert's fifth child.[6] (In September 1869 Bebel was elected the first chairman and Seifert the second chairman of the Leipzig Social Democratic Workers' Association.[7]) Dörfel and Seifert were then named godparents of Taute's child born in April 1868.[8] When Theodor Liebknecht was born at Leipzig, Braustr. 11, in April 1870, two of Wilhelm Liebknecht's Leipzig friends, the teacher Louis Haschert and the turner August Bebel, stood in as godparents and "representatives" of Wilhelmine Natalie Liebknecht's relatives living in southern Germany and Switzerland.[9] The baptismal entry of Karl Liebknecht, born on August 13, 1871, lists as godparents Dr. Karl Marx, London, and Friedrich Engels, "a

3. Liebknecht moved to Leipzig in September 1865 and organized here the nucleus of what later became a section of the IAA. See *Die I. Internationale in Deutschland (1864–1872). Dokumente und Materialien* (Berlin/GDR, 1964), pp. 94, 69ff. (correspondence with Karl Marx); pp. 888f. (Fritzsche), p. 915 (Seifert), p. 919 (Taute).

4. StadtAL, German Catholic Parish, Baptism Registries 1866/76/3. For the biography of Otto (-Walster) see: *Geschichte der deutschen Arbeiterbewegung, Biographisches Lexikon* (Berlin/GDR, 1970), pp. 360f.

5. StadtAL, German Catholic Parish, Baptism Registries 1866/77/7; the autobiographical sketch "Friedrich Wilhelm Fritzsche," *Der wahre Jacob*, no. 486, March 7, 1905.

6. St. Thomas Baptism Registry, 1868/137/759.

7. *Deutsches Wochenblatt*, no. 38, September 8, 1869.

8. StadtAL, German Catholic Parish, Baptism Registry 1868/6.

9. St. Thomas Baptism Registry, 1870/143/864.

man of private means living in London."[10] Before the introduction
of the civil registry in 1876, each birth was registered by the
appropriate church parish. Religious baptism was therefore often
merely a formality, especially among working-class families, and no
conclusions can be drawn from it alone about the workers' religious
commitment.

It was very common to choose godparents from among the
father's coworkers and their wives. This holds true for all the
occupations studied here and indicates close relations at the family
level. Table 3.1 provides objective evidence of the preeminence of
coworkers in personal relationships within the working class. Of
the 168 hours in a week, most workers in Leipzig factories and
manufacturing establishments between 1862 and 1869 spent an
average of 84 hours in the exploitative capitalist production process,
including time spent going to and coming from work. Spare time for
one's family and friends or for participation in the labor movement
or in education and culture amounted at best to 26 hours a week on
average.This could be extended only at the cost of one's health or
job performance and therefore of earnings. Because of their limited
amount of spare time, the workers' most intensive social contacts
were on the job.

For the following analysis of godparent selection in eight proletarian occupations from 1825 to 1874, a study was carried out of
3,300 baptismal entries and of the approximately 10,000 to 13,200
godparents named therein. Each of one hundred pairs of godparents
was broken down according to the godfather's occupation, and no
attempt was made to limit random variability through selection.
Tables 3.2 to 3.5 confirm that at the time and place under study,
proletarians tended on the whole to select godparents from the
proletariat. However, there was a certain percentage of socially
mixed or nonproletarian godparent pairs in every period and every
occupational category in the study. Ties to small urban or rural
manufacturers through one's own or one's spouse's family were
common at first among the proletariat, whose origins stretch back
after all to the decline of the old feudal society.

In Leipzig between 1825 and 1836, the percentage of primarily
proletarian godparents was not substantially higher than the percentage of exclusively nonproletarian. Only thirty of one hundred
journeyman printers, thirty-one of one hundred journeyman type-

10. Ibid., 1871/243/1481.

Table 3.1 *The Weekly Distribution of Time* among Leipzig Factory and Manufacturing Workers (in hours), 1862 to 1869*

Work Day (Hours)	Number of Factories	Monday to Saturday				Sunday		Entire Week		
		Work	To and from Work	Sleep	Spare-Time	Sleep	Spare-Time	Work/To and from Work	Sleep	Spare-Time
11	1	66	6	48	24	10	14	72	58	38
11 1/2	1	69	6	48	21	10	14	75	58	35
12	34	72	6	48	18	10	14	78	58	32
12 1/2	4	75	6	48	15	10	14	81	58	29
13	25	78	6	48	12	10	14	84	58	26
14	5	84	6	48	6	10	14	90	58	20

* estimated values: to and from work, 1 hour (minimum); sleep, 8 hours on a working day (maximum) and 10 hours on Sunday. Not included was frequent overtime and work on Sundays or outside regular hours

Source: StadtAl, sec. 2, F1117, vols. 1 and 2 (factory ordinances 1862–69, city of Leipzig).

Table 3.2 *Proletarian Godparents in the Families of Printers and Typesetters (per 500 Groups of Godparents)*

Social Class of the Godparents	Godparents in the Years				
Among printers:	1828–32**	1840–49	1844–49**	1850–59	1860–74
all godparents proletarian	21	44	39	46	42
proletarian godparents and those without indication	9	13	8	6	10
four godparents proletarian*	–	–	–	–	1
three godparents proletarian*	–	1	5	4	5
Total:	30	58	52	56	58
two godparents proletarian*	22	11	19	19	16
one godparent proletarian*	22	18	18	18	15
no godparents proletarian	26	13	11	7	11
Total:	100	100	100	100	100

Social Class of the Godparents	Godparents in the Years				
Among typesetters:	1825–36**	1844–49**	1850–59	1860–66	1867–72
all godparents proletarian	27	26	26	31	32
proletarian godparents and those without indication	2	7	12	3	6
four godparents proletarian*	–	–	2	2	5
three godparents proletarian*	2	5	7	8	8
Total:	31	38	47	44	51
two godparents proletarian*	23	14	17	23	20
one godparent proletarian*	25	23	20	23	16
no godparents proletarian	21	25	16	10	13
Total:	100	100	100	100	100

* others not proletarian   ** city of Leipzig, the others from the parish of Schönefeld

Source: Based on the baptism registries of the parish of Schönefeld and of the Church of St. Nicholai in Leipzig.

Table 3.3 *Proletarian Godparents in the Families of Mechanics*
(400 Groups of Godparents) and Smiths (300 Godparent Pairs)
Parish of Schönefeld

Social Class of the Godparents	Godparents in the Years			
Among mechanics:	1850–59	1860–65	1866–69	1870–73
all godparents proletarian	42	31	34	33
proletarian godparents and those without indication	21	8	7	7
four godparents proletarian*	1	3	3	4
three godparents proletarian*	6	6	7	8
Total:	70	48	51	52
two godparents proletarian*	14	17	22	21
one godparent proletarian*	8	19	14	16
no godparents proletarian	8	16	13	11
Total:	100	100	100	100
Among smiths:		1850–60	1861–68	1869–73
all godparents proletarian		26	50	35
proletarian godparents and those without indication		8	13	11
four godparents proletarian*		–	–	1
three godparents proletarian*		3	2	9
Total:		37	65	56
two godparents proletarian*		22	10	17
one godparent proletarian*		26	11	17
no godparents proletarian		15	14	10
Total:		100	100	100

* others not proletarian

Source: Based on the baptism registries of the parish of Schönefeld and of the
Church of St. Nicholai in Leipzig.

setters and thirty-three of one hundred laborers chose primarily proletarian godparents. This changed in the course of the Industrial Revolution as the number of people born into the proletariat rose and as various segments of the proletariat came into contact with one another, primarily in the large, centralized, capitalist workplaces. Increasingly, proletarians tended to choose godparents from the working class. Even among printers and typesetters, the proportion of

Table 3.4 *Proletarian Godparents in the Families of Laborers (800 Groups), Oilcloth Workers (200 Groups) and Factory Workers (100 Groups)*

Social Class of the Godparents	Godparents in the Years							
	1829–31**	1834–35	1848	1849	1858	1865	1868	1873
Among laborers:								
all godparents proletarian	26	9	43	44	39	44	42	43
proletarian godparents and those without indication	7	45	10	9	13	10	7	7
four godparents proletarian*	–	–	–	–	–	2	2	6
three godparents proletarian*	–	–	1	4	7	9	6	9
Total:	33	54	54	57	59	65	57	65
two godparents proletarian*	24	8	16	16	17	17	15	18
one godparent proletarian*	19	16	16	14	11	11	19	10
no godparents proletarian	24	22	14	13	12	7	9	7
Total:	100	100	100	100	100	100	100	100

Among oilcloth workers and factory workers (1860–72)	1840–54	1860–73	1860–72
all godparents proletarian	33	47	42
proletarian godparents and those without indication	22	12	11
four godparents proletarian*	–	1	4
three godparents proletarian*	1	7	13

Total:		
two godparents proletarian*	56	57	70
one godparent proletarian*	16	14	11
no godparents proletarian	15	15	12
no godparents proletarian	13	4	7
Total:	100	100	100

* others not proletarian ** city of Leipzig; others from parish of Schönefeld

Source: Based on the baptism registries of the parish of Schönefeld and of the Church of St. Nicholai in Leipzig.

Table 3.5 *Proletarian Godparents in the Families of Cigar Workers*
         (per 500 Groups of Godparents)
         Parish of Schönefeld

Social Class of the Godparents	Godparents in the Years				
	1840–50	1850–60	1861–65	1866–69	1870–74
all godparents proletarian	58	58	46	42	46
proletarian godparents and those without indication	9	9	4	11	6
four godparents proletarian*	–	1	4	5	2
three godparents proletarian*	2	7	2	12	14
Total:	69	75	56	70	68
two godparents proletarian*	15	8	20	17	15
one godparent proletarian*	12	7	13	7	10
no godparents proletarian	4	10	11	6	7
Total:	100	100	100	100	100

* others not proletarian

Source: Based on the baptism registries of the parish of Schönefeld and of the
        Church of St. Nicholai in Leipzig.

born proletarians and primarily proletarian godparents became
much more similar. This is evident in the selection of godparents at
the height of the Industrial Revolution (table 3.2).

The mounting inclination to restrict the choice of godparents to
fellow proletarians was only one symptom of the trend toward
strong class solidarity in the various segments of the proletariat.
This can be seen most clearly in the selection of godparents by cigar
workers, among whom in the birth years 1826 to 1835 eighty-one of
one hundred workers had been born working class and remained so.
It is only logical that the distancing trend toward nonproletarians in
the workers' social milieu continued apace as the working class
solidified. As the Industrial Revolution progressed, the number of
entirely nonproletarian groups of godparents selected by the occupations studied here sank from twenty-six to seven or eleven in a
hundred (printers), from twenty-one to thirteen in a hundred
(typesetters), from fifteen to ten in a hundred (smiths, 1845 to

1860), from twenty-four to seven in a hundred (laborers), and from thirteen to four in a hundred (oilcloth workers). Once again, it was the cigar workers who most thoroughly dissociated themselves from nonproletarians. Among a hundred groups of godparents in the years 1840 to 1850, only four could be discovered that were entirely nonproletarian. In this way we concretely demonstrated on the basis of the source material the close relationship between social origins, stability of social class, and type of social affiliations and bonds as reflected in the proletarian class movement.

In the early 1840s, a typical oilcloth worker in a factory still chose godparents from among his own occupational group, laborers, servants, and those without an occupation.[11] Twenty years later, the godparent selection of this type of worker clearly manifests expanding connections throughout the proletariat. In 1863–64, the following workers were selected as godparents by the families of the oilcloth worker Beutel from Volkmarsdorf and Mörl from Neuschönefeld: one market helper, one worsted yarn spinner, one oilcloth worker, and one bricklayer (Beutel); two typesetters, one iron lathe operator (*Eisendreher*), one carpenter, and two laborers (Mörl).[12] In 1844–45, a family of printers normally selected godparents from its own or related occupational groups,[13] although other kinds of skilled workers and even an occasional unskilled worker do appear. However by 1863–64, around the time of the mighty surge in the revolutionary labor movement in the various German states, printers working in Leipzig and living in the surrounding villages had developed intensive links through godparents to other printers and typesetters, music engravers and bookbinders, mechanics and fitters, joiners, laborers, market helpers, and servants.[14] These godparent relationships reveal strong proletarian bonding at a given time and place and make it possible to draw certain conclusions about the timing and extent of the gelling of proletarians into an emerging working class. Very few descriptive texts are able to provide this complex a view of all the various elements in the proletariat.

The following table (3.6) is entitled:"The Development of Proletarian Attachments as Reflected in the Godparent Selection of

11. Schönefeld Baptism Registries 1840/311/40; 1841/397/254; 1842/22/132.
12. Ibid., 1863/392/982; 1864/137/1169.
13. Ibid., 1844/133/10; 141/55; 160/173; 162/185; 170/233; 186/329.
14. Ibid., 1863/127; 265/218; 354/750; 354/752; 399/1020; 414/1109; 1864/1/354; 23/485; 44/612.

Table 3.6 *The Development of Proletarian Attachments as Reflected in the Godparent Selection of Leipzig Workers, 1825 to 1874*

Types of Worker
Place/Time
(godparents studied)

Godparents Selected by Printers, Typesetters, and Laborers, 1825 to 1835

Printers

Leipzig 1828–1832 (30 in 100)																			
1.	26	9	1	1	–	–	3	1	–	–	–	–	–	1	–	1	4	–	–
2.	7	–	1	–	–	1	–	1	–	–	–	1	–	–	–	–	2	–	–
3.	4	–	–	1	–	–	1	1	–	1	–	–	–	1	–	1	1	–	–
Sa.	37	9	2	2	–	3	1	2	–	1	–	1	–	1	–	1	7	–	1

Typesetters

Leipzig 1825–1836 (29 in 100)																			
1.	20	22	1	1	–	3	2	1	–	–	–	–	–	–	–	–	–	–	1
2.	6	8	–	1	–	–	1	–	–	–	–	–	–	–	–	2	–	–
3.	2	–	–	4	–	–	2	1	–	–	–	–	–	1	1	1	–	–
Sa.	28	30	1	6	–	3	5	2	–	–	–	–	–	1	3	–	1

Laborers

Leipzig 1829–1831 (33 in 100)																			
1.	–	1	6	1	–	1	11	–	1	11	–	3	–	1	3	6	–	–
2.	–	2	6	–	–	1	1	2	–	8	–	3	–	–	–	3	–	–
3.	–	–	4	1	–	1	–	2	–	6	–	–	–	–	–	1	–	–
Sa.	–	3	16	1	–	3	12	4	1	25	–	6	–	1	3	10	–	–

Laborers Par. Schönefeld																						
1.	2	–	1	5	–	1	1	2	2	4	1	23	–	–	4	–	–	15	1	3	22	–
2.	–	–	–	2	–	–	–	–	–	4	–	4	–	–	1	–	–	–	–	–	–	–
Sa.	2	–	1	7	–	1	2	2	4	1	27	–	–	5	–	–	15	1	3	22	–

(1834–1835) (54 in 100)

Key to Type of Godparent:
  1. = male and female workers
  2. = wives and widows of workers
  3. = daughters of workers (when none of this type appeared, column 3 was omitted)
Included were all godparents who fell within one of the categories listed in the heading

Source: Based on the baptism registries of the parish of Schönefeld and of the Church of St. Nicholai in Leipzig.

Leipzig Workers 1825 to 1874."Limitation to this sample appears permissible on the assumption that concentrations in godparent selection among the working class can be most clearly shown using the example of exclusively proletarian godparents. The data assume their full significance when trends in godparent selection are examined over half a century, leading to the commentary on table 3.6. It provides information about the extent of proletarian bonding, as reflected in the type of godparents selected by the families of Leipzig printers, typesetters, and laborers at the dawn of the Industrial Revolution when workers were still largely divided into guilds and still tended to isolate themselves from dissimilar occupations.

Table 3.6 seems to demonstrate the lack of strong attachments within the proletariat during its early history as a class. The method we use is the comparison of extreme groups. Laborers had figured since the 1830s among the most numerous proletarian groups in Leipzig. However, their choice of godparents – reflecting their other family contacts as well – shows that laborers remained extremely isolated from the printers and typesetters who tended to live in the city as well. Of the 200 families of printers and typesetters studied (1828 to 1836), only 59 chose exclusively proletarian godparents. They selected people of their own occupational group, including family members, in 104 cases and in only one case did they select an unskilled worker. The composition of the 44 socially mixed godparent groups, with one or two proletarian godparents, confirms this result.[15] Similarly, laborers for their part tended to select godparents from among the unskilled proletariat. Of the 200 families of laborers, 87 had entirely proletarian godparents. They included 65 unskilled workers, but only two printers and no typesetters at all. Not every laborer could have a printer or typesetter as a godparent, of course, because the two groups differed too much in size. Conversely, however, large numbers of laborers were available for selection by the families of printer and typesetters, though this still did not happen.

This substantiates, at least for Leipzig, the view that printers and typesetters remained largely segregated from the mass of unskilled workers during the 1820s and early 1830s, at a time when early

---

15. The following proletarian godparents could be discovered: 15 printers and printers' wives, 8 typesetters and typesetters' wives, one copperplate printer, one lithographic printer's wife, two shoe-making journeymen, one tailoring journeyman, one brick-laying journeyman, and five daughters of workmen, including one daughter of a manual laborer and one of a coachman.

proletarian demonstrations and the September Uprising of 1830 were occurring.

Among printers and typesetters in the years 1826 to 1836, there is no sign of any strong bonds with the rest of the proletariat, as indeed had existed during the 1770s with the wig-making journeymen in Leipzig.[16] Hair styles changed, the wig makers' guild was ruined, the social status of wig-making journeymen declined, and all the old affinities soon disappeared.

It is remarkable how very few printers and typesetters in the early 1830s chose godparents from among the horde of single journeymen. This can perhaps be explained by the highly itinerant lives of these journeymen. A godfather of this kind would inevitably leave Leipzig, losing contact with the family of his godchild. (One might mention in this context that journeymen usually developed strong bonds among themselves, since those representing two, three, or even more different trades often shared the same hostel.[17] Attempts to segregate journeymen by trade were often undertaken by the hostel wardens at the prompting of the guilds.[18]) Journeymen were more likely to become godparents to the families of laborers, a fact that can probably be ascribed to their low social status. The best they could hope for among skilled workers, apart from journeymen practicing the trades of bricklaying and carpentry, was to find godparents among the steady flow of journeymen belonging to guilds.

Even less frequent among Leipzig printers, typesetters, and indeed laborers was the choice of a servant or coachman as godparent, while the masses of female domestics hardly appear at all. This is particularly significant since some 1,213 people were in fact servants

16. J.H. Jugler, *Leipzig und seine Universität vor hundert Jahren. Aus den gleichnamigen Aufzeichnungen eines Leipziger Studenten jetzo zuerst ans Licht gestellt* (Leipzig, 1879), p. 94. According to this, Stötteritz was considered a "gathering place of wig makers, printers, etc." "Nobody who liked to keep good company" went there or to the *Brandvorwerk*, which was "nothing more than a gathering place for the poor, rough, low-born types among apprentices and wig-making journeymen, etc."

17. StadtAL, Sec. 2, H 1836, vol. 1, p. 1a (bookbinders and carpenters 1837), p. 6 (wheelwrights and bakers), p. 8 (copper founders, bronze founders, bell casters), p. 12 (glaziers, harness makers, bricklayers), p. 32 (barbers, mechanics, spur makers, and passementerie makers 1839), p. 47f. (turners, bookbinders, glaziers, armorers, brass founders, needle makers, glove makers and cloth makers 1842), p. 103 (glaziers, rope makers, bookbinders, harness makers, needle makers, glove makers, stocking weavers, brass founders, and armorers 1847).

18. Ibid., p. 49. Thus bookbinders lived in separate quarters because they were not supposed "to come into any further contact with journeymen from other guilds."

in 1832. By 1849, there were already 5,164 female domestics in Leipzig and a further 1,934 servants of both sexes (6,667 servants in 1864, 8,661 in 1871, and 9,824 in 1875), though never more than 190 males in any case.[19] These masses of young people, many of nonproletarian origin, were subject to the Leipzig Servant Ordinance of 1735 as well as to the Servant Ordinance of the state of Saxony and to the Regulations on the Police Surveillance of Servants of 1835. Servants had always originated generally from outside Leipzig, and "not just from the surrounding countryside but primarily from the Prussian province of Saxony, from Thuringia and Anhalt."[20] In the early 1830s, female servants even worked occasionally in the proletarian households of printers,[21] a relationship that largely obviated any possibility of becoming a godparent to them. The families of Leipzig laborers would not have had the wherewithal to employ servants, but they were not therefore any more inclined to establish family ties with them. Hasse was still disposed to remark that Leipzig girls tended to shun domestic service, allegedly because of their "more highly developed sense of pleasure" and "preference for personal autonomy."[22]

No less informative is the composition of the entirely nonproletarian godparents selected by the workers under study in table 3.6. It discloses that Leipzig printers and typesetters continued to maintain elements of a patriarchal relationship with their employers during the 1820s and 1830s. Among the godparents of their children can be found wealthy manufacturers and other well-to-do citizens.[23]

19. Hasse, *Die Stadt Leipzig und ihre Umgebung, geographisch und statistisch beschrieben*, (Leipzig, 1878) p. 115f.; STA Dresden, MdI, Statist. Office, no. 369/1 (city of Leipzig). In 1871, 58 percent of all households with servants required them solely for family members.

20. Hasse, *Die Stadt Leipzig*, p. 159. See as well: "Die Geburtsbezirke der weiblichen Dienstboten in Leipzig am 1. Dez. 1875," *MSBL* (1877):39.

21. StadtAl, Tit XLII, D 43 a. See the people liable to pay business and individual taxes in "Alter Hof" 5 (Reichel's garden). In the household of the printing assistant Vetter, employed in Teubner's printing shop, were an apprentice book dealer (son), a servant girl, and three subtenants: an impoverished merchant, an assistant mechanic, and a journeyman smith.

22. Hasse, *Die Stadt Leipzig*, p. 159.

23. St. Nicholas Baptismal Registry. *Printer godparents* included: the wife of C. Tauchnitz, the owner of a printing office (1829/2); G.H. Maret, owner of a printing office (1829/348); W. Staritz, owner of a printing office (1829/455); the merchant W. Fickert (1829/441); the wife of the book commissioner P.F. Schmidt (1829/455); the wives of the druggists Bärwinkel (1829/2; 1832/254) and Täschner (1829/2); the merchant C. Lampe, coproprietor of the wholesale drug company Brückner, Lampe und Comp. (1832/254); the draper Vogel (1832/254); the lawyer K.F. Vetter (1830/341). *Typesetter godparents* included: owner of a printing office

Among the clerks could still be found sons of leading capitalists, such as Friedrich Brockhaus, with godparents from a similar social background. Developments during the following decades led to a decline in patriarchal employer-employee relationships, underlining the increasing polarization between the two fundamental classes in society. The social prestige that printers and typesetters had acquired through nonproletarian godparents was now more likely to be provided by master artisans and lower-level government workers and white-collar employees (various kinds of low-level officials, supervisors of the railroad freight storage place, bookkeepers, forwarding clerks, office employees, supervisors, police sergeants, etc.) Among the exclusively nonproletarian godparents in laborers, families, those with the social standing of a Louis Chevalier (1829), the dye-industry magnate, or a Johann Gottlieb Irmler (1830), the mass manufacturer of musical instruments, were distinct exceptions by 1830.[24] Much more likely godparents in laborers' families were guild masters, who also appear around this time as godparents to the children of printers and typesetters.[25] Many sons of master craftsmen were squeezed into proletarian occupations outside the guild system or may even have become journeymen before tumbling into the unskilled proletariat. Similarly, many of their daughters married skilled or unskilled workers and formed proletarian families. Both situations had the expected consequences for godparent selection.

Small retailers and innkeepers appear frequently as godparents to the families of the printers and typesetters studied here, as well as to those of laborers. This relationship may even have resulted from the

---

C.P. Melzer (1826/415; 1836/53); bookstore owner Reclam (1829/463); bookstore owner G.H. Ayrer (1829/463); flower manufacturer and factory owner C.F. Reichardt (1828/36), who introduced artificial flower manufacturing to Leipzig and who in a factory at the market employed seventy workers as well as seventy-seven home workers in 1830 (see in this regard Karl Juckenburg, *Das Aufkommen der Großindustrie in Leipzig* (Leipzig, 1912), p. 104); paper mill owner J.G. Wittig in Forkendorf (1829/463). Further godparents could be found among students, pastors, physicians, civil servants, and, in particular, clerks.

24. St. Thomas Baptismal Registry 1829/140; 1830/187.

25. *Laborers* in the city of Leipzig: twenty-four nonproletarian godparents, including twelve guild masters or their wives and six daughters of guild masters. *Laborers* in the parish of Schönefeld: fourteen nonproletarian godparents, including eight guild masters or their wives. *Printers* in the city of Leipzig: twenty-six nonproletarian godparents, including twelve guild masters or their wives and two daughters of guild masters; typesetters in the city of Leipzig: twenty-one nonproletarian godparents, including eight guild masters or their wives and one daughter of a guild master.

"ruinous borrowing system, through which working men fell into
the clutches of small shopkeepers and publicans."[26] Government
officials and white-collar employees were found in greater numbers
among the godparents of more skilled publishing employees,[27]
while landowners appear as godparents to the children of laborers
almost exclusively in the Parish of Schönefeld as a result of their
continuing involvement in agricultural production.[28] These ties
gradually weakened and by the time the Industrial Revolution
thoroughly triumphed had completely withered away, at least in the
villages in the Schönefeld parish.[29] Certain categories of white-
collar employees also rarely became godparents in the families of
laborers. However, there were quite frequently godparents in the
families of printing and typesetting assistants, even toward the end
of the Industrial Revolution and beyond. This selection of godparents indicates both that these workers originated from and
married into white-collar families and that they encouraged their
sons, increasingly perhaps, to take up white-collar professions.

26. *Typographia*, no. 3, January 30, 1847 ("Improvements in Working-Class
Households").
27. Among twenty-six nonproletarian godparents of Leipzig *printers* there were
one bookkeeper, one business student, two trade agents, and one transcriber as well
as the wives of two transcribers, one general foreman, one police station clerk, one
lottery ticket distributor, and one court clerk. *Typesetters*: twenty-one nonproletarian godparents, including one collector of city gate taxes, one tax collector, one
tenement caretaker, and the wives of two clerks, one tax collector, and one bookkeeper. Among twenty-four nonproletarian godparents in *laborers'* families there
were one trade agent, two tenement caretakers, one waiter, two vehicle guards, and
the wives of one transcriber, two tenement caretakers, one security agent, one wool
warehouse foreman, and the daughters of one manager of a trading company, one
property manager, one foreman bricklayer and one official in charge of the town
scale.
28. Among fourteen nonproletarian godparents in 1834–35, there were four
landowners, three wives of landowners, two sons of landowners, and three private
tutors.
29. Schönefeld Baptismal Registry for 1873 (godparents to the families of laborers).

SUSANNE SCHÖTZ

On the Recruitment of Leipzig Middle Strata from the Working Class, 1830–1870

In response to a suggestion by Hartmut Zwahr, I began almost a decade ago to turn my attention to the history of classes and social strata during the bourgeois upheaval in Germany.* From the beginning I was especially interested in those persons who in the age of the Industrial Revolution became neither workers nor capitalists, but rather members of those so diverse socioeconomic intermediate entities, the middle strata. Focusing their history seemed to me indeed tempting.

My *Diplomarbeit* on the first generation of Leipzig railroad personnel was followed by a dissertation, defended four years ago, on urban middle strata in Leipzig between 1830 and 1870.[1] And although I have in the meantime worked on another small project and should have long since turned my attention to my next major project, the problem of middle strata still occupies and interests me. For me this topic is in no way closed but constantly raises new questions.

My particular interest concerned those groups within the middle

* Lecture delivered at the Max-Planck-Institut für Geschichte in Göttingen, Federal Republic of Germany, in July 1989.

1. Cf. Susanne Schötz, "Eisenbahnangestellte in Leipzig, 1837–1865. Ein Beitrag zur Genesis und Typologie von Proletariat und Kleinbürgertum in der bürgerlichen Umwälzung" (diss., Karl-Marx-Universität, 1980). Also by Susanne Schötz, "Städtische Mittelschichten in Leipzig während der bürgerlichen Umwälzung, 1830–1870, untersucht auf der Grundlage biographischer Massenquellen" (diss. A, Karl-Marx-Universität, 1985). The latter work will be published by the Akademie-Verlag, Berlin/GDR, in 1991.

strata that between 1830 and 1870 – that is, the time of the Industrial Revolution in Leipzig – successfully continued to exist or came into being. Thus I was not primarily interested in the declining groups, but rather in those middle-strata groups that established themselves simultaneously with the large-scale formation of the working class and the bourgeoisie![2]

I would like to name several questions essential to me in this connection:

1. Which vocational and functional groups within the middle strata became numerous at what time and for what reasons?
2. How and by what paths did people make their way into which middle strata? Were there specific channels of advancement?
3. Who could penetrate the intermediate social strata and thus escape the maelstrom of capitalist class polarization? Because, and this is to be distinctly emphasized, the main trend of social mobility led into the growing working class.[3] Furthermore: what share did workers and their children have in the recruitment of the middle strata? Since I consider the question of the chances for and the limits of social advancement among workers' children to be especially important and interesting, it will be the focus of the following discussion of the recruitment of the Leipzig middle strata.

But first two introductory comments, one on the documentary basis of my study, the second on the term *middle strata*.

On the documentary basis:

Like H. Zwahr, I used a biographical mass source in my study: the Schutz– und Bürgerprotokolle, which were the documents that were compiled when persons applied to become either burghers with municipal citizenship rights (*Bürger*) or simply residents without citizenship rights (*Schutzverwandte*).[4] In Leipzig

2. On the class makeup of proletariat and bourgeoisie see Hartmut Zwahr, *Zur Konstituierung des Proletariats als Klasse. Strukturuntersuchung über das Leipziger Proletariat während der industriellen Revolution* (East Berlin, 1978); "Zur Klassenanalyse der deutschen Bourgeoisie in der bürgerlichen Umwälzung," *Jahrbuch für Geschichte* 18 (1978); *Proletariat und Bourgeoisie in Deutschland: Studien zur Klassendialektik* (Cologne, 1980).
3. Cf. Zwahr, *Zur Konstituierung* (above, n. 2), p. 157.
4. On the nature of the source as well as the difference between *Schutzverwandt-*

every person who wanted to establish a household in the city was required to acquire at least the right to residence (*Schutzrecht*), and everyone who wanted to establish an independent business was required to acquire citizenship rights (*Bürgerrecht*). The personal files of almost all these persons have remained intact; they consist of short biographies, partially supplemented by birth and baptismal certificates, service and work certificates, asset vouchers, inheritance documents, passports, domestic service records, as well as medical and police certificates.

In the ideal case we can draw from these files the name and occupation of the individual, his social and territorial origin, his religious denomination, his birth date and birthplace, and the course of his life up to that point: his school years, vocational training, work experience, income/assets, in some cases even information concerning his marriage partner and plans for the future.

In a normal case one piece of information or another will be missing, but that is of course the normal working situation for a historian.[5] What the files do not make possible for all persons is the later course of their lives.[6] Alongside this mass source I used printed tax rolls and group specific material from the Leipzig *Stadtarchiv*.

From my analysis of city directories and the complete *Bürger-* and *Schutzrecht* conferrals, I came up with the following vocational and occupational groups, which on the one hand can be assumed to

---

schaft and *Bürgerrecht*, see Hartmut Zwahr, "Zur Konstituierung des Proletariats als Klasse. Strukturuntersuchung über das Leipziger Proletariat während der industriellen Revolution," in *Die großpreußisch-militaristische Reichsgründung 1871: Voraussetzungen und Folgen*, ed. Horst Barthel and Ernst Engelberg (East Berlin, 1971), 1:513.

5. In the case of persons who were born in Leipzig or married there, baptismal and wedding entries in church registers could be used as an additional sociohistorical source.

6. *Schutz-* and *Bürgerakten* only reveal the later course of a person's life when the acquisition or loss of the *Bürgerrecht* played a role in changes in that person's life. That was the case, for example,

　　a) when the person later moved away from Leipzig and thus lost the *Schutz-* or *Bürgerrecht* of the city,

　　b) when a Leipzig burger became a *Schutzverwandter* – as in the case of bankruptcy – or a *Schutzverwandter* became a burgher – as in the case of the establishment of a commercial employee as an independent merchant.

Once a person's *Schutz-* and *Bürgerakten* were opened, all of these events were duly noted with the utmost precision. Yet these files do not register the occupational changes within the categories of *Schutzverwandter* and *Bürger*. If, for example, a Leipzig innkeeper gave up his business and instead opened a grocery store without in the meantime having lost his *Bürgerrecht*, this cannot be revealed in the mass source used here. Herein lies its fundamental defect.

belong to the middle strata, and which on the other grew the most in both absolute and relative terms between 1830 and 1870: grocers, innkeepers, commercial employees, postal and railroad officials.[7] Equally rapidly growing groups were merchants and so-called manufacturers – although one can assume a stronger and more heterogeneous socioeconomic character here. I included this contrast group in my study as well.

Now for my second introductory comment, that concerning the middle strata term I am using (which naturally was not insignificant in my choice of groups): In my use of the term *middle strata* I am postulating the relatively independent existence of strata between the major classes of capitalist society – the working class and the capitalist entrepreneurial class. Since probably very few people actually fell directly in between workers and entrepreneurs, it therefore would really be more appropriate to use the term intermediate strata. Unfortunately, this term has not gained acceptance in our usage.

Both classes and strata are in my understanding structural elements of capitalist society, and a member of the middle strata cannot at the same time belong to one of the two major classes, for social classes and social strata distinguish themselves from one another in various ways.[8] The capitalist entrepreneurial and working classes owe their existence to the buying and selling of a commodity, labor power, for the production of capitalist surplus value. In this process the actual power of disposition over the means of production determines who will produce the surplus value and who can appropriate it.[9] However, the majority of middle strata members neither produce capitalist surplus value nor do they ap-

---

7. The exact figures can be found in: Schötz, "Städtische Mittelschichten" (above, n. 1), pp. 15ff.
   In my investigation of the groups under study I analyzed the vocational and occupational classifications of 19,324 *Schutzverwandte* and 13,741 *Bürger* who became residents of the city of Leipzig between 1827 and 1871.
8. Cf. the various classification criteria of social classes and strata described by Horst Handke, "Entwicklung und Struktur der Arbeiterklasse im Kapitalismus," *Jahrbuch für Wirtschaftsgeschichte* 3 (1972): 170f. See also Handke's "Einige Fragen des dialektischen Wechselverhältnisses von Klassen- und Schichtmerkmalen," in *Zur Sozialstruktur der sozialistischen Gesellschaft*, ed. Wissenschaftlicher Rat für soziologische Forschung in der DDR (East Berlin, 1974), p. 159.
9. Capitalist surplus value results for the entrepreneur from the unrecompensed surplus labor of workers. Wage laborers on the one hand perform necessary work, which reproduces the value of their labor power and corresponds to their wages, while on the other hand they produce surplus labor, which the capitalists acquire without recompense in the form of surplus value.

propriate it.[10] Thus social differentiations, which arise from the relationship to the means of production, are of subordinate importance to the peculiarities of middle strata. But what makes the middle strata into an independent structural element in capitalist society is their role – typical for neither the worker nor the entrepreneur – in both the social organization of labor and the mechanism of exploitation. This role gives rise to a broad complex of further social differentiations.[11] As I wish to show, this applies just as much to the simple goods producer, the small merchant, and other tradesmen or self-employed persons as it does to salaried employees and civil servants. (It should be mentioned that these thoughts do not represent for me a *ne plus ultra*, but are still of a tentative nature.)

The small self-employed tradesman essentially exists on the basis of simple reproduction. Through his ownership of capital or the means of production he exercises entrepreneurial functions – he plans, organizes, directs, and supervises the work process. Karl Marx identifies him as the master and owner of his working conditions. But owing to the limited nature of the capital and the means of production in his possession, the small self-employed tradesman is simultaneously his own worker.[12] In addition to certain mental functions, he performs numerous physical functions directed at the production of a commodity or the purchase and sale of commodities. The small, self-employed tradesman is characterized by a concurrence of directorial, supervisory, independent, intellectually creative as well as active physical work. In a certain sense one could also speak of a specific combination of entrepreneurial and workers' functions. The small, self-employed tradesman is an exploiter – his own – and is exploited – by himself.

The salaried employee/civil servant finds himself in a comparable situation. His activity as well distinguishes itself through a peculiar combination of entrepreneurial and workers' functions. To a certain extent it can be neither planned nor regimented and requires a high degree of participation in the organization of the work process. But at the same time this function also demands even more active work

---

10. Cf. Hartmut Zwahr, "Die Synchronisierung des Entwicklungsganges von Bourgeoisie und Proletariat als Forschungsproblem und Aufgabe," *Beiträge zur Geschichte der Arbeiterbewegung* 6 (1981): 812.
11. See n. 9.
12. Cf. Marx/Engels, "Theorien über produktive und unproduktive Arbeit," chap. 3 of *Theorien über den Mehrwert*, in *Marx-Engels-Werke* (*MEW*) (Berlin/GDR, 1956–1989), 26.1: 383. See also Karl Marx, "Theorien über den Mehrwert," vol. 4 of *Das Kapital*, in *MEW*, 26.3: 349.

with little self-determination of the sequence of operations. The less the activity of a salaried employee/civil servant is determined by physical and/or active work, and the more it consists of the assumption of directorial, planning, administrative, supervisory, and thus exploitative functions, the closer he – as a higher-salaried employee/civil servant – approaches the exploiting and power-wielding classes. Intermediate stages are, of course, also possible. Conversely, a lower-salaried employee/civil servant approaches the working class when his function takes on a primarily physical and active character. Long-term intermediate stages in the historical development of vocational groups are equally imaginable.

It is similar with the small, self-employed tradesman. The more dependent he is on capital (i.e., a master craftsman who is an outworker for a merchant or manufacturer), the less he actually behaves like the master of his working conditions and the more he resembles the worker. In other cases, through the increased employment of outside labor, he approaches the class of the capitalist entrepreneurs or even joins it.

I came up with the empirical finding that specific work situations of middle-strata members go hand in hand with specific material life situations, which again are typical for neither workers nor entrepreneurs. These peculiarities carry over into the social profiles of middle-strata members – in their social background, marriage patterns, vocational careers, etc. The middle strata of that time – despite their heterogeneity – formed a social entity distinguishable from workers and entrepreneurs without, to be sure, the existence of rigid barriers dividing it from the major classes.

Although it is not possible to go into greater detail, it must be pointed out that almost all grocers and a bare majority of Leipzig innkeepers belonged to the lowest independent middle strata (running one-man operations and with tax rates similar to those of various working-class groups). Furthermore, individual grocers, most of the remaining innkeepers, and approximately a third of both the manufacturers and the merchants belonged to the more solid independent middle strata (employing a very few workers, with tax rates above those of the working class),[13] while two-thirds of the merchants and manufacturers performed as capitalist entre-

---

13. The term "more solid middle strata" entails no moral judgment. It simply attempts to show a distinction from the lowest, economically most unstable and most fluctuating groups within the middle strata.

preneurs of various orders of magnitude. To the lowest nonindependent middle strata belonged lower postal and railroad officials and a portion of commercial employees. To the more solid nonindependent middle strata belonged middle-level postal and railroad officials as well as a majority of commercial employees. Executive commercial employees and high postal and railroad officials approached the class of capitalist entrepreneurs.[14]

What share did workers and workers' sons (the groups under study consisted overwhelmingly of male persons)[15] have in the recruitment of these groups? And thus I finally come to my real topic:

The great majority of all persons under study, from an intergenerational point of view, already came from the middle strata. They recruited themselves to a high degree from farm and master craftsmen's families. Only about a fifth of the subjects, by contrast, can be described as "social climbers."[16] The latter advanced in an intergenerational succession from the families of domestic servants and proletarian wage earners into various middle strata. This group accounts for 41 percent of lower railroad officials, 35 percent of

14. For a more detailed breakdown, see Schötz, "Städtische Mittelschichten" (above, n. 1).

15. The present study should be understood simply as a beginning in my research on Leipzig middle strata of the nineteenth century. That is why it first concentrates on those groups whose absolute and relative growth was the greatest. It turned out that men dominated these groups. Nevertheless, the analysis contains the first material about female grocers, innkeepers, and manufacturers. Cf. Schötz, "Städtische Mittelschichten" (above, n. 1), pp. 109ff, 138ff, 163. I must point out quite critically that in 1980, when I began my research, I did not yet consider that there were likewise absolutely and relatively growing, if less numerous, middle strata groups that consisted primarily of women – for example, milliners, lady companions, and school mistresses. In 1990 I plan to begin another project dedicated to these groups and hope thereby to relativize and correct the current conception of middle strata.

16. For the exact figures, see Schötz, "Städtische Mittelschichten" (above, n. 1). An international classification of the research findings is difficult since different rates of mobility naturally arise from the different assignments to the lower and middle strata made by the individual researchers. In contrast to many researchers, I do not assign lower-salaried employees and civil servants to the lower but instead to the middle strata. Genuine social advancement in my opinion lies only in the crossover into the middle strata, not in small improvements in status within, for example, the working class. For figures on international comparisons, see Hartmut Kaelble, "Regionale und soziale Mobilität. Einführung und Auswertung," in *Arbeiter im Industrialisierungsprozeß, Herkunft, Lage und Verhalten*, ed. Werner Conze and Ulrich Engelhardt (Stuttgart, 1979), pp. 18–30. Also by Kaelble, *Soziale Mobilität und Chancengleichheit im 19. und 20. Jahrhundert. Deutschland im internationalen Vergleich* (Göttingen, 1983), p. 61, ns. 4 and 5 on p. 270.

grocers, 30 percent of lower postal officials, 27 percent of middle-level railway officials, 18 percent of innkeepers, 17 percent of commercial employees, 14 percent of manufacturers, 11 percent of middle-level postal officials, and 3 percent of merchants.

I have used the classification "proletarian wage earners" (in a broad sense one could also speak of workers) for journeymen and unskilled workers. This term seemed to me appropriate in bringing together both members of the working class and those related social elements on their way into it.

In my study I found numerous manual laborers, day laborers, agricultural workers, loaders, etc., laboring as unskilled workers. As partially still free, partially already capitalistically exploited wage laborers, they can be assigned to the rising working class. It is not possible to determine the socioeconomic status of journeymen with equal clarity. If they were factory journeymen they were capitalistically exploited and, as factory workers, were a component of the working class. If they worked as journeymen under master craftsmen, then forms of noncapitalist exploitation predominated. But frequently Leipzig master craftsmen were already subjected to the capitalist relations of production as in the form of the putting-out system (shoemakers, tailors, or joiners).[17] However, many journeymen came to know their work in artisan shops dependent to a larger or lesser extent on merchant manufacturers and in the factory. All journeymen of the generation of the fathers of our upward–mobile workers had a decisive common feature, independent of the concrete relations of production: none of them succeeded in going the traditional route from apprentice to journeyman to master. Their time as journeymen did not lead to petty bourgeois independence, but instead meant life-long wage dependence. Thus there developed a new type of journeyman who distinguished himself from the "classical guild journeyman" in numerous ways: he was married, had children, no longer lived in his master's household, and provided both for himself and for his family. Leisure time gained for him new importance and new content. His conditions of reproduction resembled those of workers and led to certain related patterns of behavior.

Although likewise free from the means of production and living from the sale of their labor power, domestic servants distinguished themselves more clearly from journeymen and workers. They gen-

17. Cf. Zwahr, *Zur Konstituierung* (above, n. 3), pp. 48, 52.

erally performed nonproductive functions and performed personal services. The Gesindeordnungen (Domestic Service Regulations), hastily adjusted to the bourgeois upheaval – such as the Saxonian regulations of January 10, 1835 – sharply curtailed the personal rights and freedoms of domestic servants: they had to live in the houses of their masters, and the latter regimented the entire daily routine. If the servants exhibited "unbecoming behavior" they could be mercilessly punished without any right to legal satisfaction. But domestic service also had advantages. Basic material needs, such as room and board, were guaranteed daily. Although the annual monetary income of domestic servants lay beneath that of other wage earners, servants – as we shall see – saved more than wage laborers, who had to pay for all the necessities of life from out of their own pockets.

If one compares the share of social climbers in the recruitment of the individual groups under study, there is no room for exaggerated optimism regarding the advancement of workers: for almost three-quarters of all social climbers the advancement ended already in the lowest independent or nonindependent middle strata – in the groups of grocer, innkeeper, lower postal and railroad official. Only about a quarter of the social climbers succeeded in penetrating the more solid middle strata – the groups of commercial employees, middle-level postal and railroad officials, as well as the more well-to-do innkeepers, merchants, and manufacturers. Penetration into high officialdom, as well as the mercantile and industrial bourgeoisie, remained the great exception. In this way social advancement on a broad scale was possible only into the lowest groups of the middle strata, whose overall work and life situation resembled that of domestic servants and proletarian wage earners more closely than that of the bourgeoisie and high officialdom. However, quite interestingly, the recruitment of the newly created lower- and middle-level railroad officialdom was more open to the sons of proletarian wage earners than that of the historically older postal officialdom.

If one reviews the routes of penetration into the lower middle strata, one can identify two significant channels of advancement, and only these two can be pursued here:[18] First, there was long-term domestic service. Forty-seven percent of those journeymen's

---

18. Beyond these two there were further but altogether insignificant channels of advancement. Thus, for example, artisan journeymen who had lost any outlook in their trade switched over to the railroad or the factory: a mechanic became a

sons who later penetrated into the middle strata under study and 73 percent of the workers' sons had no vocational training. A large portion of them entered domestic service after their schooltime and began striving after so-called bourgeois independence. This could only be achieved in trades that required neither qualifications nor a high initial investment. That made the grocery and innkeeping businesses into common objectives. In the course of their independent establishment in these trades the sons of proletarian wage earners could hardly count on financial support from parents and relatives. As a rule they had to acquire by themselves the minimum start up capital of six hundred *Taler* necessary for the opening of a grocery store or inn.[19] This was more easily achieved through the position of servant in Leipzig, especially as market helpers, waiters, and manservants, than through wage-dependent proletarian functions. Thus the median start-up capital of a servant setting himself up in the innkeeping business was almost two hundred *Taler* higher than that of a journeyman with the same intentions. Not a few journeymen, after a long and unpromising wage dependence, switched over to domestic service in order to acquire the necessary means to set themselves up. Domestic servants, from an intergenerational point of view, consequently formed the primary pool of recruitment for grocers and innkeepers. Domestic service was the most significant channel of advancement into the studied groups of the lower middle strata.

But the importance of marriages to the "right" partner, i.e., to a partner of means, can in no way be underestimated. This is indicated by the timely coincidence of marriages and business openings among approximately a third of grocers and innkeepers.[20].

---

locomotive engineer and a journeyman tailor became a "manufacturer" of white gentlemen's linen. See Schötz, "Städtische Mittelschichten" (above, n. 1).

19. In order to prevent a "possible case of impoverishment and the resulting inconvenience to this community," the Leipzig city council decreed in 1828 that concessions to the grocery trade should only be granted when the applicant could prove a personal sum of at least six hundred *Taler* and had also acquired the *Bürgerrecht*. Cf. Schötz, "Städtische Mittelschichten" (above, n. 1), p. 89 and n. 8 to p. 167.

20. In this way former journeymen could often establish themselves only through the financial gifts of their brides. They not seldom married into already existing grocery businesses and inns by marrying grocers' or innkeepers' widows. Sometimes the bride was eleven, fourteen, or nineteen years older than the bridegroom! The average marriage age among innkeepers and grocers lay at thirty or thirty-one. It was higher for them than for workers because of the long-term saving necessary for their longed-for independence. Cf. Schötz, "Städtische Mittelschichten" (above, n. 1), pp. 111ff and 139ff.

Long-term military enlistment proved to be a second significant channel of advancement, although generally into the nonindependent lower-middle strata. This path reserved special positions in state service for persons who had actively served for over eight years in the military, positions such as those with the postal service, the railroad, tax and customs administration, as well as road and dike maintenance.[21] Eighty-four percent of lower postal officials and 21 percent of lower railroad officials received their positions after a ten-to-thirteen-year term of military service. As so-called *Militäranwärter* they performed simple, often primarily physical, usually mechanical tasks demanding neither scientific nor technical background training. Their long military service, which they usually performed as noncommissioned officers, had accustomed them to discipline, the unconditional performance of duty, the keeping of official secrets, but also to dealing with subordinates.

The primary channels of advancement into the lower middle strata outlined here allow an interesting conclusion: there were no insurmountable material or educational barriers to the advancement of workers' sons into the lower independent or nonindependent middle strata! The capital necessary for setting oneself up independently as an innkeeper or grocer could be acquired during a long term of domestic service, and the path of long-term military duty was in principle possible for everyone.

However, the fact that significantly more farmers' and master craftsmen's sons than workers' sons moved up through the two primary channels of advancement into the lowest middle strata resulted – and this is my thesis – from the differing experiential and functional relations of the two, determined by differing conditions of production and reproduction.

A few considerations on this:

1. Was it at all desirable for a proletarian wage earner to achieve a small civil-service position? In contrast to a wage earner, I think that even the lowest such position brought many benefits:

---

21. Cf. the administrative archives of the *Bezirkspostdirektion Leipzig*, Bestand 1/19, "Zivilversorgungsschein für den Feldwebel Otto Gustav Stegmann." In addition, §2 of the expanded postal regulations from the year 1782 contain a stipulation requiring the preferential hiring of former soldiers to parcel and letter carrier positions. Cf. Staatsarchiv Leipzig, Oberpostdirektion Leipzig, no. 5, pp. 8f. In the German Empire (1871–1918) all lower- and half of all middle-level civil servant positions were reserved for discharged noncommissioned officers.

steady, that is, permanent employment; steady, that is, regular payment; pension eligibility – to name only the most important ones. In a time of mass pauperism in which hunger, unemployment, and sickness were everyday events, these benefits must have had great value. Recognizing this, the *Erzähler an der Spree* stated in 1846: "One only has to look at how many applicants turn up whenever the smallest, most unimportant little public office comes up for grabs! What a rush when it comes time to fill the post of clerk, bailiff, or gravedigger! What pushing and shoving for positions at the railroad administrations! This morbid addiction to 'secure bread' clearly shows how precarious a middle-class livelihood has become."[22]

But might many workers not have sensed a social distance in their relationship with civil servants and higher authorities? This distance could apparently be partially overcome. This is shown at least by the relatively high proportion of the sons of proletarian wage earners in the recruitment of railroad officials: in the early years of the railroad, railroad officials were considerably less often recruited from among *Militäranwärter* than were postal officials at the same time. Apparently, long-term military service more than anything else held veterans back from striving for such a position!

2. Was the status of a small trader or innkeeper worth attaining for workers' or journeymen's sons? In view of the great fluctuations in the grocery and innkeeping businesses, which could also mean financial ruin, not every grocer or innkeeper was to be envied. But could the more "solid" grocery stores and inns become objectives? I feel that setting oneself up independently in these businesses lay outside the field of vision of most workers and journeymen. Such a move was linked to an initial capital investment that was very high for proletarian wage earners (six hundred *Taler*), and thus, on the basis of proletarian life experience, it must have in general seemed unattainable. Studies on the savings habits of Saxonian workers demonstrate that their income was too low and too irregular for any larger sums to be left over.[23] Buying on credit from shopkeepers

22. Cited from *Erzähler an der Spree*, vol. 5, no. 46, Nov. 13, 1846.

23. See Herbert Kiesewetter, "Zur Entwicklung sächsischer Sparkassen, zum Sparverhalten und zur Lebenshaltung sächsischer Arbeiter im 19. Jahrhundert, 1819–1914," in *Arbeiterexistenz im 19. Jahrhundert. Lebensstandard und Lebensgestaltung deutscher Arbeiter und Handwerker*, ed. Werner Conze and Ulrich Engelhardt (Stuttgart, 1981), pp. 446–86. See also in the same volume Günter Schulz, "'Der konnte freilich anders sparen als ich.' Untersuchungen zum Sparverhalten industrieller Arbeiter im 19. Jahrhundert," pp. 487–515.

and innkeepers was part of a worker's everyday life. In their higher earning phases (i.e., in their younger years), workers often bought household items, clothing, or some jewelry, which in emergency situations could then be sold. Savings, when they existed at all, could at most bridge over sudden emergencies. They could not help against the structural crises of working life – long or frequent bouts of unemployment, "poor people's diseases," the death of family members and especially of children, the pauperization of the elderly.[24] That made the future hard to plan for workers. Alternating phases of unemployment/insufficient support and excessive consumption were not rare among certain groups of workers.

In my view extremely uncertain working and living conditions and sporadic, excessive consumption do not contradict one another. The acquisition of jewelry or fashionable clothing, running contrary to every principle of thrift, expressed the attempt to treat oneself at least once, at least outwardly, in order to resemble the respected and well-to-do people. This was a clear example of a proletarian sense of self-esteem, the struggle for reputation.

Regular alcohol consumption and pub going, also very widespread among workers and in no way conducive to saving, were inseparable from the proletarian working and living conditions of that time. Long workdays full of hard physical work, periods of unemployment and poverty, wretched, cramped housing conditions and extremely restrictive living conditions offered poor opportunities for culturally demanding leisure activities. Many a worker probably sought out the tavern as a temporary refuge and alcohol as a painkiller. Some of them here and there certainly succumbed to drunkenness. But to many workers tavern life had the same meaning as the conviviality of the coffee houses, salons, and clubs did to the well-to-do burghers: here people were together with their own kind, here they relaxed over card and board games, here they read the newspaper and informed themselves in conversation, here they discussed the things that moved them. In the 1860s workers' educational societies and political clubs convened in taverns.[25] Despite

---

24. See Heilwig Schomerus, "Lebenszyklus und Lebenshaltung in Arbeiterhausanstalten des 19. Jahrhunderts," in *Arbeiter im Industrialisierungsprozeß* ed. Werner Conze and Ulrich Engelhardt (Stuttgart, 1979) pp. 195–200.
25. One example for this is the inn Hotel de Saxe at Klostergaße 8. Here Pastor Ludwig Würkert, who was reprimanded by the reactionaries for his activities in the revolution of 1848, ran a "refreshment room for popular education, ennoblement, and encouragement." Here the independent workers' educational society Vorwärts,

financial sacrifices, pub going and the consumption it entailed brought workers spiritual gains that should not be underestimated. Its importance for the development of solidary and proletarian community relationships must be assessed highly.[26] But it was certainly deleterious to an advancement-oriented life!

Petty-bourgeois working and living conditions demanded different consumption and savings habits. A small store, a small workshop, or a small inn could be acquired, maintained, and, if need be, expanded only through the strictest frugality. In this regard the fact of proletarian or nonproletarian birth, or the upbringing in a workers' or petty-bourgeois family, already decisively set the stage for later life.

3. Yet workers could not have been completely ignorant of the fact that domestic servants often put by considerable savings, since the latter often acted as money lenders.[27] Workers' and journeymen's sons nevertheless were less inclined than master craftsmen's and farmers' sons to enter long-term domestic service. It seems that it was just as unattractive to them to serve in the military for several years as it was to hire themselves out for domestic service for several years.

Both paths involved an extraordinarily sharp curtailment of their individual freedom and their human personality. The personal dependence on either master or superior officer was great and the possibility of achieving individual rights as a private person through special legal regulations (domestic service regulations, military jurisdiction) were limited. In domestic as in military service the entire daily routine, both work and leisure, was regulated to the tiniest detail – all the way to clothing, the type of leisure activities, and the choice of personal acquaintances. Even the gratification of normal human needs, such as love and security, partnership, and the founding of a family, were all dependent on the whims of the master/superior officer.

For many workers, as well as for many wage-earning journeymen, such a life had an unbearable, even despicable quality to it. It did not fit in with their sense of pride and honor. Thus a journey-

---

founded in 1862, also met. From it proceeded significant initiatives for the founding of the later ADAV (Allgemeiner Deutscher Arbeiter-Verein).

26. See also Siegfried Reck, *Arbeiter nach der Arbeit. Sozialhistorische Studie zu den Wandlungen des Arbeiteralltags* (Lahn-Gießen, 1977), esp. pp. 134–44. See also Zwahr, *Zur Konstituierung* (above, n. 2), p. 56.

27. Cf. Schötz, "Städtische Mittelschichten" (above n. 1), p. 136.

man's departure from the household of his master was experienced as an act of emancipation, and hardly any one ever hearkened back to his "room and board," for this always meant a simultaneous constriction of personal needs and domestic dependence.[28]

Naturally, workers did not live free from constraints and commitments either. However, the main difference between them and domestic servants and military persons was the fact that capitalist entrepreneurs sold the labor power of the worker for the purpose of the capitalist production of surplus value during set working hours, thus leaving the worker with a certain amount of leisure time. And what a worker did in his leisure time, whether or whom he married, how he dressed depended not on any regulations, but instead on his – to be sure modest – material possibilities and was of no interest to the entrepreneur.

If a worker did not enjoy great personal freedoms, he at least enjoyed the small ones. The rhythm of capitalist production and reproduction, with its dependence on working hours and leisure time, on capitalist working conditions and bourgeois living conditions, brought them about. How important these small freedoms were to him, despite all the afflictions and worries – despite the hardship, the misery, the material insecurity, and limitation of working life – in my opinion reveals itself in the fact that long-term domestic or military service represented an alternative to far fewer workers' sons than sons of the petty bourgeoisie.

The rhythm of a small commodity producer's pattern of existence demanded a different mentality. As revealed in our biographical mass source, the sons of master craftsmen and farmers struggled with all their might to continue the petty-bourgeois lifestyle of their parents in order to escape the widening maelstrom of capital and wage labor. Above all second or later-born sons (but not they alone), who had no chance of inheriting the paternal farm or workshop, seized every opportunity to achieve a status that at least resembled that of their parents and represented a step above proletarian wage dependence.[29] They put up with the cost of such a status, long years of sacrifice and curtailment of personal freedom, because they had always known it that way. Their parents and

---

28. Cf. among others Jürgen Kocka, "Einführung und Auswertung," in *Handwerker in der Industrialisierung*, ed. Ulrich Engelhardt (Stuttgart, 1984), p. 462; Zwahr, Zur Konstituierung (above, n. 2), p. 60.

29. For evidence of this, see Schötz, "Städtische Mittelschichten" (above, n. 1), esp. p. 133.

grandparents too had long submitted themselves to various kinds of dependence in order to be able to maintain their property and their independent livelihood. That might seem contradictory to many of us today. But in my opinion this discrepancy did not exist for the sons of the petty bourgeoisie in this study. Their upbringing at home and their conceptions of life scarcely permitted them to perceive any contradictions between material interests and emotions.

At this point it seems appropriate to let the biographical material speak for itself in order to illustrate – at least a little bit – the perceptions, interpretations, and reactions of those people who, as they hired themselves out for years in order to become small grocers, so rigorously restricted their human personalities. I would first like to give Heinrich Carl Karius, the son of a master butcher, a chance to speak. In 1850, when explaining the source of the six hundred *Taler* he had brought together to set himself up independently, he stated: "And because I exercised the greatest thrift over many years, thinking of nothing but of an independent existence, thus I was able – on the basis of a small paternal inheritance – to keep together my wages and every other emolument, no matter how small, through the strictest frugality. I avoided every expenditure and, through the investment with interest of my savings, I was left with a round sum of six hundred *Taler*." Before his establishment, Karius served for seventeen years as a house servant and stable groom.[30] His example reveals a complete advancement strategy, namely, always and with every action to think only of the goal, independence; with enviable consistency to save each and every bit of income and to invest it with the highest possible interest; and, above all, in pursuit of this strategy to live in the strictest frugality for seventeen years.

Christian Friedrich Zschaake, the son of a peasant farmer from Köhra near Leipzig, needed longer to establish himself as a grocer – he had worked for twenty-three years as a manservant.[31]

The path through life of Johann August Senf, a journeyman linen weaver born in 1807, the son of a master weaver, shows how intent the sons of nonproletarian parents were to carry on the petty-bourgeois lifestyle of their forefathers and to escape the ever more rapidly expanding wage labor within the capitalist relations of

30. Cf. ibid., p. 101.
31. Ibid., p. 103.

production. During his hearing before receiving citizenship in Leipzig in 1844, he stated: "Whereas the weaving industry has become more and more depressed in recent times, I thus proceeded to Leipzig in the year 1833. There I at first worked for two years in the tobacco factory of Herr Apel and Herr Brunner, after 1835 then in the shop of Herr Thiesner as well as for his successor, Herr Julius Gaitzsch, and am until now in the latter's employment as a market helper." As a market helper Senf also succeeded in saving up the six hundred *Taler* necessary for an independent existence as a grocer.[32] Senf's switch from the manufacture of tobacco to domestic service is tantamount to a break away from capitalist wage labor and can be understood as a stride toward self-demarcation from the wage laborers exploited in the putting-out system, in manufacturing or in the factory, and as a conscious self-orientation.

Twenty percent of the domestic servants streaming into the grocery business had, like Senf, first learned a trade but had then given it up and switched over to domestic service. The journeyman baker Wilhelm Daniel Fahnert belonged to this group. He confessed quite openly in his hearing in 1843: "The main object of my endeavors in the thirty years and more I have lived in this city has been my independent establishment here."[33] And if this was not possible in one's own trade, an untrained occupation could always be taken up as a last resort.

Journeymen who had been active for years as wage laborers in their trades without achieving independence and who then switched directly over to the grocery business formed, from an intergenerational point of view, the second largest pool of recruitment for grocers. A written statement by Karl Heinrich Hegenwald, explaining his switch to the grocery business in 1837, illustrates what such a path through life might have looked like: "As a journeyman soap boiler, with my trifling wages and the scant work in this area, I too, through the most strenuous efforts, could scrape together only two hundred *Taler*. Now I am already in my forty-first year, in which all hopes of a career in my profession disappear more and more, in which other sources of an honest living are frustrated. Now the opportunity offers itself to take over the grocery business of K.G. Klemm. . . . Since as a man in my forties I cannot go on the tramp in my profession, as all masters prefer to take young people,

32. Ibid.
33. Ibid., p. 104.

therefore I, as a native of this city, submit . . . the . . . urgent request
that my petition not be denied." In a time when large soap works
already existed, the independent setting up of a soap boiler depended on a high initial capital investment, which Hegewald did not
possess. The assets of his bride ultimately enabled him to open up a
grocery store.[34]

As these life stories can hardly show more clearly,[35] the entire
striving and aspiration of many farmers' and master artisans' sons
was directed toward independence, and thereby a social status
similar to that of their parents. They did everything to escape first
capitalist wage labor, and in the end any form of wage labor at all.
Inherited living patterns and values, based on so-called bourgeois
independence, continued to influence them strongly. The vitality of
such values was so great because under the changing social conditions opportunities to realize them presented themselves. One such
opportunity lay in the grocery business.

Leipzig's workers were inclined to dedicate themselves less often
to "serving their way up" than the petty bourgeoisie, perhaps
because for them other experiences, observations, and impressions
entered the equation: for example, their observation of the rapid
increase of capitalist wage labor together with railroad and factory
construction; the collective production and exploitation experience
in the putting-out system, in manufacturing, or in the factory; the
experience, perhaps the participation in collective self-help attempts
by the workers in wage disputes, in the foundation of the first
union-oriented organizations in the Vormärz and in the revolution
of 1848/49, and in the founding of the Lassallean Allgemeiner
Deutscher Arbeiter-Verein in 1863; the experience of bourgeois,
petty bourgeois, and socialist- or communist-influenced politicians
with their programs for the working class and, as the flip side of the
same coin, the experience of intensifying neighborhood, marriage,
and godparenthood relations among the workers themselves. Is it
not understandable when, on the basis of collective work and
exploitation experiences as well as deepening internal class relationships, Leipzig workers tended to hope for an improvement in their
collective situation (for example, in their occupational group) or to

34. Ibid.
35. I could verify the accuracy of the personal testimonies to the extent that many
files contain work certificates, residence and good conduct certificates, asset
vouchers, medical certificates, and other documents.

act to achieve it? And does it not seem equally plausible that the petty bourgeoisie, producing in isolation, struggling against competition – just like the domestic servant serving in isolation – sought an *individual* escape into an improvement in their situation?

Into this train of thought enters the fact that the majority of the men in the recruiting pool who were sons of domestic servants began, after their schooltime, to pursue – as shop helpers or postal and railroad officials – career paths that clearly were associated with nonproletarian orientations.[36] Even if none of the sales clerks of this background was ever able to set himself up as a merchant, mercantile training secured their existence in the more solid middle strata. While the learning of a trade frequently led into the lower middle strata, mercantile or civil service training provided access to the solid middle strata and, if the occasion arose, to the bourgeoisie and the high bureaucracy.

Compared to the advancement of workers' children, that of workers themselves was negligible. The unbroken crossover of workers' groups into middle-strata groups was apparently only marginally possible. Long-term domestic and military service indicate that an early escape from capitalist wage labor or an early nonproletarian orientation facilitated social advancement into the middle strata.

---

36. Cf. Schötz, "Städtische Mittelschichten" (above, n. 1), p. 71.

HARTMUT HARNISCH

Questions of the Mentality and Economic Circumstances of the Peasants Living on East Elbian Estates in the Final Decades before the Agrarian Reforms

1. Problems of Investigation

In "Scenes from Peasant Lives," a chapter in his well-known chef d'oeuvre of 1887 about the lives of eighteenth-century peasants on the East Elbian estates, Georg Friedrich Knapp, professor of economics at the University of Strassburg and adherent of the "modern" school of economics, wrote: "And so the peasant remained everlastingly the same, muddleheaded, dark, dissatisfied, coarse, servile, paying heed only to the warden; an unhappy cross between human being and beast of burden."[1]

This image has scarcely changed up to the present day. The dominant view of peasants remains that of downtrodden subjects of all-powerful feudal lords, struggling desperately to survive an almost hopeless situation, unable to break out of the vicious cycles of a petrified socioeconomic order, forever dependent and usually hard-pressed by their overlords. It is hardly necessary to adduce the relevant literature.

There is much truth of course to this view. But alongside many accurate assessments are some striking misconceptions, for despite

---

1. Georg Friedrich Knapp, *Die Bauernbefreiung und der Ursprung der Landarbeiter in den älteren Theilen Preußens*, (Leipzig, 1887), 1:77.

more than a century of research into the history of agriculture, the body of reliable knowledge about the peasant economy is still very fragmentary. Apart from some problematic attempts to make interregional comparisons on the basis of certain overall statistics,[2] our knowledge is based on the analysis of a meager number of individual examples. So far as the mentality of the peasantry on the East Elbian estates is concerned, virtually no studies exist at all. It is indeed no easy matter to piece together an authentic picture of the lives of the peasantry, their material circumstances as well as their typical behaviors and thought patterns.

I have attempted in previous papers to outline the evolution of peasant incomes in the final fifty years before the agrarian reforms in Prussia, primarily on the basis of material from the area around Berlin.[3] The results in short were that the incomes of tenant farmers approximately doubled between 1766–70 and 1801–5 as a result of the rising price of grain, even assuming that production remained constant. Numerous individual examples also demonstrated that many tenant farmers succeeded in bolstering their incomes even more by expanding their fields under cultivation and adapting to the demands of the market.

Nonetheless, the capacity of the peasant economy to expand and adapt remained highly circumscribed. The peasant economy was confined by the need to leave one field fallow (three-field system) in compliance with the rigid rules of the open-field system, which strangled or at least severely curtailed its ability to modernize, for instance, by growing root crops or fodder in the fallow fields. In addition, the farmers on the German lands east of the Elbe were the subjects of a feudal landholder and normally had no property rights to the farms they worked. Even their livestock and implements frequently did not belong to them, but wholly or in part to the lord of the manor. As a result, the tenant farmers had no real credit-

---

2. For instance, Friedrich Wilhelm Henning, *Dienste und Abgaben der Bauern im 18. Jahrhundert* (Stuttgart, 1969), vol. 21, *Quellen und Forschungen zur Agrargeschichte*, ed. Wilhelm Abel und Günther Franz.
3. Hartmut Harnisch, *Kapitalistische Agrarreform und Industrielle Revolution. Agrarhistorische Untersuchungen über das ostelbische Preußen zwischen Spätfeudalismus und bürgerlich-demokratischer Revolution unter besonderer Berücksichtigung der Provinz Brandenburg* (Weimar, 1984), vol. 19, *Veröff. des Staatsarchivs Potsdam*, ed. Friedrich Beck, p. 27ff.; idem, "Peasants and Markets: The Background to the Agrarian Reforms in Feudal Prussia East of the Elbe, 1760–1807," in *The German Peasantry: Conflict and Community in Rural Society from the Eighteenth to the Twentieth Centuries*, ed. Richard J. Evans and W.R. Lee (London, 1968), pp. 37ff.

worthiness and even when they acquired some money of their own, had not the slightest incentive to invest it in the farms they worked. The cardinal feature of a landed estate, as compared to other forms of property, was the prominent role played by the corvée or enforced labor on behalf of the estate, which far overshadowed the two other forms of rent. This feature of the late feudal agrarian structure had certain specific consequences. A corvée of more than two to three days a week could only be performed by large farms able to maintain two teams of draft animals. These farms were consequently compelled to employ additional laborers from outside the immediate family. The need to pay their wages as well as the heavy taxes of the Prussian state forced tenant farmers to sell their products regularly for cash. It could accordingly be said that the tenant farmers on the East Elbian estates were compelled to take part in the market economy. Long before the shift to capitalistic agriculture, these farmers had to calculate every last penny.

Tenant farmers on the East Elbian estates therefore lived curiously ambivalent lives. On the one hand, they were the menial subjects of a feudal overlord, quite at his mercy, deprived of all property rights and often even of all personal rights. The peasant laws of Prussian absolutism guaranteed that their position would continue, but did not guarantee them any right to have a family on the farm. The village community offered some protection, but it was usually very poorly developed on the East Elbian estates. Finally, the king would probably show some interest in preserving "his" peasant class. On the other hand, tenant farmers were often the heads of households numbering seven to ten people. They operated large farms and regularly marketed their products. As such, they played the role of small rural entrepreneurs, which gave them an opportunity to acquire profits and accumulate a certain "wealth." The advantages they derived from this increased substantially in the second half of the eighteenth century. In the end, this curious ambivalence in the lives of farmers on the East Elbian estates must have had a strong impact on their mentality.

My studies are based on certain definite assumptions. I presume that a peasant on the feudal estates was largely at the mercy of his overlord. I also presume that as the head of a large household responsible for paying a complicated structure of feudal dues and taxes, he must have had a good knowledge of his markets and have been able to reckon with considerable accuracy. I further presume that such a peasant had some chance of acquiring property and that inheritances and bequests therefore played a prominent role in how he planned his life and attempted to acquire some security. From these assumptions flow a whole array of questions about the peasant economy and about the tenant farmer's behavior toward his feudal master, toward his own class, and to those beneath. These questions can only be discussed on the basis of concrete regional examples. In order to do so, I have reverted to a previous study of mine,[4] which can be carried on from the viewpoint of the new interest that has arisen in the last few decades in the mentality of the laboring masses. This of course is an integral part of social history and of the history of everyday life.

2. Socioeconomic Structures in the Region

The area under study, the estate of Boitzenburg, lies in Uckermark, some 80 kilometers north of Berlin. Since the sixteenth century it had been in the possession of the von Arnim family, who were made counts in 1786. Apart from occasional small changes in ownership, the core of the estate was a fairly cohesive territory of about 300 square kilometers (exactly 287.2 square kilometers). At the end of the eighteenth century, it encompassed the eleven peasant villages of Beenz, Berkholz, Hardenbeck, Haßleben, Klaushagen, Naugarten, Rosenow, Thomsdorf, Warthe, Weggun, and Wichmannsdorf. It also included thirteen estates, the main farm of Boitzenburg as well as the farms and lands of Boisterfelde, Bröddin, Brüsenwalde, Crewitz, Cüstrinchen, Funkenhagen, Fürstenau, Götschendorf, Mahlendorf, Petznick, Wuppgarten, and Zerwelin.

If the large forested areas are included, the lands in the direct possession of the von Arnim family were considerably larger than those leased by the peasants. However, if only arable land is included – the extent of castle grounds and gardens as well as the meadowlands in the villages were not measured exactly – then the proportion of estate lands to tenant farms was 1:2.1. Tenant farms therefore still played the largest economic role in the estate.

There were 189 tenant farms and seven cottager farms attached to the eleven villages on the estate around 1800. These occasional

4. Hartmut Harnisch, *Die Herrschaft Boitzenburg, Untersuchungen zur Entwicklung der sozialökonomischen Struktur ländlicher Gebiete in der Mark Brandenburg vom 14. bis zum 19. Jahrhundert* (Weimar, 1968), vol. 6, *Veröff. des Staatsarchivs Potsdam*, ed. Friedrich Beck.

cottagers held only half as much land per head as did the tenant farmers in their village. However, they had their own team of draft animals and, so far as possible under the prevailing feudal conditions, could be considered independent, small–scale tenant farmers. On average for the entire estate, each tenant farmer worked 37.7 hectares of land, though there were substantial deviations from the norm. For instance, the average tenant farmer in Haßleben farmed 68.3 hectares of land and in Thomsdorf 56.4 hectares, but only 28.5 hectares in Weggun. The tenant farmers in each village always held pretty much exactly the same amounts of land, with the exception of the village mayor who usually held more. Finally, about as many peasants lived on Boitzenburg as generally did on East Elbian estates.

The population of the entire estate rose between 1724 and 1801 from 2,080 to 3,965, thus roughly doubling. However, the number of tenant farms remained fairly constant after about 1740. The result was that by 1800 peasants had already become a minority on the estate. According to a census of 1801, there were 513 households on the estate.[5] One hundred and eighty-nine of these belonged to tenant farmers and seven to cottagers, accounting in total for 38.2 percent of all households. *Einlieger*, or people who held no land, generally worked as day laborers, and lived in sheds rented from tenant farmers or the overlord, accounted for no fewer than 277 households or 54.0 percent of the total. The remaining forty households were those of the ruling family, who leased out the land (so far as it was leased out), pastors, a few artisans with land of their own (e.g., smiths), and finally nine *Büdner*, or owners of small strips of land, who accounted for 1.7 percent of all households.

A crucial factor in the lives of the tenant farmers was their legal position on the farm they worked and the type and amount of surplus value skimmed off by the overlord. Apart from a few remaining liege mayors and an occasional heritable-tenure farm in the village of Hardenbeck, the farmers held limited leases to their land. It and the buildings on it were the property of the overlord. The livestock and implements, however, belonged to the farmer.

Many tenant farmers were compelled upon assuming control of the farm or as a result of misfortune to borrow money from the overlord for the purchase of draft animals. Others had to borrow

---

5. Friedrich W.A. Bratring, *Statistisch-topographische Beschreibung der gesamten Kurmark* (Berlin, 1805), 2: 524ff.

because they lacked seed. These loans often weighed the farmers down for decades, though no interest was demanded.

Feudal exploitation, through the skimming off of surplus value, took two forms: monetary rentals and the corvée. Rather than having to perform a certain number of days' labor, each tenant farm on the Boitzenburg estate was required to work a certain additional area, three hectares in size, on the lord's behalf. The farmers were also required to cart the lord's produce to Berlin and, if requested, to cart dung to the estate fields. Finally, each tenant farm was required to cut the meadowlands for three days.

All this has been calculated for the village of Hardenbeck and translated into workdays per farm, amounting to seventy-eight days of work with draft animals, combined with thirty-seven days of manual labor for a man and eleven for a woman. This burden was equally high in the other villages on the estate, with the exception of Beenz and Haßleben, which were free of the corvée. If a farmer was incapable of performing these services or if a particular farm was not occupied for a time, the community as a whole was required to work the overlord's lands attached to that farm.

In comparison with labor requirements on many Prussian estates totalling three, four, or even five days a week, the tenant farmers on the Boitzenburg estate were well-off. However, they were also required to make monetary payments, described as rent. These amounted around 1800 to 28 *Reichstaler* a year in the village of Thomsdorf, where the farmers also performed the usual corvée, and to 57 *Reichstaler*[6] in Haßleben, where the farmers were not subject to the corvée. The burden imposed by these rents becomes apparent if one considers that one *Wispel* of rye (about twenty-four bushels or 972 kilograms) brought a average of 33 *Reichstaler*, 6 *Groschen* in Berlin in the years 1766 to 1770, though prices rose to an average of 71 *Reichstaler*, 10 *Groschen* between 1801 and 1805. In response to this leap in grain prices toward the end of the eighteenth century, the feudal lords also increased the annual rent, though not by nearly as much: rents increased by some 10 to 20 percent, while grain prices doubled. Very little rent was paid in kind on the Boitzenburg estate.

Enough surplus value was siphoned off to leave the peasant family with no more than it needed to reproduce itself. An estimate drawn up in 1765 for a farm in the village of Warthe has survived,

6. *Reichstaler* equalled 24 *Groschen* or 16.7025 grams of pure silver.

and it can be assumed to reflect conditions elsewhere as well. This is not the place to analyze this estimate in detail, but at least the salient points can be indicated. The farm comprised 67 hectares of land, of which only 17.53 could be farmed regularly. The harvest was estimated at 112.8 double hundredweights for the year, of which 26.9 percent would likely be marketed. Finally, a calculation of income and expenses shows that the farm was left with an annual surplus of 1 *Reichstaler*, 12 *Groschen*, and 4 *Pfennig*. This begs commentary in several different respects that cannot be delved into here. Of significance for this paper is the observation that if the market share remained constant, sales of grain in the immediate area would have earned an average of only 81 *Reichstaler*, 1 *Groschen* in the years 1766–70, but 171 *Reichstaler* as early as 1801–5.[7]

This estimate would certainly have reflected with only minimal fluctuations actual farm income in 1765. The tenant farmers went to great lengths somehow to increase this income. Since their draft animals were not fully utilized in the winter, they were commonly set to such tasks as drawing sleighs loaded with wood. For instance, a peasant widow from Beenz named Pritzkow explained in 1789 before the manorial court that she hoped during the winter to earn at least 16 to 20 *Reichstaler* hauling wood with her two horses.[8] This would enable her to pay all or a good part of the rent she owed the lord of the manor, amounting in Beenz to 20 *Reichstaler*.

The most important sources for this study were the lease records, beginning around 1770, of 165 limited-lease farms held in the manorial court. These documents contain all the information about changes in possession, in particular the contracts bestowing limited leaseholds, as well as the records of the manorial court and of the estate bailiff regarding peasant inheritances or petitions from established tenant farmers for a new lease or for their son to carry on their old lease.

These lease records provide a representative cross section of the central aspects of the lives of the peasants, or better peasant families, and show how these aspects influenced and conditioned one another. The following key aspects could be singled out:

7. Comparisons: Hartmut Harnisch, "Peasants and Markets. The Background to the Agrarian Reforms in Feudal Prussia East of the Elbe, 1760–1807," in *The German Peasantry: Conflict and Community in Rural Society from the Eighteenth to the Twentieth Centuries*, ed. Richard J. Evans and W.R. Lee (London, 1986), pp. 37ff.

8. *Staatsarchiv Potsdam*, Pr. Br. Rep. 37, Boitzenburg Estate, no. 992.

1. The authorities in general, in this case represented primarily by the von Arnim family, which owned the Boitzenburg estate. As the lords and masters of the estate, they not only embodied local feudal rule but also the authority of the Prussian state in their role as overseers of the manorial court and police force.
2. The authorities in the form of the Prussian army. Under the canton system in place since 1733, every young, male subject was liable to be conscripted until expressly released.
3. The village, without whose involvement no peasant could farm under the conditions described above and which was also largely responsible for enforcing many of the demands of the feudal lord and the Prussian state.
4. The family, within whose confines the peasantry reproduced itself and which was the primary source of succor and support.

3. Peasants' Everyday Life under Feudal Authority and in the Prussian Army

Peasant life and behaviors will be analyzed in the following from the point of view of these various key aspects.

We shall begin with the feudal authorities, who always profoundly influenced the family and the village community. The von Arnims were deeply involved in the administration of their lands. The lease records contain many directives from them about proceedings in the manorial court or the bailiff's reports.

As one glances through the records of the tenant farms, the overwhelming impression is that the leases were usually extended, or from the point of view of the lessee, that the farmers clung tenaciously to the land they tilled. Peasants directed all their efforts, it seems, toward one day assuming their fathers' farms in order to live there, reproduce there, and one day have a son or son-in-law take over the lease in their old age and provide security until they died.

For instance, when the old peasant Reinicke was forced to relinquish his farm in Haßleben in 1769 because of debt, he protested and pointed out that he had leased that farm for thirty-six years before running into difficulties through circumstances beyond his control.[9] In another case, a tenant farmer in Klaushagen asked to be

9. Ibid., no. 1104.

released from a lease he had just assumed in order to take over the farm of his brother who had died suddenly because the latter farm had been worked by his family for some two hundred years.[10] The Arnims had a strong interest of their own of course in retaining those tenant farmers who had leased and successfully managed farms for many years under the conditions laid down by the Arnims, who paid their rent punctually, performed the corvée, discharged their state taxes, and contributed their share to the village. This was the kind of submissive peasants a feudal lord needed! It was entirely in line with his own interests when Count Arnim once cut short a discussion about who would be the next lessee of a farm with the pithy comment: "I normally offer it first to the heir of the deceased peasant."[11]

The Arnims certainly did not treat their peasants brutally, but they were the overlords of a great feudal holding and were naturally concerned first and foremost with reliable payment of the rents that were due. Despite an occasional demonstration of forbearance toward farmers who were experiencing difficulties, they insisted in the main on full payment of the rent owed and on prompt performance of the corvée.

The essence of their attitude was expressed in Count Arnim's reaction in 1809 to the request of a certain Pritzkow, an old, childless peasant from Hardenbeck, that his lease be transferred to his farmhand Michael Bade, who had loyally served him for many years and to whom substantial wages were still owing. Arnim responded most ungraciously, "I don't accord any rights of reversion in respect to limited leases" and added that Bade would have to appear before the manorial court in order to seek payment of his back wages from the old peasant "because my claims on Pritzkow take precedence over those of Bade."[12] In the end, Bade did receive the farm, but Count Arnim had underscored the primacy of his claims.

Most tenant farmers managed to survive on their farms under the prevailing conditions. However, some always fell too deeply into debt and an *Exmissionsverfahren*, or bankruptcy proceedings, had to be opened. The patience of feudal lords was rapidly exhausted once a tenant farmer was clearly in serious difficulty and no longer able to pay his rents promptly and perform the corvée. For instance,

10. Ibid., no. 1131
11. Ibid., no. 1127
12. Ibid., no. 1071

Count Arnim dismissed requests for support from Christian Schulz, a tenant farmer in Rosenow who was experiencing difficulties, with the following comment: "I do not bear Christian Schulz any ill will and shall even provide for him, but a farmer who has neither money nor livestock is a miserable creature who cannot recover."[13] It should be pointed out that Prussian law required feudal lords in any case to provide for peasants who had gone bankrupt.

Bankruptcy proceedings were initiated in a number of cases because village mayors and aldermen informed the lord that certain farmers were experiencing difficulty.[14] This conduct was motivated by a clause in the lease requiring the village community to make up any shortfalls in the corvée caused by peasants unable to perform their share.[15]

On the whole, though, very few tenant farmers went bankrupt during the period covered by the records: only some fifteen to twenty between 1780 and 1810. One can safely assume that later, under capitalist agriculture, it could hardly have been any fewer.

Flight was even less common than bankruptcies. The cases that are recorded show that it was an act of desperation on the part of heavily indebted farmers on the brink of bankruptcy. The village inhabitants must have had an inkling of what was about to happen in the cases of farmers who first sold their horses and oxen.[16] These farmers evidently hoped to save at least some of their wealth before everything they owned was auctioned off after the bankruptcy proceedings in order to pay their debts. The peasant Friedrich Knop disappeared with his wife and children from the village of Warthe in 1783 after first having relocated all his livestock. But he lives on the manorial records as a "depraved bankrupt."[17]

In spite of all the risks and adversity faced by tenant farmers on limited leases, the overlords experienced no difficulty in finding a candidate for any farm that became available. In fact, there was

13. Ibid., no. 1154
14. Ibid., no. 1101; no. 1163, in which an apparent successor to the farm was described as mentally deranged in 1798, but still received a lease from overlord; no. 1137; no. 1134; no. 1240.
15. Ibid., no. 1310; the mayor and aldermen notified the overlord in 1803 that the tenant farmer had failed several times to appear to the corvée.
16. Ibid., no. 1132 and no. 1131. The Krosegk brothers from Klaushagen disappeared in the spring of 1809. It later became known that they had previously sold off livestock.
17. Ibid., no. 1245

usually more than one contender. The wives of deceased farmers were often surrounded in short order by a swarm of admirers who wished to marry them and take over the lease. Most aspirants to available farms originated from one of the villages on the estate. Since the livestock, implements, and to a certain extent the seed as well were the property of the farmer, the lessees had already to possess a certain "wealth," as the sources put it. The general impression left by these records is that the tenant farmers did not suffer from any lack of money, not to mention from poverty. The property statements, which the rulers required of the contenders before granting a new lease or which can be found in the inheritance papers of more established families, reveal that the offspring of farmers who wished to assume the family's old lease or to receive a new one were often quite capable of producing a certain "wealth." As a rule, a sum of 200 to 250 *Reichstaler* was required in order to assume a new lease. Joachim Müller, for instance, applied for a lease on a farm in 1783. He was able to show the manorial court that he had 250 *Reichstaler* in cash and "was therefore fully capable of assuming responsibility for this farm."[18] The third and fourth sons of tenant farmers often used their own savings as well as assistance from their families in order to apply for a lease on another farm.

The determination of long-term tenant farmers to hold on to their farms and the endeavors of new candidates to be awarded a lease illustrate the strategy most peasant families adopted under the prevailing socioeconomic conditions in order to gain a secure existence. Large tenant farmers with stable markets and corresponding levels of income demonstrated similar behaviors, which can be assumed to have been widespread in the late feudal era.

The accumulated wealth of a farmer in one of the villages on the Boitzenburg estate who had worked for a considerable period without experiencing any particularly extraordinary setbacks lay roughly in the neighborhood of 500 to 700 *Reichstaler*. The property of a Haßleben farmer named Wolter, who had run into financial difficulty, was evaluated in 1793 at a total of 330 *Reichstaler*. The manorial court regarded this as very low and noted that 600 *Reichstaler* was more normal in Haßleben.[19] In 1789 when a farmer named Hübner from the same village had his assets evaluated by the village court, i.e., the mayor and the aldermen, before turning his

18. Ibid., no. 1318
19. Ibid., no. 1101

farm over to his son-in-law, the total amounted to 767 *Reichstaler,* 13 *Groschen* and 4 *Pfennig.*[20]

Numerous individual evaluations produced total assets in this range. A farmer's widow named Schultz from the village of Warthe produced cash savings alone totaling 1,588 *Reichstaler,* 17 *Groschen,* in addition to all the usual livestock and equipment, but this must be regarded as extraordinarily high.[21] Equally "well-off" was the tenant farmer Gottfried Schmidt from Haßleben, who left his wife and four children 1,904 *Reichstaler,* 3 *Groschen* and 4 *Pfennig* when he died in 1794.[22]

When a farmer died and his heirs applied to carry on the lease, the Arnims usually required that the inheritance first be distributed, namely, that the value of the farmer's property be accurately assessed and the portion due to each of his heirs calculated. This was done, as Count Arnim noted in 1804 in a comment on the petition of widow Schultz in Warthe asking to be allowed to continue working the farm with her minor son and brother-in-law, "so that I might see the composition of their wealth."[23] And when a peasant applied to lease a farm for the first time in 1805, Count Arnim wrote that the lease could be approved "on condition that he possesses sufficient wealth to set up a farm."[24] The lords of the manor wanted to be absolutely certain that the farm would be worked as efficiently as possible and that all rents and services would be forthcoming.

Since the tenant farmers held no property rights to the farms, there were no firmly established customs about inheritances. In fact, the Arnims rarely interfered in the family decision about who would carry on the farm. However, every transfer to a new lessee and indeed every routine lease extension provided the overlord with an opportunity to scrutinize the behavior and submissiveness of the candidate. Every petition for a farm was made by means of "seemly entreaty,"[25] as the manorial court occasionally phrased it.

The selection of the presumptive successor to their lease was a crucial decision for an aging farmer and his wife. If the son selected proved to be a poor farmer, a peasant who had farmed successfully for decades could find himself destitute in his old age. This occurred

20. Ibid., no. 1099.
21. Ibid., no. 1248.
22. Ibid., no. 1098.
23. Ibid., no. 1248
24. Ibid., no. 1240
25. For instance, Ibid., no. 1285.

to the seventy-seven year old peasant Wolter, in Haßleben, who according to the official village records had been "a very diligent and good farmer,"[26] but whose farm deteriorated so much due to the indigence and profligacy of his wife and children that finally a new lessee had to be installed in 1793. The latter was compelled to care of the old man, while his wife, who was only fifty-five years old, was sheltered by the village, though she was required to obtain her own food.

In most families, the son who would presumptively take over the lease one day was selected long in advance. This can be seen in records of disputes over inheritances that show that these sons, though often no longer young, had left their wages still invested in the farm, as an integral part of their parents' property. For instance, the mayor of Haßleben wished in 1793 to transfer his lease to his thirty-nine-year-old son, who it turned out had wages of 280 *Reichstaler* for twenty years of labor still invested in the farm.[27] Christian Feuerstake, a longtime field hand and farmer's son in the same village, provides a similar example. He declared before the manorial court in September 1800 after the death of his mother that he had worked the farm for years with the help of two younger brothers. The overlords had assured him for a considerable time that he would be allowed one day to take over the lease. He was now thirty-six years old and his claim for back wages against his mother's estate amounted to 300 *Reichstaler*.[28]

Cases such as this were frequent. It can be assumed that peasant families counted on their overlord's well-known practice of offering close relatives first chance at a lease. As a result, the presumptive heir was designated well in advance. This assumption is supported by the fact that in the multitude of recorded distributions of estates, no other children ever claimed back wages. This cannot be ascribed to mere chance. One can therefore deduce that the axiom, frequently ascribed to peasants of the preindustrial era, "there is no keeping of accounts within the family," was either observed not at all or only in the case of the son chosen to take over the farm one day. Whether one may conclude that the other children regularly received fair compensation for their labor so long as they lived and worked on the farm is a question that has not yet been answered.

26. Ibid., no. 1101.
27. Ibid., no. 1096.
28. Ibid., no. 1106.

The ability to designate a son as the eventual successor to the farm – assuming that the lord of the manor would graciously approve the choice – greatly enhanced the present lessee's status as the head of the family, for the designated successor could be changed at any time. Reinicke, the bankrupt farmer in Haßleben, struggled before the manorial court to hold on to his farm by pointing out that he had promised to establish his son on the farm: "I had promised my eldest son that if he followed me and did well, I would give him 40 *Reichstaler* and an ox when he married."[29] In Weggun, the wife of a farmer named Hess reneged in 1789 on the intention she had expressed some years earlier to transfer the farm to her eldest son. The latter expressed his acquiescence in this and promised "none the less to support them loyally and truly."[30] In Naugarten, Liedke's widow altered the expected succession in 1812 because of irreconcilable differences with her eldest son.[31]

The phrase "to follow and do well" expresses the core belief behind the strict discipline that parents often exercised over even their adult children. They were able to do this because the life of a tenant farmer was highly prized, even under these less than easy conditions. Farmers' sons must have seen it as far more attractive and promising far greater social prestige and chances for a somewhat comfortable life than the relatively secure but meager existence of a day laborer or cottager.

The need to accumulate a certain amount of personal wealth, whether to equip the farm upon taking over a new lease or to have some reserves with which to face all the vicissitudes of farm life, meant that prospective tenant farmers could only marry women from their own social stratum. Farmers' sons naturally married farmers' daughters, who could make some monetary contribution to the partnership. The records do not reveal a single case of a prospective tenant farmer marrying the daughter of a day laborer or cottager. The most important aspect of the lives of all peasants – their relationship with the lord of the manor – became curiously bound up in this way with family life, because the overlord and the family both had an interest in ensuring that tenant farmers maintained sufficient wealth.

The importance of a substantial dowry is evident in a statement

29. Ibid., no. 1104.
30. Ibid., no. 1270.
31. Ibid., no. 1161.

made by tenant farmer Fahrenholz from Klaushagen before the
manorial court in 1796.[32] Fahrenholz had three sons and he wanted
the youngest to assume his lease. His eldest son, who worked as a
teamster on one of the estate farms, had married a woman who did
not bring any wealth into the marriage. According to Fahrenholz,
they regularly consumed what little they earned, and since this son
could not expect any further compensation from his father, he
would not be able to take over the farm. Fahrenholz's second son
was also married and he was a day laborer in Klaushagen. He too
could not possibly take over the farm because his eyesight was so
poor that he could not sow properly.

Very similar statements were given in other cases. Johann Kietz-
mann, a seventy-year-old farmer from Beenz altered the prospective
succession to his farm because his eldest son had been keeping
company with the daughter of a day laborer and now wanted to
marry her, "even though she did not have the slightest wealth, for
which reason he would not be able to stay with them."[33] It is
noteworthy that the father saw his son's romantic inclinations as
endangering a comfortable old age for himself. He therefore asked
Count Arnim to approve the transfer of the lease to his youngest
son. This son, however, was serving in the army, and Arnim
showed little inclination to seek his dismissal. Stories such as this
were occasionally concocted, to be sure, for the purpose of procur-
ing a son's release from the army.

Our sources provide little information about the relationship
between tenant farmers and the lower social orders. The mounting
social distinctions among rural folk are plainly visible in the tendency of tenant farmers to marry within their own social stratum.
However, their daughters often married *Einlieger* or day laborers,
as shown by the records of the beneficiaries of their estates, and
their sons were often forced down into the stratum of farm workers
with little or no land. However, every peasant had at least a chance
of some day becoming a tenant farmer since farms were always
becoming available as a result of individual bankruptcy or because
the widows of deceased farmers were always under pressure to
marry again soon. Numerous aspirants always hoped to obtain a
new lease. The Arnims were careful to select among the many
aspirants those who could demonstrate the greatest wealth. When

32. Ibid., no. 1124.
33. Ibid., no. 988.

farm no. 15 in Rosenow became available in 1793, for instance, three contenders applied. Köppen, a day laborer and tenant farmer's son from Klaushagen, had no chance at all because his only source of possible support was his father and father-in-law. The second aspirant was Christian Krause from Hardenbeck, whose tenant-farmer father had accumulated "substantial wealth" and who possessed an unspecified amount of cash himself. Arnim had already decided on Christian Krause when a third aspirant appeared: Martin Friedrich Goetsch, also the son of a tenant farmer. He had 300 *Reichstaler* in cash and further announced his intention "to marry a daughter of tenant farmer Berzin in Rosenow who has 200 *Reichstaler* in cash, if your gracious excellency would be so kind as to accord him a farm."[34]

Many cases indicate that successful farmers were eager to acquire a farm for their sons or sons-in-law. Thus farmer Hoppenrath from Hardenbeck successfully applied in 1809 for a lease on farm no. 18 in Rosenow on behalf of his son, who worked for him as a farmhand, saying that "he wanted to establish him on a farm somewhere."[35] In 1805, a farmer named Dahms from Warthe secured a lease on a farm in Weggun for his younger son and provided him with an additional sum of 500 *Reichstaler*.[36] The mayor of Naugarten leased a farm for his eldest son in 1803 and gave him 200 *Reichstaler* in addition to the 200 *Reichstaler* he had received as a dowry from his bride, the daughter of a tenant farmer and innkeeper.[37]

Many more examples could easily be given. Various interests came into play in these attempts to secure available farms. For a peasant's son who already had or was likely to acquire sufficient money, a lease provided a chance to secure his future and possibly even a final exemption from military service. The family as a whole had an interest in establishing as many family members as possible on farms. Records of the beneficiaries of estates show that many a peasant father had three or four sons or daughters established on farms. This engendered influence in the village and could be vital in difficult times if credit was withdrawn.

The remarriage rate among the widows of deceased farmers shows how coveted the position of farmer was, despite all the

34. Ibid., no. 1191.
35. Ibid., no. 1194.
36. Ibid., no. 1283.
37. Ibid., no. 1152.

tribulation and coercion. Marrying a widow became a typical stepping-stone to independence for the sons of tenant farmers who did not take over their father's lease. This was also a common means of social advancement among day laborers and field hands. For many young men who had been conscripted into the army but spent most of the year on leave in their home villages, who worked there, and still considered themselves part of the village community, marriage to a such a widow could also spell lifelong release from military service.

Widows were often compelled by force of circumstance to re-marry as promptly as possible if they wished to remain on their farms. Thus Dorothea Roloff, a widow from Beenz, advised the manorial court in 1796 that her deceased husband had left her in debt and that she could only carry on the farm if she married a fitting suitor – namely, Lexow, a mayor's son from a neighboring royal administrative village whose wealth amounted to 200 *Reichstaler*.[38]

The difficulties of operating a farm provided another compelling reason for widows to remarry quickly. In 1800, a widow named Blies from the village of Wichmannsdorf requested approval of her marriage to her deceased husband's brother with the argument that she "could not manage the outdoors operations of the farm with only the help of an unrelated field hand."[39] This logic is not infrequent and illustrates the degree of trust needed to run a farm and the way in which the family relied on one another.

It is generally assumed that there was little room for mutual affection in the choice of a marriage partner among the peasantry. This was probably especially true of the second marriages of wid-ows. Our sources confirm that both parties often looked upon their marriage primarily as an avenue to personal security or greater social status. There are numerous examples of this. In order to preserve her farm, a widow from Thomsdorf named Schilling requested approval in July 1801 of her prospective marriage to Mandelkow, a farmer's son whose wealth amounted to 150 *Reichstaler* and who had served for fourteen years in the sovereign's own regiment in Prenzlau. Count Arnim gave his assent, on condition that Mandelkow could secure his release from the army. Arnim added that he did not wish to see the widow driven off her farm, and

38. Ibid., no. 997.
39. Ibid., no. 1323.

if Mandelkow was unsuccessful in securing his release, "she should then look around for another farmer of some means."[40] Schilling did in fact reappear before the manorial court in October 1801 to announce that Mandelkow had not been able to secure his release and that she now wished to marry Johann Ide, a field hand from Hardenbeck with savings amounting to 100 *Reichstaler*. Ide was very short in stature, she added, and likely to escape military service.

Only a short note is needed about village organizations as an important aspect in the lives of the peasantry. In so far as they are mentioned at all in the records, they appear only as a tool for enforcing the will of the authorities, whether the absolutist state or Count Arnim. These were not the organs of a self-confident village, asserting the interests of its residents. It was mentioned above that the village organizations took action to inform the overlord of the difficulties which had befallen a particular farmer.[41] The village also kept the books on rental payments, which were evidently paid collectively to the overlord, as well as on state taxes. Under these conditions, the village community did not afford its members any protection against the feudal lord. It played an essential role however in determining the work year of all those who labored on the lands attached to the village.

Prussia's standing army or "the regiment," as it was tersely labelled in the manorial court records, played a crucial role in the lives of the rural population.[42] All family strategies had to assume that any sons might well have to serve time in the regiment. Every adult male subject who had not yet received his "discharge," or written confirmation that he would no longer be required for active service, was expected to present himself every year at the cantonal review. Every petition for a lease had to include the candidate's age and height, in inches over five feet. Short peasants could reasonably hope for early dismissal from "the regiment."

Petitions for a lease were almost always accompanied by a request that the overlord seek the petitioner's dismissal from the regiment. Count Arnim therefore determined whether the petitioner would be placed on the list of those whose dismissal was sought, which the

40. Ibid., no. 1212.
41. see above p. 123.
42. Otto Büsch, *Militärsystem und Sozialleben im alten Preussen* (West Berlin, 1962), vol. 7, *Veröff. der Berliner historischen Commission* of the Friedrich-Meinecke Institute of the Free University of Berlin.

bailiff annually turned over to the district administration.[43] The overlord therefore decided who could lease a farm and who could marry whom, in addition to exercising considerable influence over whether a particular peasant had to serve in the army. It can truly be said that the lord of the manor had the lives of the peasants firmly in his grasp.

If a peasant had several grown sons, it was a virtual certainty that at least one of them would have to serve in the army. This can be seen in the lists of beneficiaries drawn up for the distribution of estates. Some peasants saw two of their sons conscripted – for instance, a peasant named Schröder from Klaushagen. One of his four sons served in the Guards and another in the grenadier batallion in Templin.[44]

The rural population could scarcely escape its blood debt to the king of Prussia. A family had to assume that it had begotten and raised one son, often enough the physically strongest, for the king. If one assumes that the rural population was already practicing forms of family planning in the eighteenth century,[45] the unanswerable question arises of the extent to which this blood debt influenced its reproductive behavior.

The records of the Boitzenburg estate divulge that the peasants were very anxious to escape the life of a soldier, even though this was rarely articulated. Behaviors speak loudly enough. There were very few statements as forthright as that of a peasant woman from Weggun named Heß, who in 1789 advanced as one reason for revoking an already firm decision to transfer the farm to her eldest son the fact that "she and her husband had only intended at the time to shield their son from the life of a soldier."[46]

Peasant families had some assurance, however, that some of their sons would escape military service or at least would be dismissed when their father became unable to work or when they inherited a farm. Parents therefore had some hope, even under the Prussian cantonal system, that they would be cared for in their old age.

There are numerous examples of families struggling with con-

43. The cantonal review commission consisted of one representative of the district administration and a staff of the regiment.

44. Staatsarchiv Potsdam, Pr. Br. Rep. 37, Boitzenburg Estate, no. 1126.

45. Arthur E. Imhof considers in *Einführung in die historische Demographie* (Munich, 1977), p. 89f. that mounting family planning has been demonstrated in France before 1789.

46. Staatsarchiv Potsdam, Pr. Br. Rep. 37, Boitzenburg Estate, no. 1270.

siderable craft and tenacity to secure the release of sons already conscripted into the army. This was motivated, besides by parental concern and an aversion to the army, by the desire mentioned above to have as many sons as possible established on their own farms in order to enhance the family's influence in the village. The strategy of a peasant family was usually to place one son on a farm somehow, whether through marriage or through a successful petition for an available farm. The next step was to declare the next son (who may have been on the army rolls, though still at home, or already actually conscripted) to be the sole possible heir to the family farm, whose final release from military service was absolutely essential. This was probably the strategy pursued by Fahrenholz, the peasant from Klaushagen alluded to above, who declared his first two sons unsuitable to take over his lease and requested that the third become his support in old age.[47] Without even bothering to check the arguments regarding the first two sons, Count Arnim decried the fact that the son who had been conscripted was precisely the son chosen to carry on the farm. Arnim nonetheless applied for the dismissal of this son.

Equally instructive is the story of a family named Klockow from Thomsdorf.[48] Old Klockow appeared before the lord of the manor in 1789 and requested that the lord seek the dismissal of his son who had served in the regiment for nine years because this particular son was now needed to carry on the farm. Klockow added that his eldest son already held a lease, and his second son was already a cottager in Thomsdorf. Arnim noted that the eldest son had already been dismissed from the army several years earlier in order to take over the family farm and continued: "I cannot support this application. This son should have moved onto the farm. To secure the release of all three sons is too much, especially as this one is 5' 3/4."[49] However, the Klockows did not give up and eventually they secured the release of their youngest son who took over his father's farm. Arnim, however, had shown himself by no means blind to the Klockow family tactics. The army of course was irritated by all attempts to secure the dismissal of family members who were "under arms."

47. See above p. 128.
48. Staatsarchiv Potsdam, Pr. Br. Rep. 37, Boitzenburg Estate, no. 1222.
49. Ibid.

4. Conclusions – Comparisons

Let us now return to the opening observations of S.F. Knapp. Peasants around 1800 still served indeed as beasts of burden for the entire feudal society. Estate peasants in particular had no other choice but to behave in a "servile" fashion toward their overlord for only those who appeared to be obedient subjects could hope to escape all manner of harassment and molestation. "Muddle-headed," on the other hand, can hardly be considered a typical characteristic of the tenant farmers. Permitted only to work land they did not own, they had to struggle doggedly in order to survive under the conditions described above. It was a precarious existence, but most farmers adapted well, as the sources show. The need to market their goods intensively meant that they had to know how to calculate down to the last penny, and most evidently succeeded. They learned how to take advantage of market opportunities and managed to accumulate considerable savings.

Quickly accessible savings were essential if a farmer was to survive very long on his lands. Even the most successful of farmers could not escape failed harvests, outbreaks of disease among his livestock, fires, etc., and substantial credit was often not available. The attempts of farmers to lease lands for close relatives in their own or neighboring villages were therefore an integral part of their effort to plan their lives and secure their existence.

By 1800, tenant farmers no longer lived as a rule in bitter poverty. The sources disclose a surprising level of savings in many cases. Equally evident is the increasing social differentiation of the peasantry into one stratum of independent tenant farmers, acting as small-scale entrepreneurs with real opportunities to generate a profit and accumulate savings, and other strata with little or no land and few opportunities for advancement. While the latter grew increasingly impoverished because they had to purchase at least some of their food at a time when wages were stagnant, the former were clearly enjoying an economic upswing. The view, still frequently expressed, that the peasantry in general on the East Elbian estates lived on the edge of dire poverty is simply not true around 1800, at least in so far as the Boitzenburg estate is concerned.[50]

---

50. Hanna Schissler, *Preussische Agrargesellschaft im Wandel. Wirtschaftliche, gesellschaftliche und politische Transformationsprozesse von 1763 bis 1847* (Göttingen, 1978), vol. 33, *Kritische Studien zur Geschichtswissenschaft*, ed. Helmut

Here too, however, obstacles to progress that were part and parcel of the feudal system were very much in evidence: the system of land tenure, the lack of any substantial credit for peasants, and the lack of a free market in land. As a result, though farmers accumulated savings, they had no reason to invest in their farms. Some successful farmers tried to escape their narrow economic existence by leasing a second farm,[51] but this was only permitted for a few years. A few succeeded in bursting the bounds of peasant life by leasing entire estates.[52] One could mention in this context that the peasants simply put aside their savings, which could amount by their old age to several hundred *Taler*, rather than placing them in a bank. From an economic point of view, this was of course highly unproductive and even harmful.

To what extent can these findings in regard to Boitzenburg be considered generally applicable? The most startling discovery was probably the amount of money accumulated by peasant families. Was this peculiar to Boitzenburg and the circumstances prevailing there or can it be considered common among the masses of farmers holding thirty to seventy hectares of land as a consequence of increasing grain prices? More in-depth studies are needed in this regard. Conditions were doubtless more difficult elsewhere.

It seems to me, on the basis of the average size of the farms and of the need (and opportunity) to market goods intensively in order to earn money to pay the rent, that a considerable portion of the tenant farmers began to break out of the poverty cycle around 1800. This appears to have happened primarily in regions that were adjacent to good markets, for instance, in the Berlin area or in central Silesia.

Berding, Jürgen Kocka, Hans-Ulrich Wehler, p. 95. Friedrich Wilhelm Henning, *Dienste und Abgaben der Bauern im 18. Jahrhundert* (Stuttgart, 1969), vol. 21, *Quellen und Forschungen zur Agrargeschichte*, ed. Wilhelm Abel and Günther Franz, p. 166.

51. For instance, a tenant farmer named Wollenberg on farm no. 5 in Hassleben requested in 1813 that he be allowed to share the lease on farm no. 10, of which his wife was the sole heir (Staatsarchiv Potsdam, Pr. Br. Rep. 37, Boitzenburg Estate, no. 1100). In 1812 Carl Springborn asked to be allowed to share the lease on farm no. 14, which was currently available, adding that he had 120 *Reichstaler* in cash in a Berlin bank (ibid., no. 1191). A peasant from Wichmannsdorf named Schnock sought permission in 1809 to operate farm no. 22 in addition to his own. He had only daughters and expected that a son-in-law would soon turn up (ibid., no. 1323).

52. For instance, a peasant from Warthe named Stabe requested in 1797 that the overlord seek the release of his son from the army so that he could take over the farm. The elder Stabe had leased the seigniorial estate of Metzelthin and therefore wished to leave the original farm (ibid., no. 1244, Warthe, no. 3).

This is not to deny, of course, that some tenant farmers were always falling into financial difficulty and were forced off their farms or that more remote regions saw little of this economic upswing. In addition, the economic prosperity of this social stratum was often gained at least partially at the expense of the rural poor. All in all, the experience of Boitzenburg was probably typical of developments across much of Prussia east of the Elbe.

The second conclusion of more general significance is that tenant farmers, though very insecure in many ways, did not behave any differently as a group than farmers with some property rights to the land they tilled. The tenant farmers on the Boitzenburg estate behaved like any group of landowners who saw an opportunity to profit by running their farms efficiently. In this they did not differ from farmers with an inheritable tenancy or property right. Their behaviors were also identical in regard to maintaining possession of their farms and strengthening their family's position in the village. Their responses to the pressures of the militaristic Prussian state were also probably much the same.

However, the precarious property rights of these peasants resulted in greater servility and acquiescence in the prevailing social order than in areas west of the Elbe where the village communities were much stronger. This confirms our belief that social history cannot inquire into the mentality of the peasantry in general in the late feudal era but must always take into account local economic, legal, and social conditions.

HANS-HEINRICH MÜLLER

Crown Leaseholders in the Nineteenth Century

Well-known historians, economists, and agronomists have always been fairly unanimous in their view of crown estates and crown leaseholders. Gustav Schmoller lauded the crown estates as an "advanced course for more capable farmers," and he praised the leaseholders for successfully combining "advanced techniques, large amounts of capital, and a modern flair for entrepreneurship with certain qualities of the civil service."[1] While Schmoller was referring to conditions in the eighteenth century, Friedrich Aereboe, the foremost representative of agricultural business administration, stated that after the agricultural reforms of 1807 "the rapidly evolving class of crown leaseholders made a substantial contribution to the upswing in German agriculture, especially in Prussia."[2] According to the agricultural historian Theodor von Goltz, "the crown leaseholders always played a leading role; the organization and leadership of crown estates were usually better than that of other operations"[3] – a comment aimed not primarily at peasant-run farms but at estates managed by the nobility.

Not only historians and agricultural economists held crown leaseholders in high esteem; newspapers also praised them for their exceptional achievements and efficiency. In the May 1841 edition of the *Leipziger Allgemeine Zeitung*, the author of an article about "Prussia's leaseholders" praised crown leaseholders in particular for

---

1. Gustav Schmoller, *Umrisse und Untersuchungen zur Verfassungs-, Verwaltungs-und Wirtschaftsgeschichte besonders des Preussischen Staates im 17. und 18. Jahrhundert* (Leipzig, 1898), pp. 169 and 607.
2. Friedrich Aereboe, *Agrarpolitik* (Berlin, 1928), p. 190.
3. Theodor Freiherr von der Goltz, *Agrarwesen und Agrarpolitik* (Jena, 1904), p. 73.

"showing the way to the entire farming community during the present mighty surge in all rural activities."[4] Finally, we would like to add the voices of two representatives of the Prussian state, which was intimately involved in agriculture because of the extensive domains under state control. Dr. Robert Lucius, minister of agriculture, crown estates and forests, declared in 1885 that crown leaseholders had always been "the pioneers of agricultural progress."[5] Hugo Thiel, an outstanding agricultural manager who became secretary-general of the Prussian College of Rural Economics and a senior bureaucrat in the Ministry of Agriculture in 1873 and then director of the Crown Estates Department in 1893, lauded the estates under his control as "model farms" and stated that the leaseholders demonstrated "how economic success can be achieved even under the most trying circumstances."[6]

There were actually very few of these crown leaseholders, who numbered among "the rural elite" and whose accomplishments could not be applauded enough in the specialized agrarian literature of the nineteenth century.[7] Prussia, the state with the most extensive holdings, counted 503 crown estates in 1849, including 879 *Vorwerke* (smaller farmsteads at the edge of a larger estate but belonging to it) of which by far the greatest number were in the eastern provinces. Only 110 estates were situated west of the Elbe, 96 of them in the districts of Magdeburg and Merseburg. The amount of arable land on all crown estates totalled 1,285,228 *Morgen*[8] (approximately the same number of acres), accounting for 1.2 percent of all arable land in the country.[9] The number of crown estates and the amount of land they comprised had therefore declined sharply since the end of the eighteenth century when some 700 estates still existed on a total of 2,517,800 *Morgen* of arable land or almost 4.5 percent of the total.[10] As a result of the heavy

4. *Leipziger Allgemeine Zeitung*, no. 128 of May 8, 1841, p. 1479.
5. See Franz Berghoff-Ising, *Die Entwicklung des landwirtschaftlichen Pachtwesens in Preußen* (Leipzig, 1887).
6. *Stenographische Berichte* of the Prussian House of Deputies, 1900 (Berlin, 1901), 1:332.
7. Berghoff-Ising (above, n. 5), 75ff.
8. Adolf Frantz, *Preußens Staats-Domänengüter nach Umfang, Wert und Ertrag* (Jena, 1864), p. 44; Franz Berghoff-Ising (above, n. 5), p. 72.
9. See Günther Franz, "Landwirtschaft, 1800–1850," in Hermann Aubin and Wolfgang Zorn, eds., *Handbuch der deutschen Wirtschafts- und Sozialgeschichte* (Stuttgart, 1976), 2:295.
10. Georg Dähne, "Die wirtschaftlichen Verhältnisse in Preußen vor und in den Befreiungskriegen" (Ph.D. diss., Berlin, 1928), p. 82.

reparations extracted from Prussia during the Napoleonic Wars as well as the high state debt incurred during the first half of the nineteenth century, Prussia was compelled to sell some of the crown estates it had previously considered inalienable national possessions. By 1820 estates worth 60 million marks had been sold; between 1820 and 1866 estates valued at another 211 million marks were sold and between 1867 and 1890 estates worth another 50 million marks.[11] Often these estates ended up in the hands of their former leaseholders. Occasionally "meritorious generals" such as Neithardt von Gneisenau, Tauentzien von Wittenberg, or Karl Friedrich von Knesebeck were granted crown estates as gifts. At the same time, however, the state was continually acquiring new domains. After the war of 1866 and the annexation of Hannover, Schleswig-Holstein, and Hessen-Nassau, Prussia added many more crown estates consisting of 301 *Vorwerke* with arable land totalling 51,949 hectares.[12] By 1884 Prussia possessed 813 estates (1,072 *Vorwerke*) comprising 339,578 hectares of land and another 2.3 million hectares of forests.[13] Thereafter, the number of individual estates declined slightly, while total land possessions increased somewhat.[14] There were crown estates in the other German states as well. Before the First World War, Mecklenburg-Schwerin held 235 crown estates and Mecklenburg-Strelitz, 77. The Thuringian states counted 113 crown estates extending over 23,705 hectares, and in Baden 19,400 hectares belonged to the state, of which 14,200 were rented out. Württemberg held 42 crown estates covering 4,400 hectares. Hessen reckoned its crown estates at 17,680 hectares, and Saxony in 1882 held 16 estates covering 3,768 hectares, not including forests, vineyards, and fish ponds.[15]

I have already written extensively about farming on the Prussian estates: about technical progress, rental conditions, the length of the leases and their renewals, rental charges and the security required;

11. Fauser, "Domänen," in *Handwörterbuch der Staatswissenschaften* (Jena, 1926), 3:263; G. Strutz, *Der Staatshaushalt und die Finanzen Preußens*, (Berlin, 1900), 1:22ff.; Ludwig von Rönne, *Das Domainen-, Forst- und Jagd-Wesen des Preußischen Staates* (Berlin, 1854), pt. 9, *Die Verfassung und Verwaltung des Preußischen Staates*, pp. 125ff.
12. Berghoff-Ising (above, n.5), p. 74.
13. Preußische Landesverwaltung in den Jahren 1881, 1882, 1883, pt. 3 (Berlin, 1885), pp. 617ff.
14. Fauser (above, n. 11), p. 275.
15. Ibid.; K. von Langsdorff, *Die Landwirtschaft im Königreich Sachsen, ihre Entwicklung bis einschl. 1885* (Dresden, 1889), p. 62.

about the leaseholders, their origins, wealth, education, and entrepreneurial spirit; about the evolution of the estates into "family
farms" and the relationship between the chamber of estates and the
leaseholders; and finally about the dual role of leaseholders during
the eighteenth century as both agricultural entrepreneurs and functionaries of the Prussian state.[16] In broad summary, this research
shows that a class of capitalistic leaseholders had begun to emerge
by 1800.[17] It possessed substantial wealth, had taken over many
manors previously belonging to the knighthood, and accounted for
a sizeable portion of the emerging bourgeoisie. A memorandum of
1799 entitled "Observations on the Condition of the Brandenburg
Nobility" noted: "The class that could be a richer source of
support . . . is the upper bourgeoisie, or more precisely, merchants
and crown leaseholders."[18] A decade later Friedrich von Cölln, a
radical journalist and one of the severest critics of socioeconomic
conditions in Prussia, adopted a very similar point of view in one of
his much feared "Confidential Letters": "It is seldom that leaseholders do not become wealthy men; and the more wealthy people
of this sort there are, the more sources of money the government
can tap when a crisis arises."[19]

Many of the conditions and circumstances characterizing crown
leaseholders in the 1700s carried over into the following century,
and a few grew even more pronounced under a capitalist economic
structure and consequent rationalization. However, some reversals
were evident. The universal leasing system common before the
agrarian reforms of 1807[20] was abandoned, and the collection of
dues, rents, and taxes from district villages was separated from the
rental of estate farms. The collection and administration of fees,
rents, and taxes were henceforth transferred to special functionaries
– Domänenrentmeister or Amtsintendanten – and crown leaseholders were only responsible for farming operations. Only in

---

16. Hans-Heinrich Müller, "Domänen und Domänenpächter in Brandenburg-
Preußen im 18. Jahrhundert," in *Jahrbuch für Wirtschaftsgeschichte* (1965), pt. 4, pp.
152ff.
17. See also Ulla Machlitt, "Die anhalt-dessauischen Domänen in der Periode des
Übergangs von der feudalen zur kapitalistischen Produktionsweise (etwa 1700 bis
1800)," (Ph.D. diss., Halle, 1971), pp. 174ff.; Hanna Schissler, *Preußische
Agrargesellschaft im Wandel. Wirtschaftliche, gesellschaftliche und politische Transformationsprozesse von 1763 bis 1847* (Göttingen, 1978), pp. 87ff.
18. Staatsarchiv (StA) Magdeburg, Rep. H, Erxleben II, no. 3707, pp. 5, 7.
19. Friedrich von Cölln, *Vertraute Briefe* (Amsterdam-Cölln, 1808), 1:46.
20. See Müller (above, n. 16), pp. 153f.

occasional cases did the lease entail collection of estate taxes.[21] Thus crown leaseholders largely became pure farmers and capitalist entrepreneurs. Normal lease durations also changed. Prior to 1807, leases usually ran for six years and required the leaseholder to accept the conditions laid down by the estate chamber regarding both the operations and profits of the farms and the relationship of the local population to the estate department. Leaseholders could assume that their rental agreements would be renewed so long as they farmed efficiently and promptly paid all monies due, though this did not obviate the sense of insecurity surrounding six-year leases.[22] Toward the end of the eighteenth century, nine-year leases became common under certain conditions, and in places even twelve-year leases. After the agrarian reforms, estate administrations finally began to realize as a result of the influence of the "rational school" of Albrecht Thaers[23] and after years of experience (especially with the outstanding results achieved by the crown leaseholders under their control) that short rental periods "impede good farming practices" and should be avoided.[24] Convinced of "the benefits to be derived from long rental periods," they converted to leases with a usual duration of eighteen years, though leases of twenty-four or even more years were not uncommon.[25] As a result, crown leaseholders were much more willing to invest and introduce new techniques to enhance productivity.

Production on the crown estates continued to progress steadily throughout the nineteenth century. At first, leaseholders persevered with measures already introduced prior to 1800. They reduced or eliminated the fallow-field system, expanded the production of fodder and of root crops and tubers, improved their tilling techniques, and in many cases alternated or rotated crops. They selected their seeds and bred their animals very carefully and increased the size of their cattle herds in order to obtain more dung. Sheep strains

21. H. Oelrichs, *Die Domainen-Verwaltung des Preußischen Staates* (Breslau, 1883), p. 19f.; StA Potsdam, Rep. 2A, IIID, no. 515, report of February 10, 1830.
22. Müller (above, n. 16), p. 170.
23. See Thaer, "Über die Werthschätzung der Landgüter," in *Annalen des Acker-baues* (Berlin, 1807), 5:678f.
24. Lorenz von Stein, *Lehrbuch der Finanzen für Staats- und Selbstverwaltung* (Leipzig, 1878), p. 270.
25. Rönne (above, n. 11), p. 510.

were improved by crossing with merinos and wool production increased. The raising of merinos and wool exports represented a substantial portion of estate income until the 1840s. At the advice of the estate administration or on their own initiative, leaseholders soon began to divide up common fields and property, eliminating joint use of meadows, crop fields, and stubble fields.

Crown leaseholders also recognized the great advantages to be derived from employing free labor, which they had already utilized in part prior to 1800 while in some cases completely eliminating statute labor. Many leaseholders shared the views and methods of August Karbe, a leaseholder on the Ukermark estate of Weselitz, who publicly proclaimed in 1802 that he did not run his farm like "a little shop with something of everything" but operated instead "in accordance with factory principles." Such a farm did not require forced labor "or bonuses because it produces the bonus itself" and "raises spirits." He said that he employed day laborers on a piece-work basis, in that each laborer was fully responsible for working fifteen *Morgen* of land. In this way, the self-interest of the day laborers was brought "into play." Experience showed that they "race through their work without any supervisors or judges. . . . They utilize every available hour, many of which would have been wasted by day laborers. . . . Their energies are redoubled by the desire for high earnings."[26] In the course of time, this experience was confirmed by other leaseholders, who thereby provide additional evidence of the triumph of capitalist production methods.[27]

After 1835, sugar beet factories were constructed in the Magdeburg district by estates in Barby, Calbe, Dreileben, Etgersleben, Gottesgnaden, Schlanstedt, Stassfurt, Ummendorf, and Westerhüsen, and later in Egeln, Gröningen, Groß Ammensleben, Unseburg, and Wolmirstedt.[28] In 1837 Koppe in Kienitz (Oderbruch) built a sugar beet factory that was able to produce 2,450,000 kilograms of sugar by 1856.[29] Crown leaseholders in other regions

26. August Karbe, *Die in der Mark Brandenburg und anderen deutschen Provinzen mögliche und nützliche Einführung der englischen Wechselwirtschaft* (Prenzlau, 1802), pp. 118, 156, 236.

27. See Johann Gottlieb Koppe, *Unterricht in Ackerbau und in der Viehzucht*, pt. 1 (Berlin, 1845), pp. 47ff.

28. J.A.F. Hermes and M.J. Weigelt, eds., *Historisch-geographisch-statistisch-topographisches Handbuch vom Regierungsbezirk Magdeburg*, pt. 1 (Magdeburg, 1843), pp. 114f.; pt. 2 (1842), pp. 34ff.; A. Keber, *Der Regierungsbezirk Magdeburg* (Halberstadt, 1843), passim.

29. StA Potsdam, Rep. 7, Amt Wollup no. 6, pp. 40f.

also began to produce sugar, and sugar beets became a much more frequent crop. It required considerable care in tilling the soil and tending to the plants and also needed large amounts of fertilizer. On the Schlanstedt estate, for instance, 800 of a total 2,200 *Morgen* of land were planted with sugar beets. In 1840 some 2,500,000 kilograms of beets were processed into sugar and in the following two decades capacity was expanded to 7,500,000 kilograms.[30] If sugar beets were "excellent for business," as Gustav Wahnschaffe, the leaseholder of the Gorgast estate in the Lebus region, confided, so too were the distilleries, which were lucrative operations on almost all estates. "The distillery gives us a great deal of pleasure," it is "doing well" and will "soon have paid off the capital invested," Wahnschaffe informed his father-in-law, leaseholder Kühne in Wanzleben. The leaseholder of the Lebus estate grew and "purchased mountains of potatoes for the distillery" in order to turn them into alcohol. Potatoes and spirits provided "high pure profit levels" and helped offset poor grain harvests.[31]

As distilleries, sugar and starch factories, and other processing operations spread, the crown estates entered the industrial world to a certain extent. It supplied them with machinery, boilers, steam engines, and fuels, provided them with technical information, and made them aware of scientific advances. Many crown estates, at least in the province of Saxony, already possessed by 1840 steam-driven threshing, sowing, and drilling machines, new, efficient plows, and other equipment for working the land.[32] East Prussian estates made lasting improvements in their cattle- and horse-breeding techniques. The Klein-Tapiau leaseholder purchased some English shorthorn cattle, and later some Dutch cattle as well, and thereby succeeded in building up a valuable breeding herd. The cattle he sold contributed appreciably to an increase in milk production on other estates and his full-blooded stallions were in high demand on state stud farms.[33]

The crown leaseholders kept abreast of the latest scientific discoveries, and they all seemed to ascribe to the view expressed by the

30. Wilhelm Rimpau, *Die Bewirtschaftung der Domaine Schlanstedt* (Braunschweig, 1859), pp. 21ff.

31. StA Magdeburg, R.H., Wanzleben, no. 88, letters from September 20, 1830, April 14, 1836, December 14, 1839, and April 15, 1840.

32. Rimpau (above, n. 30), pp. 27, 31; StA Magdeburg, Rep. Da Schlandstedt, Generalia, no. 5, p. 15.

33. Von Dade, ed., *Die deutsche Landwirtschaft unter Kaiser Wilhelm II.* (Halle, 1913), 1:47.

Schlanstedt leaseholder August Wilhelm Rimpau in 1840 (probably under the influence of Liebig's new book, *Applications of Organic Chemistry to Agriculture and Physiology*): "Onward is the battlecry of the day, and this is as true in agriculture as in all other realms of human endeavor. Faith has been supplanted by research. The task of modern agriculture is to apply the principles of physics, chemistry, and mechanics to the practical world. Much has been achieved in this direction; but infinitely more remains to be accomplished."[34]

Technical progress on the estates brought mounting net proceeds. They amounted in Prussia's eastern provinces to the following per hectare: 13.90 marks in 1849, 31.18 marks in 1869, 35.63 marks in 1879, and 38.96 marks in 1890, before falling back by 1907 to 32.26 marks as a result of the chronic agricultural crisis due to falling prices for grains, wool, and sugar combined with mounting production costs (higher wages).[35] However, net proceeds declined less on crown estates than on estates operated by the nobility. They fell much further in Prussia's eastern provinces than in the western reaches, though they remained approximately 2.3 times as high as the equivalent proceeds in 1850. The crown leaseholders earned impressive profits particularly in the periods between 1840–50 and 1880–90. This was not only a consequence of rising prices during the "golden years of agriculture" but also of increased application of scientific and technical discoveries and of developments such as machines, mineral fertilizers, new breeding techniques for plants and animals and the use of efficient business methods which intensified and increased productivity. The increase in the average grain yield (in kilograms per hectare) on the Gerlebogk estate in Anhalt, farmed by the teacher of economics, Adolf Säuberlich, will serve as an example. (See Table 6.1).

Equally impressive were the increasing yields of potatoes and sugar beets and the achievements in cattle breeding, distilling, and sugar production. For the five farms on the estate (1,042 hectares), Säuberlich paid annual rents amounting to 36,500 marks after 1857, a sum which was increased in 1884 to 90,000 marks and then reduced in 1902 to 87,000 marks. In the years from 1901 to 1911, farm receipts amounted to an annual average of 416,586 marks and livestock receipts to 105,200 marks. In so far as expenses are concerned, 38,429 marks were spent annually on artificial fertilizers,

34. StA Magdeburg, Rep. Da Schlandstedt, Generalia, no. 5, p. 48.
35. Fauser (above, n. 11), p. 276; Goltz (above, n.3), p. 70.

Table 6.1 *Increase in Average Grain Yield (kg/ha) on Gerlebogk Estate*

Period	Winter Wheat	Summer Wheat	Rye	Barley	Oats	Peas
1851–1860	1538	–	1800	1630	1360	674
1861–1870	2022	–	1700	2180	1698	2160
1871–1880	2452	–	1572	2208	1844	2062
1881–1890	2624	1582	1622	2320	2062	1963
1891–1900	2520	2202	1846	2296	2246	1986
1901–1910	2742	2158	2076	1980	2496	2556

Source: von Dade, ed., *Die deutsche Landwirtschaft unter Kaiser Wilhelm II.* (Halle, 1913), 2:445.

61,159 marks on fodder, and 124,156 marks on salaries and wages. This calculation leaves a profit of some 121,000 marks, not including the profits from the distillery and sugar factory. In addition, Säuberlich leased the estate of Gröbzig (669 hectares), which produced similar profits.[36]

Farming large crown estates required technical knowledge, experience, capital, organizational skills, a willingness to take risks, and a flair for entrepreneurship and decision making. The crown leaseholders were therefore "recognized to be among the most intelligent and successful farmers."[37] According to their contemporaries, they were an essential "foundation of rural life."[38] Some of the leaseholders stemmed from urban families with histories as merchants, tradesmen, and industrialists, backgrounds that helped introduce an entrepreneurial, business spirit into agriculture. These classes were accustomed to working with free wage earners and adapting to the ups and downs of the market, skills that stood them in good stead in the realm of agriculture, even though many of them had little experience on farms. They knew how to call in experts and gather experienced help, and together with their personnel they managed to build rational, highly profitable operations.[39] Above all, leaseholders possessed sufficient capital to acquire leases on additional estates that became free, whether through auction (highest offer) or cession (relinquishment of the lease before it expired). In

36. Ibid., pp. 435, 441f.
37. Theodor Freiherr von der Goltz, *Geschichte der deutschen Landwirtschaft* (Stuttgart-Berlin, 1903), 2:349.
38. *Leipziger Allgemeine Zeitung*, no. 128 of May 8, 1841, p. 1479.
39. See Aereboe (above, n. 2), pp. 190f.

any case, substantial rents had to be paid year after year. Around 1880 these amounted, for instance, to an average of 14,000 marks in the district of Königsberg, 19,000 marks in the district of Potsdam, 21,000 marks in the district of Frankfurt an der Oder, 15,300 marks in the district of Stettin, 12,000 marks in the district of Stralsund, 24,000 marks in the district of Breslau, 19,300 marks in the district of Hannover, and 48,000 marks in the district of Magdeburg – though only to 5,200 marks in Aurich and 8,700 marks in Kassel. Some crown estates rented for far more than the average, for instance, 32,600 marks for Ragnit (Gumbinnen), 45,068 marks for Brüssow (Potsdam), 55,200 marks for Cottbus, and, in the district of Magdeburg, 87,410 for the estate of Barby, 90,465 for Calbe, 108,999 for Egeln, and 120,815 for Wanzleben.[40] In addition a deposit had to be made, amounting usually from 25 to 33 percent of the annual rental, though this later rose to from 100 to 200 percent of the annual rental, before plummeting after the turn of the century to 10 percent. This deposit was paid at the appropriate financial office either in the form of government securities or in cash, in return for 4 percent interest.[41] Leaseholders consequently had to have strong financial reserves in order to assume control of an estate. The circle of potential leaseholders was severely limited by the steep rental fees and deposits and by the cost of animals, equipment, and other investments that the leaseholder was expected to pay.

A large proportion of leaseholders stemmed from the ranks of the leaseholding class. The state attempted to ensure the economic stability of its landholdings by encouraging a kind of "family farm." Only rarely were estates offered to the highest bidder; instead, leaseholders who had proved their worth were usually allowed to extend their lease if they agreed to a rent increase of some 5 percent after a certain number of years, usually five to ten.[42] One of the largest leaseholders in the middle of the nineteenth century, Johann Gottlieb Koppe, who farmed the estates of Wollup and Kienitz in Oderbruch, described the general practice as follows:

40. See the rents of the individual crown estates in: Oelrichs (above, n. 21), pp. 217ff.
41. See Rönne (above, n. 11), p. 550; Kurt Liebich, *Allgemeine Pachtbedingungen für die Preußischen Staatsdomänen* (Berlin, 1928), pp. 195ff.; K. Steinbrück, "Pacht," in *Handwörterbuch der Staatswissenschaften* (Jena, 1925), 6:791.
42. See Heinrich Berghaus, *Landbuch der Mark Brandenburg und des Markgrafthums Nieder-Lausitz* (Brandenburg, 1855), 2:623ff.

Confidence in the management of the estates was so . . . high that a leaseholder with a clean conscience (i.e., one who had paid his rent on time and had not only conserved but improved his land) could be quite confident that his lease would be renewed after an appropriate increase in the rent. This sense of trust and confidence is the reason why the royal Prussian estates are usually in better condition than estates in private hands.

Crown leaseholders also enjoyed the backing of government officials because "it was a matter of conscience with them to attempt to advance the state of agriculture in the province that they administered. The solicitude they showed for me sprang from their desire to encourage agriculture because they recognized that this was in the best interests of the common weal."[43] One of these government officials, the liberal Baron Ludwig von Vincke (who was the first president of Westphalia and who had worked during the reform period in the Brandenburg estate chamber, even becoming its president) stated outright that crown estate leases not only provided "a lifelong living" but also constituted "a family benefice" that was "passed along from father to son to grandson."[44]

Very little changed thereafter in the leasing system. Many families leased the same crown estates for generations, and there are numerous examples of estates that remained in the hands of the same family from the final third of the eighteenth century until 1945. For instance, Friedrich Ludwig Philipp Kühne, a former senior "official in the Unseburg office of the Duke of Brunswick . . . with wealth totaling 160,000 *Taler*" took over the estate of Wanzleben on December 24, 1778, and it remained in the hands of his descendants until 1945.[45] The following families, whose histories I have followed back through the various sources, remained the leaseholders of the estates cited in parenthesis from at least 1830–40 – and in some cases from prior to 1800 – until the end of the Second World War: Rosenstiel (Gorgast, Marienwalde), Koppe (Wollup, Kienitz), Schröter (Alvensleben), Bennecke (Athensleben, Löderburg), Dietze (Barby, Gottesgnaden), Dietrich (Egeln), Klamroth (Egeln),

43. Johann Gottlieb Koppe, *Lebenserinnerungen* (1866), pp. 51 and 62 (in StA Potsdam).
44. Ernst von Bodelschwingh, *Leben des Ober-Präsidenten Freiherrn von Vincke* (Berlin, 1853), p. 88.
45. StA Magdeburg, Rep. Da Wanzleben, IV, no. 27, p. 11; Friedrich Hoffmann, *Geschichte des Königlichen Domänen-Amts und der Kreisstadt Groß-Wanzleben* (Berlin, 1863), p. 69; Kurt Liebich (above, n. 41), p. 298.

Elsner (Rosenburg), Rimpau (Schlanstedt), Wahnschaffe (Wester-
burg), Friese (Wolmirstedt), and Iffland (Zellin), in order to cite
only a few cases drawn from Brandenburg and the province of
Saxony.[46]
Under these conditions, it is hardly surprising that the leaseholders felt themselves to be proprietors and behaved accordingly.
They were therefore in a position to weather many a crisis. Both the
estate administrations and contemporaries in general recognized the
enormous influence of long-term leases on farm production and on
the socioeconomic condition of crown leaseholders. "A leaseholder
who can count on the profits accruing to his operation over a
number of years and who can therefore hope to withstand the lean
years at least approaches the comfortable position of an owner."[47]
In fact, crown leaseholders were "often in a stronger position than
owners because their investments in the land made it practically
impossible for the state to cancel the lease without incurring enormous redemption payments. . . . The state demonstrated its esteem
for crown leaseholders as a mainspring of agrarian progress not only
by maintaining rents at moderate levels but also by demonstrating
particular concern for these leaseholders during times of economic
crisis. The favoritism occasionally accorded crown leaseholders
during the 1820s is well known, for instance when Finance Minister
von Motz not only repeatedly postponed and canceled their rents
but also ordered that they be granted special bank credits and
advance payments on their future wool deliveries to the Prussian
merchant marine."[48] A letter written in 1837 by Agnes Kühne (wife
of Gustav Wahnschaffe, a leaseholder in Gorgast) to her father in
Wanzleben, who was thinking of leaving his estate because of "poor
health" and temporary economic difficulties, reads like a gloss to all
this:

> May heaven drive from your mind, dear father, the idea of leaving
> Wanzleben. Anyone who has farmed there will never find pleasure in any
> other estate. . . . It cannot be denied that our occupation, despite all the
> vexations and associated risks, is still the most pleasant and the most

46. See StA Magdeburg, Rep. Da Athensleben, no. 11; Rep. Da Rosenburg, I,
no. 50, 51; XXI, no. 12, 14; Rep. Da Schraplau, no. 5; Rep. Da Schlanstedt,
Generalia, no. 5; StA Potsdam, Rep. 7, Amt Wollup, nos. 2, 4, 5; Heinrich Berghaus
(above, n. 42), 2:622ff., (1856), 3:771ff.; Kurt Liebich (above, n. 41), pp. 270ff., 295ff.
47. Rönne (above, n. 11), p. 509.
48. Herbert Pruns, *Staat und Agrarwirtschaft, 1800–1865* (Textband Hamburg-
West Berlin, 1978), p. 223.

rewarding. Even if we could achieve a return of 10 instead of 4 percent on our capital, were it not invested in the farm, we still would not have anything like all the pleasures we now enjoy. You are now a happy and very respected man. How could you bear to fritter away empty days with nothing to do? So my good, dear father, let yourself be dissuaded from even thinking about leaving Wanzleben, let alone talking about it.[49]

Whether old man Kühne intended to "fritter away empty days" is somewhat doubtful since he still was the proprietor of an impressive manor.

Despite many difficulties and setbacks, crown leaseholders were often highly successful, enjoyed considerable security, and grew prosperous or even wealthy,[50] thanks to lengthy rental agreements at moderate prices, lifelong occupancy of their estates, the goodwill of the Prussian state, intensive and progressive farming of the land, their experience at carefully assessing economic conditions, the knowledge that their material well-being was directly proportional to their own efforts, and the sizeable cunning and craft that they brought to the task at hand. However, there were always some leaseholders who ran into difficulties and were forced to relinquish their leases after a single rental period. In some cases, they were not sufficiently capable farmers or were unable to handle the management of a large estate; in others, they ran into a spell of bad luck and were not provided adequate assistance by the estate administration for various reasons. This was the experience, for instance, of Robert Wilhelm Gotzkowsky, who leased the crown estate of Fahrland near Potsdam from 1835 to 1855. He was a grandson of the successful and well-known Berlin merchant, Johann Ernst Gotzkowsky, who had established several manufacturing enterprises in the time of Frederick II, and he was also a cousin of the composer Albert Lortzing, who was often a guest at Fahrland. After Gotzkowsky provided evidence of "available wealth amounting to 12,500 *Taler*," he was granted a crown estate at an annual rent of 1,580 *Taler*. However, several water mills near Brandenburg and Rathenow had a damming effect on the Havel River, and Gotzkowsky's pastures and meadows were repeatedly flooded. The crop was ruined and Gotzkowsky was forced to purchase hay. Moreover, some of his livestock was killed off by "lung plague," financial reserves fell dangerously low, and rental payments could

49. StA Magdeburg, Rep. H, Wanzleben, no. 88, letter of May 28, 1837.
50. Goltz, *Geschichte der deutschen Landwirtschaft* (above, n. 37), p. 349.

not be met. The estates administration failed to provide adequate support, bureaucratic quarrels and delays ensued, and finally Gotzkowsky was forced off the lands before the lease had elapsed because of bankruptcy and the refusal of the authorities to forego the rent – all this despite help and financial assistance from his brother-in-law, Grosse, who leased the nearby estate of Bornstedt.[51]

Nonetheless, most crown leaseholders seem to have been most fortunate, if one equates good fortune with diligence, perseverance, skill, intelligence, a burning desire to produce and earn profits, and last but not least, capitalist exploitation of the rural proletariat. Otherwise, many households would scarcely have survived for generations on their estates, growing to consider them "family benefices."

What is most surprising, however, is that the crown estates were not only "family benefices" that were "passed from father to son to grandson," but that they tended to be held within the same extended families. Individual families held dozens of estates, and the emergence of a class of crown estate leaseholders can even be discerned, which was socially hermetic and difficult for "outside" farmers and leaseholders to penetrate.[52] For instance, the crown estate of Athensleben in the district of Calbe was held by the Bennecke family from the mid-eighteenth century until 1945. At the same time, this same family leased the Stassfurt estate. Bennecke sons and daughters, grandsons and granddaughters also married, often with the artful connivance of the family, into the estates of Amelunxborn, Arendsee, Bernburg, Canstein, Egeln, Gorgast, Groß-Oerner, Hoym, Hunnesrück, Marienwalde, Rethmar, Rosenburg, Sandau, Schlanstedt, Schönfeld, Strelno, Unseburg, Wanzleben, Westeregeln, and Winningen. The leaseholders of the Athensleben estate thus had family ties to at least twenty other estates farmed by leaseholders with excellent reputations in crown estate circles and German agriculture in general: Fritz, Gansauge, Gropius, Honig, Kamlah, Koerber, Krahmer, Kühne, Reuter, Rosenstiel, Stolz, and Wahnschaffe.[53]

---

51. Hans Höltje, "Aus dem Leben des Urgroßvaters Robert Wilhelm Gotzkowsky, 3.9.1804–4.1.1860. Königlicher Oberamtmann und Pächter der Domäne Fahrland bei Potsdam, 1835–1855" (West Berlin, 1980), ms.
52. See in this regard Machlitt (above, n. 17), p. 174.
53. *Charlotte Louise Bennecke und ihr Kreis. Familienbild für Verwandte und Freunde*, comp. Gertrud Jonas (Berlin, 1910), with a genealogical overview in the appendix.

The Wanzleben estate in the hands of the Kühne family had close family ties to the crown estates of Blankenburg, Heimburg, and Sülldorf, to Bleesern, Gorgast, Kienitz, Lebus, Strelno, Schönfeld, Thänsdorf, and Vessra. The Gansauge family, which had many family connections with the aforementioned estates, also had family ties with the estates of Bornstedt, Frauendorf, Neugattersleben, and Sachsendorf.[54] Johann Gottlieb Koppe on Wollup and on Kienitz had sons-in-law on the estates of Klein-Rosenburg and Patzetz (M. Elsner), Sorau (G.F. Peyer) and Wanzleben (Ph. Kühne) and a daughter-in-law on the Lebus estate (S. von Gansauge).[55] All these examples could be multiplied many times over.

The interconnected families on the crown estates informed one another about operations, prices, various upswings and downswings, the weather, new purchases, and the latest technical innovations. They arranged visits and swapped experiences about crops and livestock. Crown leaseholders also had strong social connections with many elements in society. They received representatives of the estates administration, with whom they had professional dealings. They hosted hunts, in which ministers of the crown, army officers, civil servants, and the artistic community participated. For instance, *Amtsrat* Kühne in Wanzleben hosted a hunt attended by von Itzenplatz, the chief administrative officer of the district, von Angern, a minister of the crown, Baron von Stolzenburg, the minister of forests, Colonel von der Marwitz, and Prince William. Kühne also frequently entertained the renowned painter of horses, Franz Krüger, who also painted a portrait of his host. A letter Krüger sent to Kühne leaves the impression that he even preferred visiting Wanzleben to visiting the king of Hannover: "I left my arrival time in Hannover indeterminate, for I am willing to let the king of Hannover wait a few days in order once again to have the pleasure of visiting Wanzleben."[56] Kühne provided Herr von Münchhausen, Herrengossersted, with seed and agricultural advice and carried on a correspondence with Albrecht Thaer, whom he asked for some clover seed and English farm implements. He also expressed his pleasure to Thaer when the latter decided to take up residence in Prussia. Kühne's son continued this tradition, corre-

---

54. Ibid.

55. Helga Tucek, *Fur den Fortschritt der Agrarwissenschaften. Johann Gottlieb Koppe, 1782–1863* (Luckau, 1982), pp. 32 and 33f.

56. StA Magdeburg, Rep. H, Wanzleben, no. 80, letter of December 31, 1838.

sponding with many different people including merchants, manufacturers, and leaseholders throughout Germany. He supplied President von Flottwell with potatoes, invited members of high society to hunts, and played cards with generals and colonels.[57] Many other crown leaseholders carried on a similar lifestyle, though their exact connections were somewhat different depending on location and other circumstances.

While crown leaseholders cultivated an active social life, they also constituted a kind of agricultural "academy." Leaseholders educated their own children by sending them to their relatives' farms for thorough training in practical and theoretical aspects of agriculture. The state also encouraged crown leaseholders to accept "pupils for thorough training in agriculture" and paid them correspondingly for "a successful performance in this regard." Many crown leaseholders proved excellent instructors for neophyte farmers and leaseholders from business and industrial circles as well as the middle and upper levels of the civil service. Sons of the landed nobility also sojourned on crown estates in order to gain a thorough training in agriculture, probably well aware that these "bourgeois master farmers" could provide more stimulating information and better insights into the rational operation and management of a large estate than could the landed nobility. The "pupils" who paid an extended visit to the Gramzow estate in Ukermark leased by Hermann Karbe, a farmer of outstanding reputation, included a Count Bernstorff and a Herr von Arnswald from the district of Hannover, a Count Kielmannsegg and a Herr Hengstenberg from Westphalia, a von Bielow from Pomerania, a Herr von Gareis from Bavaria, and a von Senfft from eastern Brandenburg.[58] Friedrich von Bodelschwingh was a pupil on Koppe's estate at Wollup from 1849 to 1851.[59]

The crown leaseholders were certainly the bearers of economic progress. They were well educated, had attended secondary schools, technical schools, and universities, and undertook educational trips, especially to Great Britain. The Magdeburg estates administration said that the "caste of crown leaseholders is celebrated for its knowledge and experience in rational, highly practical agri-

57. Ibid., no. 88, letter of December 13, 1832; no. 94, p. 44; no. 217, report of March 18, 1844.
58. StA Potsdam, Pr. Br. Rep. 2A, III D, no. 1058, report of January 21, 1845; July 8, 1851; July 20, 1856; January 11, 1859; January 2, 1861.
59. Tucek (above, n. 57), p. 16.

culture,"[60] and it certainly was influential. Progressive and at times even revolutionary from an economic point of view, crown leaseholders tended politically to be liberal-conservative and extremely loyal to the royal family to which they felt closely connected. This attitude was never better demonstrated than during the revolution of 1848–49. For instance, the Wollup leaseholder Koppe, a diligent and astute entrepreneur who operated "a factory-like farm" in which "the division of labor is as successful as in other branches of the economy,"[61] frowned on the "rebellion" and solemnly affirmed the sense of gratitude he "bore in his heart for the king and the royal family."[62] However, Koppe also deplored the way Prussia demeaned its citizens and demanded that the authorities remove "the obstacles to freedom of occupation" and "adequately protect the individual citizen."[63] All in all, crown leaseholders numbered among those strata of the bourgeoisie that wished to eliminate the abuses in society and encourage the emergence of a civil order, though they hoped to achieve all this without the necessary struggles and new contradictions.

The royal family, the Ministry of Agriculture and the estates administration knew how to reward the achievements and the loyalty of the crown leaseholders. After "many years of diligent farming and prompt fulfillment of the lease conditions," they awarded the titles of *Amtmann, Oberamtmann,* or *Amtsrat,* always preceded by the attribute royal. The title of *Amtsrat* required the express approval of the king himself, who also remitted a letter and official certificate.[64] The leaseholders set great store by these distinctions, which significantly enhanced their prestige and standing in the community. Leaseholder Kienitz on the Vehlefanz estate declared in a letter of gratitude that this honor was "more gratifying than anything else possibly could be."[65] Numerous crown leaseholders were raised to the ranks of the nobility, for instance Blacha, Diebitsch, Frankenberg, Frantzius, Gansauge, Gersdorf, Honig, Kries, Lenske, Oppen, Rosenstiel, Schultz, and Schweinichen, in order to name only a few.[66] Carl Ernst von Freier in Goldbeck

---

60. StA Magdeburg, Rep. Da Rosenburg, I, no. 51, p. 124.
61. Johann Gottlieb Koppe, *Sind große oder kleine Landgüter zweckmäßiger für das allgemein Beste?* (Berlin, 1847), p. 4.
62. Zentrales Staatsarchiv der DDR, Abt. Merseburg, Rep. 87 B, no. 10675, p. 37 v.
63. Ibid., Rep. 164 a, no. 96, vol. 2, p. 3 v.
64. See StA Potsdam, Pr. Br. Rep. 2A, III D, no. 515.
65. Ibid., letter of December 29, 1829.
66. Oelrichs (above, n. 21), pp. 218ff.

(Prignitz) was granted the title of *Amtsrat* and raised to the nobility because he "at great expense to himself" undertook major improvements to the farms adjacent to the estates of Goldbeck, Wittstock, and Scharfenberg, established meadows irrigated by sewage, and instituted "rational horse breeding" among other things. He thereby acquired "the reputation of being one of the best farmers in the district."[67] Crown leaseholders or their offspring sometimes married into noble families, though they were regarded by most of the reactionary nobility as intruders and parvenus. This prompted the highly self-confident Johann Gottlieb Koppe to remark condescendingly: "One often observes rich daughters of the bourgeoisie marrying impecunious nobles in order to become ladies."[68]

Ennoblement and other honors for crown leaseholders were also to a certain extent a recognition of their affluence and wealth. One characteristic trait of wealthy crown leaseholders was their tendency to purchase what often had been indebted and debilitated estates previously belonging to the nobility and to transform them into flourishing farms at the leading edge of advances in agriculture. This phenomenon could be observed throughout the nineteenth century. The leaseholders usually continued to operate their previous leasehold estates as well "because their low capital cost meant that they were more profitable than properties that had been purchased."[69] For instance, in 1810 *Oberamtmann* Palm of the Schraplau crown estate purchased for 181,965 marks the estates of Schafsee and Stedten, previously belonging to Prince August of the Prussian royal family. Palm then resold these estates to a merchant in 1833.[70] *Amtsrat* Hagemann, leaseholder of the Oranienburg estate, purchased in 1803 the manors of Merz and Ragow, located in the district of Beeskow and including a total of some 11,000 *Morgen* of land, from the wholesale speculator Lieutenant-General von Schmettau for 600,000 marks.[71] Measured by today's standards, Hagemann would have been a millionaire several times over.

Koppe, who has already been mentioned frequently throughout this article, was the son of a cottager and day laborer under the

---

67. StA Potsdam, Pr. Br. Rep. 2A, III D, no. 515, letter of December 29, 1824; May 3, 1832; November 29, 1843.

68. Koppe, *Lebenserinnerungen* (above, n. 43), p. 107; ZStA Merseburg, Geheimes Zivilkabinett, Landwirtschaft, Rep. 2.2.1, no. 30081, p. 47.

69. Pruns (above, n. 48), p. 223.

70. StA Magdeburg, Rep. Da Schraplau, nos. 65 and 87.

71. StA Potsdam, Rep. 37, Ragow estate archive, no. 7.

feudal regime. He became the steward on several manors and a colleague of Thaer in Möglin. In 1827 he leased the estate of Wollup, with the help of a 40,000 *Taler* loan from Baron von Eckhardstein, and in 1830 he leased Kienitz as well. In 1841 he became the proprietor of the manors of Beesdau und Crinitz (Luckau district), for which he paid the son of his former employer, Major von Thümen, 330,000 marks.[72] His children continued in his footsteps as crown leaseholders and also purchased the manors of Liebenfelde, Lindow, and Vossberg. Typical of this intense interest in money and accumulation of property was the question Koppe addressed to his future son-in-law, Franz Guenther, on the occasion of the latter's engagement to his daughter, Marianne: "So dear Guenther, tell me now, what is your total wealth?" Guenther responded, "about 20,000 *Taler*," to which Koppe replied, "That to be sure is not very much."[73]

Schröder, the leaseholder of the crown estates of Alvensleben and Tundersleben, received a letter in 1883 from a certain Herr A. von Waldenburg: "I wish to compliment you on your acquisition of the best estate in the area of Mansfelder See, whose sole proprietor you now are. I congratulate you on this excellent transaction . . ., for in my estimate the purchase of Elzdorf has made you 450,000 marks richer."[74]

Finally we should mentioned the Karbe "leaseholding family," a genuine dynasty. Already well known at the end of the eighteenth century as highly successful crown leaseholders, they farmed the Brandenburg estates of Neuendorf for 104 years, Gramzow for 82 years, Chorin for 37 years, Weselitz for 20 years, Biegen for 48 years, Mahlisch for 20 years, and Potzlow for 57 years as well as the Pomeranian estate of Jacobsdorf for 35 years. They also worked other estates that they leased for only a few years before shifting to new estates or purchasing lands for themselves. By 1945 this "leaseholding dynasty" held leases for longer or shorter durations on eighteen crown estates and estates belonging to the schools, as well as seventeen other estates. They owned twenty-six manors or other lands. By 1840 they already possessed at least 50,000 *Morgen* of land, of which a large proportion remained in the hands of the

---

72. Tucek (above, n. 55), p. 17; StA Magdeburg, Rep. H, Wanzleben, letter of October 18, 1832; StA Potsdam, Rep. 7, Amt Wollup, no. 2.
73. Cited in Pruns (above, n. 48), app. vol., pp. 30f.
74. StA Magdeburg, Rep. Da Schraplau, no. 738, letter of January 20, 1883.

Karbe family for many years, representing an enormous capital investment.[75]

These wealthy, property-accumulating, bourgeois-capitalist lease-holders did much to advance Prussian agriculture. They participated in many different clubs and associations, took part in committees and exhibitions, and went on special assignments. They were entrusted by the government with an enormous variety of tasks, held many public offices, published books and articles, and engaged in many different activities in the service of agriculture. We encounter them as tax collectors on manors or rent-free estates. State authorities commissioned them to estimate the value of lands ceded to the railroads and asked them to arbitrate the separation of fields and the division of common properties. Crown leaseholders appear as leading members of fire and hail insurance companies, as experts on dikes, as founders and supporters of agricultural schools, or as chairmen of sales and purchasing cooperatives. Many attained the position of *Landrat* or chief administrative officer and thereby represented the state in their district. They were also much in demand as judges at regional trade and agricultural exhibitions, at livestock shows, or horse races.

During the agrarian reforms, highly capable crown leaseholders, for instance, Carl Friedrich Baath, an *Amtsrat* in Sachsendorf and a proponent of Albrecht Thaer, were called upon as consultants and asked to help formulate new laws. August Karbe, an *Amtsrat* in Blankenburg, who helped pave the way for Thaer to settle in Prussia, was asked for his opinion on laws pertaining to agriculture and taxation.[76] Koppe in the district of Wollup was entrusted with manifold duties. He gave instruction to the three Prussian princes, reported on agricultural conditions on estates that the princes were considering purchasing, and assessed the economic circumstances of various estates that the Crown wished to lease out. The minister of the interior asked this "skilfull and contented farmer," who was well known as an "agricultural authority," to look over proposals for, and the bylaws of, an agricultural college to be built by the

75. For extensive information about various proprietors and family trees, see Harald Riechert, "Brandenburgische Landwirtschaftsgeschlechter und ihre genealogischen Verflechtungen," *Archiv für Sippenforschung und alle verwandten Gebiete mit Praktischer Forschungstätigkeit* 22, no. 32 (1960), pp. 504ff.; *Deutsches Geschlechterbuch*, vol. 150, *Brandenburgisches Geschlechterbuch*, (Limburg an der Lahn, 1969), pp. 1ff.

76. See H.A. Pierer, ed., *Universal-Lexikon* (Altenburg, 1840), under "Karbe."

state. The college was completed in 1842 and Koppe was named one of its first members. This agricultural college became the most important source of information and advice for Prussian agriculture and a key intermediary between the government and the rural community. King Frederick William IV even offered Koppe the position of minister of agriculture, though he declined because "aristocrats in the hinterland" would scarcely be willing to accept "a man of plebian birth."[77]

When the Association for the Assembly of Agricultural Machines was founded in Magdeburg in 1838, three crown leaseholders from Alsleben, Alvensleben, and Wegelegen were elected to its six-person technical directorate.[78] (This association organized in the same year a machine exhibition that was the first on the European continent and only the second anywhere after the 1837 exhibition in Oxford and did much to test and encourage the use of agricultural machinery.) Numerous crown leaseholders later participated in this "technical association" and gave "addresses on practical agriculture."[79] Moritz Elsner, the crown leaseholder of the Rosenburg estate and a model farmer who was always in the forefront of applying new scientific advances to agriculture and who was a member of the board of a sugar factory, was appointed a member of Prussia's official commission for the Parisian World Exhibition of 1854.[80] Elsner's son Gottfried was responsible for managing the traveling exhibitions of the German Agricultural Association,[81] which greatly helped to encourage the technical and economic advance of German agriculture and to broaden the horizons of many farmers and estate owners. Many crown leaseholders were members of the Agricultural Association, founded by Max Eyth, and a number of them made considerable contributions to the advancement of German agriculture by serving on specialist commissions and on the board of exhibitions.[82]

One crown leaseholder named Weyhe, who lived in Wegeleben near Halberstadt, was placed in charge of the agricultural academy

77. Koppe, *Lebenserinnerungen* (above, n. 43), pp. 56, 87 and 102f.; ZStA Merseburg, Geheimes Zivilkabinett, Landwirtschaft, Rep. 2.2.1, no. 30081, p. 47.
78. StA Magdeburg, Rep. Da Schlanstedt, Generalia, I, no. 5, p. 17.
79. Ibid., Rep Da Rosenburg, XXI, no. 11, p. 87.
80. Ibid., no. 9, p. 218.
81. Ibid., no. 11, p. 56.
82. See J. Hansen and G. Fischer, *Geschichte der Deutschen Landwirtschafts-Gesellschaft* (Berlin, 1936).

in Bonn-Poppelsdorf from 1851 until 1856.[83] This appointment serves to symbolize the marriage of science and applied agriculture as practiced by many crown leaseholders. Not only did they attend science courses at colleges and universities and successfully employ what they had learned in everyday farming, but they themselves actually developed and applied new techniques, carried out active research programs, collected and interpreted the data, and thereby contributed initial building blocks and later important foundations of the agricultural sciences in Germany. Only a few names can be mentioned here: F.F. Gottlob Holzhausen, for instance, leaseholder of the Gröbzig estate in Anhalt, who contributed greatly around 1800 to the introduction and expansion of clover cultivation and to improved feed for sheep. At the same time he sparked a lively debate about his new methods.[84] Johann Heinrich Fink, a successful farmer who leased the Petersburg estate near Halle in the 1790s, also made substantial contributions to sheep breeding. In 1797 he founded a sheep-farming school, and his breeding of merinos attracted the attention of other breeders and the government. Fink achieved much recognition, even during his own lifetime, thanks to the many business associations of which he was a member and to the tasks he carried out on behalf of the Prussian state.[85] Later as well, there were many well-known sheep breeders among the crown leaseholders. One of them was Rudolf Thilo of the Mecklenburg estate of Ballin, who was renowned for his breeding farm of full-blooded merino sheep. It was he who bred the German strain of Merino worsted-wool sheep.[86]

A plant breeder of some distinction was Wilhelm Rimpau (1842–1903), leaseholder of the Schlanstedt estate and proprietor of the manors of Langenstein, Emersleben, and Anderbeck, who is honored as the "father of German plant breeding." He hybridized numerous plants, building on and criticizing the works of Darwin, Vilmorin, Nägeli, and Da Vries. Rimpau's research led to the development of "Schlanstedt rye," famous for its high yield, and various varieties of wheat. "Rimpau's Early Bastard," which combined English squarehead wheat with the frost resistance of German

---

83. Eduard Hartstein, *Die landwirtschaftliche Akademie Poopelsdorf* (Bonn, 1864), p. 21.

84. See Ulla Machlitt (above, n. 17), p. 174f.; Hans-Heinrich Müller, *Akademie und Wirtschaft im 18. Jahrhundert* (Berlin/GDR, 1975), p. 210.

85. Pruns (above, n. 48), app. vol., p. 36.

86. *Die deutsche Landwirtschaft unter Kaiser Wilhelm II.* (above, n. 33), 2:329f.

and American varieties, was one of the leading German varieties for some fifty years. Rimpau was not only an outstanding plant breeder but also a prominent farmer, livestock breeder, business administrator, and advocate of agricultural technology who was one of the first to introduce steam power onto his estates.[87]

Finally we should mention *Domänenrat* Eduard Meyer, leaseholder of the Friedrichswerth and Neufrankenrode estates near Gotha. Meyer was one of the leading breeders of *Edelschwein* (a large, white strain of German pigs) and a farmer who evaluated all the latest achievements of science and technology in order to improve his domains. He developed a strain of intensively bred white *Edelschwein* that combined early maturity with good fattening qualities. By 1912 Meyer had sold 25,000 breeding pigs, of which substantial numbers were shipped abroad to Austria-Hungary, the Balkans, Russia, Switzerland, Asia, Africa, and South America – living evidence of the worldwide renown of Friedrichswert pig breeding.[88]

The crown leaseholders were truly pioneers of agriculture. They were technical, agricultural, and economic paragons of their day, a progressive and enlightened element in German agriculture. They contributed a considerable "sum of intelligence and capital."[89] Their estates in many cases were model farms, exemplars of modern agriculture from which the peasantry and landed nobility alike learned a great deal, especially as many improvements and innovations were not highly expensive. Crown estates and leaseholders also provided the state with a means through which it could and did influence agricultural conditions in its own interests. Von der Goltz, an agricultural historian who himself administered large estates and was well acquainted with nineteenth-century agriculture, once noted that the high standards that German agriculture had attained by the end of the century would scarcely have been possible "if we had not had the crown leaseholders."[90] This is an opinion that we too affirm without any hesitation.

There is still no comprehensive history of crown leaseholders, or

---

87. Konrad Meyer, "Wilhelm Rimpau," in Günther Franz and Heinz Haushofer, eds., *Große Landwirte* (Frankfurt a.M., 1970), pp. 271ff.

88. *Die deutsche Landwirtschaft unter Kaiser Wilhelm II.* (above, n. 33), 2:415ff.

89. Berghoff-Ising (above, n. 5), p. 76; see as well H. Rimpler, *Domänenpolitik und Grundeigentumsverteilung* (Leipzig, 1888), pp. 57ff.

90. Goltz, *Agrarwesen und Agrarpolitik* (above, n. 3), p. 73; Aereboe (above, n. 2), p. 191.

even of leaseholders in general, who played such an important role in the development of German agriculture. This paper is an attempt to illuminate some social and economic aspects, though it represents no more than a beginning. Social and economic historians still face an urgent need for more thorough research into the origins, agricultural techniques, and financial resources of the crown leaseholders and into their relationship with rural laborers and other farm personnel.

JAN PETERS

One's Place in Church:
Hierarchical Attitudes in the Late Feudal Period

1. Seating

In 1637 in the Church of St. Augustine in Gotha, the keepers of the Church Seating Registry noted with some relief that after a period of "great quarreling and snapping, cursing and blaspheming," "the war" had finally drawn to an end.[1*] During a discussion in Ruhla in 1648 about reassigned seating arrangements in church, a peasant declared that "he would let himself be carved into pieces on the church floor before being removed from his seat."[2] An investigation into a dispute between two communities over seating in the church of Groß-Luja (district of Niederlausitz) produced the comment that "the spirit was more like that of a pub than of a church."[3] The parish councillors of the Church of St. Nikolai in Greifswald complained in 1730 that there was hardly "a pew remaining in the church whose occupants are not warring back and forth."[4] During a dispute over a particular pew in Barth, the consistory urged the parish councillors in 1740 to consider that "since this pew is in front of the council pew, it stands in an honored position in the church. Its use should reflect this fact and it

---

* from *Jahrbuch für Volkskunde und Kulturgeschichte* 28 (13 in new series), 235 (1985: 77–106 condensed.

1. Staatsarchiv Weimar (StAW), Oberkonsistorium Stadt Gotha, no. 131, loc. 3, no. 2.
2. StAW, Oberkonsistorium, Gericht Thal, no. 194. Report of February 4, 1648.
3. Staatsarchiv Potsdam (StAP), Rep. 40 C, Niederlausitzisches Konsistorium, Kr. Calau, no. 27. Articuli probatoriales of March 8, 1710.
4. Staatsarchiv Greifswald (StAG), Rep. 35, no. 693. Note of September 26, 1730.

should not be assigned indiscriminately to anyone at all."[5] In Wolgast, a seaman struggled to win a seat in the seamen's choir of St. Peter's. He too, he said, had been a sailor for a time and the others on the bench did "not have the slightest reason to be ashamed of me."[6] In Beuster in Brandenburg, two freeholders erected a balconylike structure for themselves in the local church in 1749 and "were foolish enough to have their names and aristocratic coats of arms painted on their new gallery."[7] In the town of Leina in Thuringia, it was not uncommon around 1811 for aspirants to a newly vacated pew "to awaken the parson at three o'clock in the morning in order to be first in line."[8]

Examples of this kind can be adduced at will for they were not in the least unusual. In the late feudal era one's place in church was a critical consideration that often consumed people's thoughts and determined their behavior. This paper is intended to demonstrate why this was so. Using the social distinctions in seating, it seeks to clarify the relations between social structure and personal prestige, between one's position in church and daily life. In doing so, it will also help to illuminate the late feudal mentality from a viewpoint that is seldom considered.

The church and the view of human existence propagated there exerted an enormous influence over the mentality and behavior of the peasantry in the late feudal period. In a religiously charged atmosphere, regular attendance at church, communion, and confession served as important stabilizing and disciplining factors, as essential in the spiritual realm as work in the fields and in the shops was in the material realm. The Sunday sermon was a key method of communication and attendance at church was the social highlight of the week. It was here that one demonstrated one's importance, observed and compared – especially the clothes of the other wives. It was here that values were established and propagated. From the standpoint of our current understanding of religiosity and social values, the importance of the church service during the late feudal period can scarcely be imagined. Weekly church attendance (and the seat one occupied on this occasion) had a decisive influence on the basic needs and emotional responses of all social classes and strata,

5. StAG, Rep. 35, no. 634. Judgment of July 29, 1740.
6. StAG, Rep. 35, no. 676. Note of March 21, 1753.
7. StAP, Pr. Br. Rep. 40 A, no. 229. *Amtmann's* letter of January 16, 1749.
8. StAW, Oberkonsistorium Stadt Gotha, Amt Tenneberg, no. 340. Note of November 27, 1811.

even though individual sensitivities did vary somewhat.

What follows can only be properly appreciated if one understands that participating in the church service – especially seeing and being seen – was essential to everything that mattered in life. The luminous Gothic wall paintings, the winged altarpieces with movable Biblical motives, the moving wooden statues of the saints, and even the triumphant crucifix of pre-Reformation times were all lovingly preserved for many years, especially in village churches. The joy derived from such visual impressions ran deep and they were a valuable didactic tool. Opulently painted pews (whether for the nobility or the peasants), brightly colored baptismal angels, golden altar pieces, and star-spangled heavens lavished across the church ceiling provided parishoners in both Protestant and Catholic Baroque churches of the seventeenth and eighteenth centuries with an immediate "impression of the heavens."[9] Church interiors were bright and colorful – at once exciting, soothing, and awe inspiring. The importance attached to visual impressions was always first and foremost in the minds of the people whenever the discussion turned to seating arrangements.

The seating arrangements in church (in this case the Protestant church, which is the subject of this study) always reflected the social barriers and boundaries in outside society. Both the feudal lords in the countryside and the upper classes in the city, ruling through wealth, had special pews built to mark their superiority over the common folk through their size, positioning (near the pulpit and altar), elevation, decoration, and seclusion.[10] Social distinctions first found expression in "open" pews and "closable" pews, which could be locked shut. This was the primary means through which pews were distinguished in the church rules of the sixteenth century.[11] Soon, however, the external differences grew more marked: Where "peers and personages in authority customarily sit," according to the *Krünitz Encyclopedia* of 1786, "particularly large and highly decorated pews are installed, which are enclosed like separate little chambers."[12] This august seating was often outfitted with all creature

9. *Dorfkirchen* (Dresden, 1957), p. 10.
10. They are also easy to confuse with confessionals (stemming in some cases from the eighteenth century), which can still be found, for instance, in some village churches on Rügen.
11. Emil Sehling, ed., *Die evangelischen Kirchenordnungen des XVI. Jahrhunderts* (Leipzig, 1902), 4:209; 5:421.
12. Johann Georg Krünitz, *Oekonomisch-technologische Encyklopädie*, pt. 38 (Berlin, 1786), p. 168.

comforts: heaters, cushioned seats, tables, mirrors, and sometimes even a library.[13] Glassed-in "praying chambers," latticework galleries, or decoratively painted benches on a balcony overlooking the pulpit and general congregation were common manifestations of feudal rule. Some regional differences did exist. An aristocratic pew in a village church that was shared by several noble families was generally more modest than the seating of a particularly eminent member of the landed nobility. The seats in a residential city of a prince ruling over one of the many German principalities were even more impressive, with a large separate gallery and private entrance, which could sometimes even be reached directly from his castle or residence. Since nobles were inclined to adopt status symbols from further up the feudal chain of command, even village churches soon sported separate, external entrances to boxlike seats that were reachable by stairs, glassed-in, highly decorated, and "hung" in the area of the pulpit. In the nineteenth century, seating such as this as well as individual seats in the choir were often torn out in response to the bourgeois-democratic sense of equality and later to the desire for more light inside the church. Box seating with separate entrances has now all but disappeared.[14]

In the tradition of the old church, men and women sat on opposite sides "for modesty's sake,"[15] with the men usually on the right, which was considered the more privileged position.[16] In churches with larger galleries, especially in Thuringia, the men sat upstairs while the women sat downstairs. However, the entire family of nobles or other "persons of rank" often sat together in their "prayer chambers" with only a hint of sexual separation, for instance, women might "be in the first pew, topped with a latticework, while the cavaliers were behind."[17]

Besides privileged positions for those with economic power, there was also special seating for functional reasons for the officials

13. Siegfried Scharfe, *Dorfkirchen in Europa* (Leipzig, 1973), pp. 6f.
14. An excellent example can be found in Dedelow, District of Prenzlau. Cf. Heinrich Ehl, *Norddeutsche Feldsteinkirchen* (Braunschweig/Hamburg, 1926), p. 19. For Saxony, see O. Gruner, *Die Dorfkirche im Königreich Sachsen* (Leipzig, 1904), p. 32.
15. Krünitz, (above, no. 12) pt. 38, p. 781.
16. Especially widespread in Sweden: Berndt Gustafsson, *Manligt-kvinnligt i 1800 – talets svenska folkliv* (Lund, 1956), pp. 46ff. For the origins of this lengthwise division of the church and deviations from it, see Iso Müller, "Frauen rechts, Männer links. Historische Platzverteilung in der Kirche," *Schweizerisches Archiv für Volkskunde* 57 (1961): 65–81.
17. StAP, Rep. 40 C, no. 28. Niederlausitzisches Konsistorium (Drebkau, 1705).

and leaseholders of the local lord. The special seating of the parson and his family belonged to this category. The parson had a definite place to occupy in the church, as in the feudal system as a whole, and his seating often consisted of a relatively unimposing rebuilt latticework confessional that was situated near the altar and also served as the sacristry. This seating often still exists today.[18] Parsons with large families sometimes required an entire little choir for themselves.[19] Officials and leaseholders tended to prefer more impressive seating, and the leaseholder usually assumed the seats of the local lord if they were vacant.

Also accorded special seating, though not especially dignified, were the teacher and the organist (these two positions were usually combined in one person who occupied a seat in the organ loft and also conducted the student choir with the help of an adult assistant), as well as the sextons, vergers, sacristans, and parish councillors. The latter could be counted among the ruling class to a certain extent, because they usually belonged to the upper social strata, at least in the cities. The city council always enjoyed privileged seating in church, as did the members of the government and the chancery in residential cities.

In the absence of any other ordering principle, even the ordinary seating in church was assigned according to social status, usually more strictly and permanently in villages as compared to cities and more distinctly in the *Gutsherrschaften* as compared to the *Grund-herrschaften* in Saxony and Thuringia. The best seats (which always meant the most prominent seats near the pulpit) were occupied by wealthier peasants, especially freeholders, followed by other occupations in order of declining income. Cottagers, day laborers, and farmhands came last. In villages they usually sat at the back, that is at the entrance or in the organ loft, and in Thuringia in particular, they sat in the back rows of the side galleries. The servant classes in the city often brought folding chairs with them (called *Kreckstühlgen* in Pomerania),[20] which they placed somewhere in the central aisle or at the back. In addition, folding seats were often

---

18. Examples just on Rügen: Bobbin, Gustow, Landow, Neuenkirchen, Patzig, Poseritz, Rambin, Rappin, Schaprode, Trent, Vilmnitz, Wiek, and Zirkow. For Saxony, see Gruner (above, n. 14), pp. 43f.

19. StAG, Rep. 10, no. 3857. Note of September 20, 1773.

20. J. C. Dähnert, *Sammlung gemeiner und besonderer Pommerscher und Rügischer Landes-Urkunden, Gesetze, Privilegien, Verträge, Constitutiones und Ordnungen* (Stralsund, 1767), 2:695.

attached to the sides of the pews and occasionally still remain today.[21] Male and female servants usually sat apart,[22] though in their role as status symbols they could be found quite frequently alongside their master or in the pew of wealthy peasants, though of course "they must never draw attention to themselves."[23] The servants of aristocrats generally took precedence over peasants, at communion, for example.

A larger separation between pews is a sign that "persons of rank" had been pushed down into the regular seating and wished to avoid rising to their feet when allowing others to pass in front of them. When the seats face one another, they could be exchangeable seats[24] (one moved from one to the other in order to see better as the parson moved between the pulpit and the altar), or possibly seats for children.

In the areas where *Gutsherrschaften* predominated, the women's seating was divided along exactly the same social lines as the men's (in contrast to Thuringia, for example, where the men often sat in the galleries). In villages, the wives of parsons, sextons, and teachers therefore came first (in Thuringia the wives of community shepherds were also often included). The women's seating was always on the ground floor and was highly visible from everywhere in the church. It was here, therefore, that the battles for social status usually erupted. The socially more prestigious "upper seats" or "preferred seats" (locations on the central aisle within each row of pews) were prized especially highly, because it was always "better to sit on the upper end."[25] These seats should "not be sold to very little people to the great annoyance and vexation of all the others."[26] When the church began to charge a little more for the "highest and best situated seats," they soon fell in any case into the hands of the wealthier classes.[27] However, there was still no end to "irksome quarreling and jockeying for position."[28]

---

21. The mountain church of Oybin, district of Zittau, is an especially impressive example (eighteenth century).
22. StAG, Rep. 35, no. 812. Note of March 26, 1727.
23. Krünitz (above, n. 12), pt. 38, pp. 788f.
24. Petersdorf, district of Strasburg; Fürstenwerder, district of Prenzlau.
25. Letter of Joh. Chr. Prehn, living in Apenburg, on January 19, 1754. Staatsarchiv Magdeburg (StAM), Rep. H. Beetzendorf, A IIIb, no. 99, fol. 67f.
26. Church seating arrangement for Neustadt Brandenburg/H. of March 17, 1710. Archive of the Brandenburg cathedral canons' chapter, BKa 563.
27. Church seating arrangement for Neustadt Brandenburg/H. of 1712. Ibid.
28. Seating arrangement for the cathedral of Schwerin of September 8, 1697.

The following diagram illustrates a typical seating arrangement by social rank (though churches in Thuringia and parts of Saxony had somewhat different plans).[29] This schema varied according to the floor plan of the church, the social structure of the parish, and the presence of one or more ruling families. It was also altered somewhat by the number of galleries, the construction of individual choir seats, etc. Paradoxically enough, seating was usually arranged most strictly by social rank in those parishes that were politically weak and had few members of real rank and position. This was especially true in the areas where *Gutsherrschaften* predominated, and the struggle between aristocrats over seating reflected their uninhibited contempt for the village inhabitants. The latter followed the example set by their "betters" and sought to assert their own rather repressed sense of self-respect by engaging in the same sort of struggle in their own modest arena – regardless of how ridiculous many individual cases may seem today. Vestiges of these struggles

Altar

Pastor	Parish
Sexton	Councillors
	Pulpit
District	Nobles
Councillors	Leaseholders
Women:	Men:
Farmers	Farmers
Half Farmers	Half Farmers
Small Farmers	Small Farmers
Cottagers/	Cottagers/
Day Laborers	Day Laborers
Servants	Servants

Gesetzessammlung für die Mecklenburg-Schwerinschen Lande (Wismar/Ludwigslust, 1865), 2:392.

29. See Krünitz (above, n. 12), vol. 38, app. no. 2083. The model offered here of a "typical" village church with the division of pews (p. 248) is unusual in that the organ gallery with "pews for children" was in the apse of the church, the ruling family sat on an isolated single gallery in the western part of the church, and men and women did not sit on different sides of the church but only on separate benches.

can still be seen today in pews that are elevated or embellished with a trelliswork in village churches in Uckermark or in what was north-western Pomerania.

The struggle among aristocrats for more prestigious seating was more restrained in Thuringia and parts of Saxony and Brandenburg, where rural parishes long remained quite intact. This was due not only to the Christian doctrine of equality before God (which everywhere stood in stark contrast to the extreme concern for prestige and status), but also to the survival of self-confident parish councils in these areas. Here too, of course, the peasants were very conscious of social rank, but they were more willing to forego external manifestations of status because their sense of self-respect was not under the same kind of relentless assault as on the great estates. The same held true for small towns within strong rural parishes (with the exception of residence towns where the struggle over one's place in the hierarchy reached outlandish proportions). In Saxony-Thuringia and Brandenburg, seating in church was often determined by age, at least among the men in the galleries, while the women sat in the same order as their farms or houses in the village, i.e., their "pews in church followed the order of their homes in the civic realm."[30]

2. Seating Differences in Church as an Expression of the Mentality of the Times and the Preoccupation with Hierarchy

a) The Struggle among Aristocrats

Strife and overweening pride in the house of God – an obvious contradiction and yet not so difficult to understand when one considers that Christianity was firmly integrated into the feudal world and was shaped and twisted accordingly. The feudal world was hierarchical in structure with everything in its place. Social distinctions and barriers were omnipresent. There was therefore enormous social pressure to think in terms of social rank, even among the peasantry, and it usually sufficed to outweigh any biblical injunctions of equality before God. The landed gentry in particular felt no compunction vis-à-vis the Christian ethic and the

30. Letter of Joh. Chr. Prehn, living in Apenburg, on January 19, 1754. Staatsarchiv Magdeburg, Rep. H. Beetzendorf, A IIIb, no. 99, fol. 67f.

Sermon on the Mount. Anyone who questioned the social hierarchy in church hit a vital nerve in the society that triggered great alarm. Conflict was inevitable whenever more than one grandee attended a given church and desired "a place of honor" in accordance with the time-honored principle of "see and be seen." This occurred first and foremost in residence towns where swarms of government officials competed with one another as well as upper-level townsmen to obtain what was regularly termed "a right comfortable and reputable position." Many thick tomes in the churches of St. Margaret and St. Augustin in the residence city of Gotha were filled with the records of disputes of this kind. Arrogance and social envy were at the root of these mountains of documents generated throughout the eighteenth century by countless court advocates, privy councillors, apothecaries, closet advisers, gentlemen-in-waiting, government officials, and superintendant-generals engaged in the battles of the painted chapels and glassed-in pews.[31] "A town in the foothills of the Harz offers the example of the collector of excise Siewecke from Dardesheim, who wanted a prominent seat in the gallery for his wife, "because the rabble would not be able to see and adequately admire the stylish outfit of his dear wife in a latticework chair of the kind installed on the ground floor of the church."[32]

Spats between nobles were unusual in the villages of Thuringia, the Duchy of Magdeburg, and much of Saxony and Brandenburg. Strong rural parishes evidently limited the scope for aristocratic "vanity." However, this constraint vanished when the parishes were deprived of their power and functioned merely as a rubber stamp for the local potentate.

Squabbles over pews were therefore frequent among aristocrats in Pomerania. Envy and jostling for position were inevitable when, as in Zudar on the island of Rügen, seven aristocratic families built closed boxes in the same small church in order to set themselves off from the peasant seating.[33] Long epistles ensued over the disputed seating arrangements, which were only settled when the squabbling lords and ladies drew lots.[34] Disputes regularly erupted over the aristocratic seating when an estate was taken over by a leaseholder even though some heirs of the landed family remained in the area.

31. StAW, Oberkonsistorium Stadt Gotha, nos. 134, 136–41.
32. StAM, Rep. A 12, Spezialia, Dardesheim, no. 15 a. Note of January 6, 1791.
33. Easily visible in a photograph of the church (before the renovation).
34. StAG, Rep. 10, no. 4088. Record of August 25, 1727.

This occurred, for instance, in Wusterhusen. A tenant farmer named Müller leased the estate of Ernsthof belonging to the Hakevitz family, married a Hakevitz daughter, and soon found himself engaged in a pitched battle with other family members for the right to sit in the places set aside for the lord of the manor.[35] Müller's predecessor, a certain Herr Kruse, had already laid claim to this seating, though the Hakevitz family heirs let it be known that this would appear "very petty before the entire congregation." They added, rather caustically and quite confident of the power of their argument, that "an old noble family hopefully merits sufficient consideration that it will not be expected to leave a plebeian, whose worth one is otherwise happy to recognize, with the upper hand in the community."[36] These scions of the nobility saw a world of difference between those of gentle breeding and mere bourgeois leaseholders. The "old noble family" won out in Wusterhusen, as it also did in Weitenhagen in the district of Greifswald where the leaseholder of the Grubenhagen estate was forbidden to sit in the pew of the previous leaseholder because the latter had obtained only "a usufruct to this seat."[37]

Not only the seating itself but all the servants and farmhands who used it were thought to belong to the aristocratic family and to reflect on it. Their prominence, as well as that of the pew, provided concrete visual evidence of the social standing of its owner. Highborn families therefore often fell to squabbling over the places of their servants and retainers. A protracted dispute about the place of their respective retainers arose in the 1720s between Lieutenant Johann Carl von Kitzleben (proprietor of Warsin among other properties after his father-in-law Franz Albrecht v. Hakevitz) and the Müller brothers mentioned above who leased the Ernsthof estate. The parties feuded over the Hakevitz choir in the Wusterhusen church, each claiming its own people should occupy some positions in the aisle leading to the choir. Kitzleben claimed that his father-in-law, von Hakevitz, had built the choir and that the aisle leading to it commenced with "a castle door decorated with the arms of the Hakevitz family and the name Frantz Albrecht."[38] The Müller brothers responded that the choir had been "built from Ernsthoff, belonged to it, and must again be appended to it." The unmarried

---

35. StAG, Rep. 6, Tit. 18, no. 1127. Note of September 20, 1714.
36. StAG, Rep. 6, Tit. 18, no. 715. Note of October 5, 1702.
37. StAG, Rep. 35, no. 495. Court record of October 5, 1768.
38. StAG, Rep. 35, no. 812. Note of Kitzleben, undated.

Hakevitz daughters, according to the leaseholders, should therefore be permitted only to pass through the choir until they married and thereby acquired the "seating associated with their estates."[39] The situation was legally very complicated and raised questions of established rights. The farmhands of the Ernsthof estate had always used the disputed aisle, and when possession of the estate changed they "had not been assigned separate seats like some others."[40] The Byzantine problems raised by divided usage, "reduction," and various legal rights were by no means unusual in Pomerania,[41] and the church consistory (whose competence in matters of seating arrangements was also in dispute)[42] had its hands full dealing with all the claims, counterclaims, hearing of witnessess, and writing of reports. The situation was further complicated by the fact that the retainers became involved in the disputes of their overlords. There were approximately twelve seats on the two disputed benches in the aisle, and they soon began to entice not only the original two groups of retainers but others as well. The Müller farmhands, Kitzleben complained, "were so thick in this aisle on Sundays that one can scarcely reach the choir."[43] It was especially scandalous, he said, that outside farmhands "after raising complaints crowd so stubbornly into the aisle that they cannot be moved."[44] Various witnesses reported: "Before the dispute there was pushing on the pew, but no real fighting. But afterwards there was much more pushing."[45] The aisle, Kitzleben said with some logic, should be considered part of the choir because it "is impossible to fly up to the choir."[46] The Müller brothers, however, insisted on the rights of their retainers and mocked their adversary who "fills sheet after sheet with writing but says nothing about the heart of the matter."[47] The coat of arms by the door would not be particularly important, in their view, even if von Hakevitz had "had every one of his ancestors painted on it."[48]

39. Ibid. Notes of the Müller brothers of January 29, 1727, and March 26, 1727.
40. Ibid. Note of March 26, 1727.
41. See the squabble over church seating among aristocrats in Pütnitz in 1729. StAG, Rep. 10, no. 3874.
42. See StAG, Rep. 35, no. 899.
43. Ibid. Note of Kitzleben, undated.
44. Ibid. Note of Kitzleben on December 16, 1727.
45. Ibid. Record of May 28, 1727.
46. Ibid. Note of Kitzleben on December 16, 1727.
47. Ibid. Note of Müller brothers on February 13, 1728.
48. Ibid. Note of Müller brothers on June 15, 1728.

The pastor took action with his yardstick, measuring the width of the pews and the distance between them and concluding that there was place enough for all if only the field hands "did not wish to stir up emnity and create obstacles."[49] Such pious hopes were unlikely to be fulfilled, however, both here and in similar cases elsewhere. The field hands were eager to take advantage of the dispute between their overlords because it alone afforded them an opportunity to express their pent-up irritation without fear of the consequences. Some field hands wished to act as spokesmen and champions of "their" overlord, while others wished only to be on their best obedient behavior. These tendencies were probably not so widespread, however, as the delight in seizing a risk-free opportunity to vent hostility toward overlords. All in all, the situation was a curious mixture of quarrelsome backwardness (not unusual in areas of large landed estates), aristocratic wrangling (totally oblivious to Christian principles and to the need to preserve the ideological stabilizing function of the church), and the warped aggressiveness of the poor, suppressed rural population.

In their struggles for social prestige, the ruling families often came into conflict with churchmen who were not equally oblivious to the incidental damage inflicted on the moral stature of the church. Pomeranian aristocrats in particular were most eager to enhance the trappings of their own prestige (or to acquire new trappings to match those of their rivals), but at the same time they tended to be miserly. Pastors and church officials certainly often assisted the local ruler or other embattled grandees but also crossed swords with them when it came time to collect money for the church. Aristocrats were willing to pay handsomely for the construction of their own seating but thereafter often refused to pay their annual fee in order to "bestow" occasional "gifts" on the church of any value they pleased (or even to build certain parts of the church, though this was usually quite expensive).

The conflict between the material interests of the church and those of the local nobility also played a role in those disputes in which the contentious issue was not so much the seating itself as the impression it gave of the importance of its occupant. The wife of General von Schoultz desired new seating in the Franzburg church in 1727, allegedly because her seat in the choir was unsuitable because of "all the drafts there." Her new seat was to be glassed-in

49. Ibid. Report of Pastor Behren on June 10, 1727.

and enclosed, with a separate outside entrance, and after her death she would bestow it upon the church as a confessional. The pastor realized that the view from his own seat would be impeded by this bulky new showpiece, and he must have protested because the responsible administrator rejected the seating. A high commission was then established to investigate, though it determined that if the pastor "bent a little to his left while sitting in his seat, he could adequately see past the seat of the *Frau Generalin*" and out over the congregation.[50] The pew therefore remained.

Such spats strike us as rather ridiculous, for to the modern sensibility any quarrel over status and rank tends toward comedy. In Fehrbellin, a postmaster and customs official who was feuding with the pastor over a socially suitable position for his wife finally "had a large easy chair carried into the church."[51] A similarly motivated dispute in Brandenburg reached its climax when a girl "was forcibly thrust" into the chair in question, "landing on top of my daughter," as the socially humiliated party complained.[52]

From the wives of the general and the privy councillor to those of the merchant and chamberlain, this feuding over "appropriate" seating must have simmered away incessantly, though rarely breaking into the open. Even when one had obtained the prized possession, the quarrels were not likely to end. Instead they continued over plans to heighten the pew or decorate it with latticework, windows, pictures, or coats of arms. Disputes were incessant, especially in the cities with their more fluid social structures. Not only the installation of choirs "over our heads"[53] but also the heightening of pews on the ground floor were a never-ending source of controversy.

Von Üsedom, a gentleman-in-waiting, had his seat in the church in Barth so elevated in 1782 that people sitting behind him could neither see nor properly hear the sermon.[54] The status consciousness of church officials themselves gave rise to further dissension, for instance, in 1736 when Provost Wudrian in Barth had his wife's pew near the altar "encircled with a large, carved latticework

50. StAG, Rep. 10, no. 2839. Notes of May 16, 1727, and May 26, 1727.

51. Record of September 27, 1701. Brandenburg cathedral canons' chapter, Fe 162.

52. Note of May 9, 1724, in regard to the Church of St. Peter in Brandenburg, Brandenburg cathedral canons' chapter, Fe 6280.

53. StAG, Rep. 6, Tit. 18, no. 816.

54. StAG, Rep. 35, no. 817. Record of February 12, 1782.

intended only as a pompous display of vanity." This, according to the evidently offended city council, could only have "vexatious consequences": first, the congregation was deprived of its "entire view of the altar," and secondly, others would behave similarly, such as the wife of Lieutenant-Colonel von Klinckowström whose pew had been decorated "for many years with only a small lattice-work," but who now had commissioned a larger one.[55]

Instances of this kind were especially frequent in Pomeranian cities but also occurred in larger cities in areas where *Grundherr-schaften* predominated, particularly in residential towns. However, there were marked differences between areas dominated by *Gutsherrschaften* and those dominated by *Grundherrschaften*. In Thuringia, the pastors were less dependent on the church patron and they fought for the right to collect fees from the nobility as well.[56] In addition, the local grandees were compelled to restrain their struggle to outdo one another. In Pomerania, however, the battle for prestige raged unchecked, including of course seating in church.

b) The Struggle for Prestige in the General Congregation

The strength of the tendency to think in hierarchical terms, even among peasants and similar strata, and the pervasiveness of this attitude, even in church where all were supposed to be equal, had many curious consequences. The concern of underlings, peasants, for instance, about their position in society was unique in some ways because their status was so precarious and dependent on the whims of an arbitrary ruler. Peasants sought to underline and entrench their social standing by means of visual symbols, and their desire to obtain these symbols therefore had a definite rationale. The struggle became rather tragic, however, when it was directed against fellow peasants in an identical or similar position, that is, when the objective common cause of the peasants vis-à-vis the nobility and their desire to display affirmative symbols were perverted by feelings of inferiority into an acceptance of the hierarchical thought of these feudal lords and a battle with other peasants for increased status. Not surprisingly, this phenomenon was most

---

55. StAG, Rep. 35, no. 904. Note of November 17, 1736.
56. StAW, Oberkonsistorium, Wangenheimsche Gerichte, a. Wangenheim, no. 271 (1745–46).

frequent in the late feudal era in areas where *Gutsherrschaften* predominated.

An instructive example can be found in the Neumark town of Regenthin[57] – which also provides evidence that the principle of assigning church seating by the order of farms could clearly have a social dimension when the farms were laid out around the village according to social groups. When it was decided in 1764 that seats would be not be assigned "by lot," but rather "according to the order of the farms in the village," the peasant Daniel Wohlfeil's wife landed on the fifth bench at the very back "where the half farmers and cottagers sit." The "Wohlfeil woman" and two others immediately complained about the social humiliation to which they had been subjected by being seated next to women of the "lower" social orders. Previously, they grumbled, the pews "had always remained unalterable according to the farms," but now the distribution was commenced at the end of the town instead of in the middle. The pastor maintained on the other hand that the reassignment had been made "in the order in which the persons lived from the house of the village mayor. Furthermore, Daniel Wohlfeil's wife was "the only one who is full of foolish peasant pride." She "considers it an affront that she is expected to share a bench with a half farmer's wife" and a cottager's wife. A hearing was held, and several peasants (who according to legal practice spoke on behalf of their wives) criticized the "foolish pride and obstinacy" of the three women and declared that they had forbidden their wives (who in any case had been assigned more "suitable" seating) to become involved in this matter because it was "of no consequence." All this occurred in the second half of the eighteenth century, and the extent to which this socially "belittling" seating arrangement disturbed Frau Wohlfeil's concentration on the service is astounding. The three women declared that they wanted "only peace of mind in order to attend church with truly devout thoughts." Social "misplacement," however, undermined this intent: "We also lose the means to happiness, the word of God, and the Lord's Supper."

It is clearly implied that such an unbearable social slight cast doubt on further church attendance itself. The weakness of this argument, in view of the absolute social compulsion to attend church, is quite apparent, though there were explanations as well for

---

57. For what follows: StAP, Pr. Br. Rep. 40 B, Neumärkisches Konsistorium, no. 217/1.

this weakness: "Whether we can hear the word of the Lord as well-we are at the entrance to the door or beside the altar, we sit far back in the hall or on the square- everyone nonetheless seeks to defend and preserve his rights. Moreover, we are also human beings and although we wish to submit equally to the perfect rules of our God, we have still not rid ourselves of all the weaknesses that humanity is subject to and we would listen with much annoyance to the words of the sermon and not be able to see any improvement."

The deep roots of such hierarchical thinking are easy to comprehend, even though such behavior grew less prevalent in strictly orthodox circles in the second half of the eighteenth century. A majority of the peasants in Regenthin considered it "great foolishness" that "Daniel Wohlfeilen's wife considered herself superior to other farmer's wives" (though the critics to be sure had suffered no disadvantage from the new seating arrangements). The teacher who composed the letter of complaint was perhaps able to articulate the arguments of the three women much more clearly than they themselves could have done, and the government dismissed the complaint. As in other backward areas where *Gutsherrschaften* predominated and the social structure was similar, the peasants advanced two arguments, indisputable in themselves, in order to save what little sense of social prestige the East Elbian Junkers left them: the defense of one's rights, namely a socially "appropriate" seat in church, was an inevitable component of peasant behavior, and the weaknesses of the flesh, though admittedly present in the struggle for social prestige, were described in the Bible itself.

In Thuringia, where rural parishes had lost little of their strength and self-confidence, the struggle to enhance one's social prestige within the parish was not very pronounced. When it did occur, it tended to focus on the rights of guardianship of the community council and occasionally prompted conflict with the pastors. A conflict over the seating of the councillors in Gossel (district of Arnstadt) dragged on for ten years. Pastor Oschmann described Lang, the local mayor, as a man "who wants to do everything his own way, whether in the parish or in the church." Oschmann agreed that the councillors who sat scattered throughout the congregation should be "brought together in one section," but he opposed seating them beside the pulpit. The councillors, according to the pastor, had begun "putting their heads together in various pubs" and were becoming uncooperative. The seven members of the community council agreed with the pastor that they should not "be scattered about in the church . . . because it is customary in all churches for the councillors to be seated with one another," but they also insisted, contrary to the wishes of the pastor, that they be accorded a place "on the side near the pulpit." This dispute, which seems rather trite but which would have appreciably enhanced the prestige of the council, was motivated, at least according to the councillors (and possibly quite accurately), by some rather unusual considerations: "Everything can be explained by the obstinacy of our pastor who simply does not want us in the section beside the pulpit, probably because we would have a somewhat closer look at his outdated concepts."[58]

Conflicts among commoners over their places in church were more frequent in urban parishes. Though our records stem almost exclusively from *Gutsherrschaften*, quarrels among commoners were certainly not unusual in the cities. In the church of St. Margaret in Gotha, where aristocrats quarreled incessantly, parishioners of much less gentle birth were very careful early in the seventeenth century that "a simple servant girl" not be allowed to go to the front "into the chairs" but was instead required to remain at the back "out of respect for the others."[59]

The bitterest squabbles among commoners took place in the urban parishes of Pomerania, where "there were hardly any pews at all whose possessors were not engaged in combat and dispute."[60] Years of war, destruction, and shifting populations contributed to the frequent eruption of "public scandals . . . in churches, caused when someone decides to resort to violence in order to maintain his possessions." Because there were greater demographic and social changes in the cities than in the villages, "strangers and indigenous persons alike who had become members of the parish had continually to be accommodated according to their social rank primarily by crowding in more chairs."[61] Numerous church documents from Wolgast, Greifswald, and Stralsund bear witness to the resulting disputes. Sometimes the use of a seat alternated, for instance, in Wolgast where, after the Church of St. Peter burned down in 1713, "the local inhabitants joined together and rebuilt the seating because

---

58. StAW, Oberkonsistorium, Amt Ichtershausen, no. 51. Notes of June 2, 1769; June 17, 1769; March 21, 1770; July 15, 1775.
59. StAW, Oberkonsistorium, Stadt Gotha, no. 130. Note of December 18, 1644.
60. StAG, Rep. 35, no. 693. Note of September 26, 1730.
61. StAG, Rep. 35, no. 1085. Note of February 12, 1749 (Wolgast).

of the penury of the church."[62] Space was short, the atmosphere tense, and conflict inevitable, especially since the struggle for social prestige still played a prominent role.

After the Great Nordic War (which had a particularly devastating effect on Wolgast), St. Peter's was filled with portable benches, and folding chairs were attached to them or to fixed pews. As usual "the lower orders were located" here. Innumerable wrangles ensued however because these chairs covered over various carvings on the pews intended to enhance the prestige of those who sat there. A commission was established to calm the atmosphere, though the bedeviled church authorities had no idea "what we can do in the midst of all this strife without giving offense." Various citizens were invited to the inspection but refused to appear, for instance, the powerful spice merchant Loysevitz who declared that he had already arranged everything with the prefect. Those who did attend noted that in Wolgast, as elsewhere, "benches or folding chairs had been attached even to the seating of prominent *"collegiorum,"* and that the people who sat here had no other available space. The Company of Carpenters observed that "the decorations on their pews, which had been added at great expense and effort, were covered over by folding chairs and benches that had been pushed against them, though these decorations were made to be seen and were intended to embellish the entire church." It was therefore suggested to the carpenters that they elevate their pews and attach the folding chairs further down where they "would not cover the adornment on the pews." The carpenters remonstrated that this would make it necessary to raise all the pews on this side, including that of the Loysevitz brothers. The "commissioners" thereupon admitted that all their efforts had been in vain, "especially because the Loysevitz brothers, who had initiated the entire dispute, . . . diligently refrained from taking part in any of the proceedings."[63] The dispute in Wolgast dragged on for a considerable length of time[64] and was characteristic in many ways of the stubbornly hierarchical outlook even of commoners, of the importance of the visual effect one made in church, and of the need to modify the entire seating arrangement in order to accommodate small, individual changes.

62. Ibid.
63. StAG, Rep. 35, no. 748. Note of October 9, 1720, record of December 10, 1720.
64. See StAG, Rep. 35, no. 676, 1079; Rep. 10, no. 4039.

In Wolgast as elsewhere, the plight of the most downtrodden remained but a secondary consideration in settling "normal" seating disputes. Those who hoped for a folding chair were also concerned about the salvation of their souls and had to be accommodated somewhere in the church. But no one doubted that theirs should be the worst seating: "Those who have not can stand in the steeple."[65]

Equally unenviable was the predicament of people who, though they had "fallen into poverty," fought bitterly to retain their former seats in church.[66] Society, in keeping with its rigidly hierarchical outlook, was merciless in its demands that they should now occupy a less eminent position in church. The fundamental principle governing all other considerations was that a person's outer attributes must reflect his real situation in life. The strict observance of this rule gave feudal society its stability. Even the lower social orders ensured that this principle was upheld, and no peasant could safely ignore it. This explains the collective hard-heartedness toward those who had been expelled from their former positions in church but refused to accept their new seats.

The only pleasure left to those at the bottom of the social hierarchy was to observe the squabbles among those further up the social ladder. A brewer named Dickman afforded them such an opportunity in 1655 when he had five pews destroyed and carted away from the church in Treptow near Kolberg. They allegedly were blocking access to his family's tomb in the church where he wished to lay his deceased mother to rest. (The position of one's grave in the cemetery or church was also much influenced by the hierarchical social order.) The outraged parish councillors interpreted Dickman's actions as stemming from the fact that he "wishes his wife to have a pew near the nobles' pew only out of ostentation, ambition, and devilish avidity for she is suitably seated where she is now." Dickman disputed this and accused the councillors of contravening the command of the prince "to remove the pews in the middle of the church and to admit the servant classes into the middle" where they could use the folding chairs that they brought along. According to the self-confident brewer, the church councillors had, quite to the contrary, left the pews in the middle, thereby blocking access to the tomb. Dickman's arguments proved rather

---

65. Undated note (c. 1690) about the general opinion regarding a church seating dispute in Fehrbellin. Brandenburg cathedral canons' chapter, Fe 162.
66. StAS, Rep. 28, no. 769; StAM, Rep. A 12, Spezialia, Wolmirstedt, no. 36.

specious in that the pews did not really need to be moved in order to provide access to the tomb (a procedure that in itself was not unusual at the time), and he quite evidently had removed them only as a joke on some highborn parishioners. The *provisores* (the presiding officers of the church) emphasized that some of the brewer's adherents "were laughing and snickering that he had exposed a number of highborn ladies in the church to ridicule and derision by taking away their pews."[67]

Women in Pomeranian cities waged an incessant struggle, usually covert though occasionally erupting into the open, for the highly prized uppermost position on the nave. These "outward devotees of the church service" loved to sit in the uppermost position on the great holidays because "an aisle seat and an upper position in the church would lend them prestige in the eyes of others." Attempts to persuade the "chair sisters . . . to make room for those who came later by sliding along" failed because of their "inflated hearts" and "their imagined honor and superiority."[68] Hierarchical attitudes were too deeply ingrained, and the temptations to compensate for constant social humiliation through outward displays of superiority were too strong.

An ugly dispute over seating arrangements in church erupted in 1731 in the village of Pütte (Stralsund area) between the wives of Carsten, the mayor, and Ludehase, a smith. When the mayor's wife refused to allow the Ludehase maid to pass in front of her, "although the customary practice is that girls pass before the women and sit below," the maid was enraged because "she could previously have married a wheelwright, as the Carsten woman had done, who herself was a former servant girl." The mayor's wife thereupon declared that "the smith girl was the daughter of a dirty bitch." The women began quarreling and fighting even though the people sitting behind the smith girl "hit her in the neck with their muff" and the pastor "knocked on the confessional." Both women had to pay a fine and the mayor's wife was also "jailed for eight days" and beaten. The verbal battle between the women persisted ("whore," "sow," etc.), and the case wended its way from the city council and the consistory to the courts.[69] If a moral judgment is permitted about such events, the perverted way in which the self-

67. StAG, Rep. 7, no. 4692. Notes of February 26, 1655, and February 28, 1655.
68. StAG, Rep. 10, no. 3803 (church seating dispute in Loitz, 1767).
69. StAS, Rep. 28, no. 1258. Notes of June 12, 1731, and June 25, 1731.

esteem of the "little people" on the *Gutsherrschaften* found expression can only be called tragic.

This attitude seemed to change only at the very bottom of the social scale, among the very poor. Here the prevalent attitude was opposition and defiance toward those "above," even in questions of church seating. It must be added, however, that if these people worked for an aristocrat or a farmer and were allowed to sit in their employer's pew, they usually became jealous of their status and quickly rallied to their employer's cause in case of any disputes. We have seen several examples of this, in addition to the case just mentioned above. This could produce unusual sets of allies. For instance, a tenant farmer and a pastor crossed swords in Velgast in 1697, each supported by his own coterie of rural laborers. A maid named Düntzig, who had allegedly caused a commotion in church, responded to the remonstrances of the pastor: "Whatever you say to me and however you say it, you know who I am and that is how I shall stay. You cannot change me." The pastor then ordered that the benches used by the farmers' supporters be removed so that they would have to stand during the service. Since the farmer was particularly eager to have his workers well rested, he provided them with portable chairs. Soon after the next church service began, the pastor's supporters "arose from their pews with a great tumult and to the great exasperation of the congregation and tore away from under her the chair that Dorothea Düntzig had brought from home."[70] The farm laborers had certainly been "unruly and insubordinate," but the fronts in the conflict were bizarre and hardly ran along class lines.

The rural poor were confined to the edges of the church more relentlessly and uncompromisingly than any other social cohort, especially when they were not local people. This held true for Thuringia as well, with the proviso that field hands, servants, and day laborers were usually assigned a definite place in a particular gallery. Toward the end of the eighteenth century, the natural high spirits of the younger field hands, especially those who did not live nearby, made these galleries rather disorderly and tumultuous. "The younger people, especially the numerous laborers, pushed forward on all side,"[71] causing disturbances. This leads us to those church disputes that had little to do with social class.

70. StAM, Rep. A 12, Spezialia, Egeln, no. 40. Note of April 23, 1801.
71. StAW, Oberkonsistorium, Amt Ichtershausen, no. 56. Note of January 19, 1838.

c) Disputes Unrelated to Social Class

Although we have concentrated on disputes revolving around social status, there were some other reasons as well for quarrels over positions in church. It is important to investigate these motives as well in order to shed additional light on the mentality of the time and to avoid a one-sided view of people's motivations. Some of these disputes were rooted in serious physical and emotional needs. In the late feudal period, the urge to express a collective identity through local social groups was still very strong and often resulted in the ostracization of individuals who deviated in some way from the norm. Many people must have lived in constant fear of becoming an object of public ridicule. The church provided a focal point of much social observation and passing of judgments, and here the collective scorn could rain down in any especially childish and brutal fashion. The danger of social ostracization drove those with a physical disability or the emotionally less confident into the dark corners and recesses of the church. An older woman fought desperately in 1748 to save her place in a recess of the Church of St. Nicholas in Greifswald, claiming that it "is somewhat secluded and I can sit there quite alone and listen to the service with more devotion than if I had to sit in full view of the entire congregation in my weak old age and notoriously indigent condition and expose myself to the mockery and derision of this person and that."[72] Considerable discord resulted when older people sought a new seat because of impaired hearing. A shoemaker's widow in Wolgast requested a different position "because age has deprived me of most of my hearing and I am unable to hear the preacher." In an ensuing quarrel with a church councillor, she allegedly began "to scold and snore and pound and insult him, even in the coarsest of terms."[73] Those who grew unable to hear the church service were often deeply disturbed by this and reacted in an emotional way. Disputes over the right to inherit a particular pew frequently "disturbed one's devotions" and were also largely psychological in origin. Again there were furious scenes, especially in the case of one particular daughter "who goes into convulsions when she becomes angry."[74]

72. StAG, Rep. 35, no. 865.
73. StAG, Rep. 35, no. 1085. Note of April 29, 1749.
74. StAM, Rep. A 12, Spezialia, Amt Croppenstedt, no. 30. Note of October 18, 1796.

Maintaining a socially appropriate place in church was essential for one's prestige, while the retention of any place at all was an existential necessity. Both touched vital nerves and the resulting struggles could be extremely intense. The explosive character of the struggle (to a large extent characteristic of the feudal period generally) was also an expression of the feeling of powerlessness and isolation of those concerned. In our case, the rural poor and the urban journeymen at best had the support of a community without which their individual rights could not have been maintained against the rights of the others. We have seen many examples of the explosiveness of the ensuing struggle. People could react with apparently irrational rage, for instance, a man from Stralsund named Werneke who was removed from his seat in the choir of the church in 1612 because the space was needed for pupils and school personnel. According to a councillor of the church of St. Mary, Wernecke responded "like a mad, demented beast," threatened "to kill me by stabbing me in the heart" and "began to disturb and molest the school people in their pew, to climb over it to great consternation and to reoccupy it, not without much cursing and blaspheming." This "bird" with his "vulgar song" and "wanton wretchedness" complained before the courts that he had suddenly been deprived of his pew after twenty years, though he did apologize that his anger had caused him "to drink so heavily that I even insulted their lordships the judges."[75] Individual temperaments may partially explain such behavior, but not the frequency with which such outbursts occurred in relation to church seating.

Another unending source of conflict unrelated to class considerations was passage to one's seat in front of other people on the pew or bench. Clothes could be soiled and passageways blocked or made difficult. A "great perturbatio cultus divini publici" that occurred in Barth in 1722 was largely motivated by sheer antipathy. When "the wife of guild officer Jacob Vicken attempted to pass through in her usual way, Caspar Schulte's wife did not wish to allow it. Vicken's wife delivered herself of some oaths, and an exchange of words ensued in the middle of the singing." Schulte's wife defended herself before the consistory, claiming that the guild officer's daughter had said, "Make way or I'll walk all over you" and that his wife had

75. StAS, Rep. 3, no. 3453.
76. StAG, Rep. 35, no. 477. Note of August 7, 1722, records of September 23, 1722.

added, "These women are like sows lying around here." The exchange of words culminated when Vicken's wife said, "Woman, here's something else for you," turned her backside and lifted her skirt.[76] Extreme sensitivity in all matters touching on social prestige naturally played an important role here as well.

Seating disputes unrelated to class were also prompted by regional considerations. This kind of quarrel was especially likely when several communities were squeezed together in a single church. Such situations were frequent and interregional hostilites often smoldered beneath the surface, occasionally exploding into the open.

A typical example of intercommunal feuding erupted in 1708 in the Church of Groß-Luja (Spremberg district).[77] As a result of the arrival of a new aristocrat, General von Oertzen zu Bagenz, some peasants were compelled to move into the choir of the church where the retainers of Major von Stutterheim from Groß- and Klein-Luja normally sat. "Two or three of the strongest" of Bagenz's men had been "squeezing in with the people from Klein-Luitz [Luja]" in the balcony so that "the spirit there was more like a pub than a church." The major refused the general's retainers any room in the choir until the latter finally pushed their way in and "shoved my people causing a tumult. One's of Bagenz's peasants by the name of Krüger boxed the ears of a man from Luitz and knocked his hat off." There was "a danger that the entire choir would be knocked down." The pastor thereupon denounced the major's retainers (who still owed their church taxes) "in the most violent way as oxen, louts, etc." This controversy, which dragged on for years, clearly pitted one community against another and was totally unaffected by class considerations. The opposing sides were led by the major and the general, together as they claimed "with my people." The communities of Bagenz and Groß-Luja even quarreled independently under the leadership of their own councils, when not under the direction of the major and general. Such struggles between communities was a potent force for diminishing class consciousness.

3. Conclusions

The following conclusions can be reached at the end of this investigation into church seating as a barometer of social

---

77. StAP, Pr. Br. Rep. 40 C, Niederlausitzisches Konsistorium, Calau district, no. 27.

attitudes and mentalities, especially hierarchical attitudes, in the late feudal period in the territories now occupied by the GDR.

People were extremely concerned about their seating in church – seats that they were likely to have built, inherited, purchased, leased, won by lot, or assumed by long-standing tradition. Their seats may have been purely functional or may have been a visible symbol of their standing in society. Seating arrangements in church reflected the social barriers and distinctions in society at large. Seating that seemed inappropriate to an individual or to the congregation as a whole could easily provoke violent confrontations. In ensuring that a person's seating corresponded to his position in the strict feudal hierarchy, particular importance was attached to the visual impact of the seating and whether it afforded an unimpeded view of the service.

There were many different gradations in the seating, reflecting the pyramidal social structure. The nobility was especially sensitive to these gradations, though peasants and artisans also adopted them, especially in areas where they were particularly oppressed by the ruling class and attempted to uphold their sense of social worth through petty struggles over rank. In the villages of Thuringia, Saxony, and the *Altmark*, where the rights of peasants were better developed, social prestige played a much less prominent role in the assignment of seats and in differences between pews.

Church seating arrangements also reflected the great feudal counteroffensive that began in Germany in the sixteenth century. This led, in broad terms and with many regional variations, from the private pews of the sixteenth century to the rented pews of the seventeenth century to the predominantly purchased pews of the eighteenth century. The church as proprietor decided how seating would be allocated.

Disputes over seating were virtually inevitable whenever several aristocrats attended the same church, all desiring the best pew, or in residential cities where envious and suspicious government officials vied with one another and the upper classes in the town for "suitable" seating. In the countryside, firmly entrenched parishes were often able to curb the strife between competing aristocrats. When this did not occur, bruising struggles erupted in full view of the congregation. A nobleman's servants and field hands (and above all his wife) served as status symbols in the struggle for prestige and could therefore derive some advantages from the battle over the best seating. The only other advantage for the rural poor was the pleasure it derived from observing the local grandees clawing at one another and from taking advantage of an opportunity to express its opposition to the ruling class by voicing its antipathy toward those on the other side of the dispute. Conflicts with church authorities and their taxation policies often played a role in these conflicts. The aristocracy fully expected the local parson to arrange for a strong visual distinction between its seating and that of the populace.

The repressed peasants in areas of pronounced *Gutsherrschaft* were often particularly concerned about upholding their social status, and this concern often found warped expression in an embrace of the hierarchical outlook of their overlords. However in areas such as Thuringia, for instance, internal conflicts within churches were usually confined to questions of the appropriate seating for parish councillors. The cities had a more fluid social structure and disputes among "the common people" over church seating were more common. These disputes were especially explosive in Pomerania. Those who occupied the lowest rungs on the social ladder were in danger in the cities of losing their places altogether, while in the countryside they were usually simply confined to the most undesirable locations. Urban workers appear to have been the only social cohort to undertake a collective struggle to ensure the best possible conditions for the salvation of their souls, fully conscious of the social ties that bound them and freed them from hierarchical attitudes.

Besides these social causes, disputes over church seating could also be prompted by physical and spiritual factors as well as one's general sense of worth. Those who became engaged in controversy (with the exception of the urban and rural poor) usually did so as individuals, defending their rights against all the others. The resulting sense of social isolation and helplessness often led to explosions of uncontainable rage.

These conditions created a climate in which strong class consciousness could not arise, with the possible exception of a general sense of discontent with the rulers, especially when excessive attempts to enhance their status impeded "the view and the hearing" of the entire congregation. The aristocracy's insistence on upholding at all times the strict social hierarchy (which of course was not limited to the late feudal period) represented a kind of class consciousness based on maintaining the feudal estates and the strict separation between them (distance from the common folk, disputes among aristocrats as a reflection of the struggle for power within the feudal elite). The controversies over church seating in which farmers and artisans engaged appear to reflect partly their adoption of the social outlook of the ruling class and partly a genuine need to defend their place in society. Strata that were disadvantaged by the obsession with the social hierarchy therefore often embraced it, to such an extent that it erupted with elemental force even in church, where all were theoretically equal before God. This shows that these disadvantaged strata nevertheless had their own hierarchy – a social structure that helped to fuel the social disease of hierarchical attitudes and status seeking. As a result, struggles over one's place in the social hierarchy became common in the late feudal period, even among those strata that one would expect to struggle against feudalism itself rather than against one another within the categories feudalism imposed. Quarrels over church seating therefore served to reduce class consciousness in the late feudal period.

HELGA SCHULTZ

The Chronicle of the
Berlin Master Baker
Johann Friedrich Heyde

If we ask history where we have come from and where
we are going, we are not only interested in the essential points of the
processes and events but in the real lives of the people.* We would
like to be face to face with our forefathers and want to understand
the motives for their actions and the situations in their lives. We
want to understand the basically different conditions of their existence and the ways in which it is similar to ours.

There we soon come to the limits of our resources. The majority
of the working people in past societies did not write autobiogra-
phies and did not carry on correspondences. Written accounts of
their lives were produced – if at all – by state authorities or by the
church and not by themselves. Therefore, every single autobiography is valuable if it is handed down to us by craftsmen, farmers, or
wageworkers.

In the eighteenth century, besides the nobility, the trading and
manufacturing bourgeoisie, and the intellectuals, only the craftsmen
in guilds were able to write.[1] From these circles there exist some
autobiographical documents concerning Berlin. We have the auto-

---

* Delivered as a lecture at the University of Buffalo, State University of New
York, in October 1987; based on her *Der Roggenpreis und die Kriege des großen
Königs. Chronik und Rezeptsammlung des Berliner Bäckermeisters Johann Friedrich
Heyde, 1740 bis 1786* (Berlin/GDR, 1988)

1. R. Stadelmann and W. Fischer, *Die Bildungswelt des deutschen Handwerkers
um 1800* (West Berlin, 1955).

188

biographical stories of a barber journeyman, Johann Deitz,[2] who later became a master of his trade in Halle, of the soldier Ulrich Bräker,[3] later a manufacturer in his home country of Switzerland, and the biography of the noncommissioned officer's son, goldsmith's apprentice, and later first director of the Berlin Trade School Karl Friedrich Klöden.[4] The chronicle of the master baker Johann Friedrich Heyde, which is kept in the Berlin city archives, is in many aspects different from these accounts.[5] First of all, it does not claim to be a work of art, but is a direct, naive reflection of what he saw or learned. The author is also firmly rooted in his craft in Berlin. His life did not take him to other social classes or strata nor lead him away from Berlin. Therefore, his records are especially informative about the mentality of important parts of the Berlin working population. In contrast to the other accounts mentioned above, it was not written as a final account of a successful career, but grew directly out of everyday life.

It frankly reflects changing positions and attitudes. The records of the baker Johann Friedrich Heyde do not follow the tradition of the older Berlin chronicles. In contrast to the officer who drew up the *Berlin Garrison Chronicle*,[6] which was probably written as a commercial assignment, and the *Chronicle of 1704 to 1758*,[7] he did not concentrate on the uncommented reports of criminal cases and court events. He introduces his own experiences and value judgments, so that an actual, subjective picture of the time results. With his account he intended to give future generations – and this means above all his own children – "a memorial and good memories." This required a high degree of reflection and self-assurance.

In order to discover the roots of this self-assurance, one has to look into the personality and the circumstances of the chronicler's

2. E. Consentius, ed., *Meister Johann Dietz erzählt sein Leben* (Ebenhausen, 1915).

3. U. Braeker, *Das Leben und die Abenteuer des armen Mannes im Tockenburg*, ed. A. Willbrandt (Berlin, 1910); H. Böning, *Ulrich Bräker. Der arme Mann aus dem Toggenburg. Leben, Werk und Zeitgeschichte* (Königstein/Taunus, 1985).

4. K.F. Klöden, *Von Berlin nach Berlin. Erinnerungen, 1786–1824*, ed. R. Weber, 2d ed. (Berlin/GDR, 1978).

5. Stadtarchiv Berlin: Bestand Amtsbücher, HS 117; H. Schultz, ed., *Der Roggenpreis und die Kriege des großen Königs. Chronik und Rezeptsammlung des Berliner Bäckermeisters Johann Friedrich Heyde, 1740 bis 1786* (Berlin/GDR, 1988).

6. E. Friedlaender, ed., *Berliner Garnison-Chronik, zugleich Stadt-Berlinische Chronik für die Jahre 1727–1739* (Berlin, 1873).

7. F. Holtze, ed., "Chronistische Aufzeichnungen eines Berliners von 1704–1758," *Schriften des Vereins für die Geschichte Berlins* 36 (1899): 95–114.

life. Johann Friedrich Heyde tells us much about himself and his family. In addition, supplements are provided by the church registers[8] and the civil registers.[9] The chronicler's father was Gottfried Heyde who came to Cölln on the Spree River from the village of Stolpe near Angermünde in the Mark Brandenburg. He obtained the rights of citizenship and became a master tailor in 1698, when he was twenty-seven years old. His younger brother Martin, who was recognized as a baker in 1706, soon followed him to the city, which was the seat of the government, and bought a home in Markgrafenstraße. Marriage to well-to-do widows enabled both brothers to establish themselves in Berlin. The first wife of Gottfried Heyde, the chronicler's mother, was the widow of someone with the family name Zilcher, first name unknown, an assistant judge. She was seven years older than her husband. Johann Friedrich Heyde was born in 1703 when his mother was thirty-nine years old, and he remained the only surviving child from that marriage. He grew up together with his half brother Daniel Zilcher, who was eight years older than he. Johann Friedrich may often have been in Markgrafenstraße at his uncle's where he met his cousins Johann Friedrich, Christian Friedrich, and Martin Friedrich. Even if they could not be equal playfellows to him – they were four to seven years younger than he – he maintained close contacts with them and with his half brother all his life. This was proven by the numerous mutual appointments of godparents. The five boys and also the youngest cousin, who was born in 1722, became master bakers in Berlin.

For the development of the chronicler, his mother was obviously of great importance. As the former wife of a lawyer, she probably had enjoyed a better education than the average baker's wife, who still always signed with three crosses. She must have raised her children in the simple living conditions in which she was placed. This makes the baker's eloquence remarkable. Although we may be struck by the peculiarities of his orthography and the lack of punctuation marks in the chronicle, his son's clumsy entries at the end of the account show us by contrast the chronicler's great skill in

---

8. Zentralstelle für Genealogie, Leipzig: Kirchenbücher der Gemeinde Dorotheenstadt, Filmkopien.
9. E. Kaeber, ed., *Die Bürgerbücher und die Bürgerprotokollbücher Berlins, 1701–1750* (Berlin, 1934); P. Gebhardt, ed., *Die Bürgerbücher von Cölln, 1508–1611 und 1689–1709, und die chronikalischen Nachrichten des ältesten Cöllner Bürgerbuchs, 1542–1610* (Berlin, 1930); idem, ed., *Das älteste Berliner Bürgerbuch, 1453–1700* (Berlin, 1927).

reading and writing that distinguished him from other craftsmen. Further impressive evidence along the same lines is provided by the files of the butcher's guild and the journeyman's book of the blacksmiths' guild in the Berlin city archives.

The extent and the quality of elementary school education in Berlin in the first third of the eighteenth century was not adequate for an active command of reading and writing. The sons of the craftsmen were educated in the parochial schools of the various churches. At that time, to be sure, at the turn of the seventeenth to the eighteenth century and under the influence of the pietist Philipp Jacob Spener, those schools offered besides catechism, instruction in reading the Bible and also in writing and in arithmetic,[10] but the boys in most cases forgot later on what they had learned there only superficially. Between the ages of thirteen and fifteen, after confirmation, Johann Friedrich Heyde was apprenticed to a baker as was his brother Daniel Zilcher. The father surely chose this trade for his sons to provide them with a secure and profitable livelihood. Just like the butchers, the bakers everywhere were among the most well-to-do craftsmen, independent of economic crises. A baker in the middle of the eighteenth century could earn five hundred to six hundred *Taler* annually,[11] triple the amount earned by a weaver or a tailor. The paternal tailor shop did not provide a living because there were too many tailors in the capital. Many tailors from the Brandenburg villages and small towns moved to Berlin, as did Gottfried Heyde, because tailoring was the most common craft in the countryside. Therefore, Gottfried finally gave up the tailoring business and opened an inn. From 1731 on he is called an innkeeper in civil and church registers. In his father's inn, the chronicler obviously became interested in brandy distillation and liqueur production. The many relevant, tasty, and sweet recipes that he wrote down in his album at least point to a secondary occupation as a distiller for domestic use. The prospering bakery of Martin Heyde may have contributed considerably to the boy's choice of apprenticeship. Perhaps Johann Friedrich passed his apprenticeship at his uncle's bakery, but it may also be that the uncle brought him to his fellow guild member Michael Wilcke, who was a baker in Dorotheenstadt. When the chronicler, after a long time as an apprentice

---

10. W. Lemm, et al., *Schulgeschichte in Berlin* (Berlin/GDR, 1987), pp. 30–33.
11. H. Rachel, *Das Berliner Wirtschaftsleben im Zeitalter des Frühkapitalismus* (Berlin, 1931), p. 235.

and a journeyman, settled down and became a master baker, he married the sixteen-year-old daughter of Master Wilcke. Such a young bride as Eva Maria was unusual for that time. The average age for a woman to be married was higher than today. The bridegroom's age, on the other hand, was usually in conformity with the average age at which Berlin craftsmen married. Marriage was closely connected with the establishment of an independent livelihood as a master. Because of the difficulties in establishing a livelihood, poorer craftsmen and factory workers could not marry until they were older or had to refrain from marriage altogether. It was not easy for Johann Friedrich Heyde to become a master baker in the capital. The number of bakers in each of the town's districts was restricted by the municipal council so that they all could make a living. These limits were extended with the growing number of inhabitants. Therefore, we read in the civil register on the occasion of the chronicler's establishment as a citizen in 1731: "Things are now quite right with this trade because he has been granted by the royal rescript of November 10, the fifteenth baker's spot in Dorotheenstadt." The civil fee was reduced from four to three *Taler* because "his father was an old citizen and contributed much to the public welfare."

The establishment of a bakery required considerable financial means. The tailoring trade, for example, could be carried on in any room, which could be rented yearly for ten to twenty *Taler* and which could also serve as a living- and bedroom for a family. For a bakery, it was necessary to have a special room with an oven, a room to store flour and rye, and a lot of equipment. The bakers normally had their own houses. At this time the Berlin land register shows that seven bakers' houses were sold for between 1800 and 3500 *Taler*, that is to say an average of 2586 *Taler*.[12] Our chronicler could not have earned that amount of money as an apprentice and as a journeyman, and even his wife's dowry and his father's help could not have made up those sums. First he had to rent a house with a baking room. It was only in 1744 that he bought the house at 27 Mittelstraße. It was situated on the corner of Neustädtische Kirchstraße opposite the Dorotheenstadt church. He and his family lived in the narrow space between the baking room and the church. From there he saw the world and recorded its ways in his chronicle.

12. R. Lüdicke, *Geschichte der Berliner Stadtgrundstücke seit der Einführung der Grundbücher Ende des 17. Jahrhunderts. Nach den Hypotheken- und Grundbüchern* (Berlin, 1933).

The social relations of Johann Friedrich Heyde were determined by his relatives and by the bakery trade. Family relations and relations in the trade merged; they seemed to be mutually dependent on each other. The entire extended Heyde family became a real Berlin baker's dynasty. The bakers obviously established a closed marriage circle of their own. This was in keeping with the living conditions and traditions of classes and strata of feudal society (a Marxist term, here referring to the precapitalist period before the political, social, and economic reforms initiated by the French Revolution). It took a long time for the coming bourgeois society to break through this isolation. The more prosperous the trade was, the stronger were the relations and traditions in it. The Berlin bakers and butchers were able to keep them longer than any other trade in the city.[13] The guild determined the marriage, the choice of a trade, and the social life of the craftsman from birth to death. The solidarity of the craftsmen was limited to the guild, but this isolation gave the members somewhat more security in a world marked by illness, unemployment, hunger, and war. This community was the source of a guild consciousness, but also of a bourgeois one. Within the relative security of a guild, the chronicler, a master baker in the Brandenburg-Prussian capital, succeeded in founding and supporting a large family. This was neither common nor easy at a time when the death rate in Berlin was higher than the birth rate. Heyde proudly recorded the birth of his eight children in the normal stereotypical phraseology. This is the oldest part of the record, which he began before the actual chronicle entries. He marked the years simply by the price of rye. The price of rye was determined for the baker by hailstorms, war, drought, and biting cold, or by the absence of such catastrophes. This description expressed his personal view of the world. In recording the births and deaths of the children, the chronicle tells us something of the life of Eva Maria Heyde, who was still almost a child when she married. The chronicle does not mention her with a single word later on. She must have patiently carried the burden connected with the births and care of the children and with the running of a large household, which surely also included an apprentice and one or two journeymen. Certainly she was not an equal partner of her husband, who was twelve years older than she, and who was broadly educated with many intellectual interests. She did not participate in his

13. H. Schultz, *Berlin, 1650–1800. Sozialgeschichte einer Residenz* (Berlin/GDR, 1987).

public life in the church or the trade. The position of the women in the trades was restricted to the house and the family. Their task was the maintenance of relations among the relatives, as the numerous godparentships of wives prove. Eva Maria Heyde had their first child, a son who was given the name of his father, when she was seventeen years old. At regular intervals of two years, she bore another five children. The last two were born after an interval of three years; when the youngest was born, the mother was thirty-three years old. Meanwhile, she buried three children. When the last of them married, she was fifty years old. She survived her husband by eleven years. For that time one could regard her eighty-six-year-long life as a successful one. She was able to raise and marry off five of her children and escaped an early widowhood. In old age she did not depend on support from the guild or on public charity but lived sheltered and respected in the family of her son Gottfried.

The family of Johann Friedrich Heyde with its many children was a lucky one under the circumstances of that time. Infant mortality, which could actually diminish families in Berlin as in other big cities by between a third and half of all infants and toddlers, can also be clearly seen in the Heyde family: a sister and three younger half brothers and sisters of the chronicler as well as four siblings and half siblings of his wife died, as did all five children of his son Gottfried and two of his grandchildren. Four times death was caused by smallpox, which spread as an epidemic with unrelenting severity all over the country every two to four years. Three times "the teeth" were given as the cause of death – a diagnosis of medical ignorance and powerlessness. These deaths occurred in a family with enough food at all times, where the women were able to breast-feed their infants and where extreme ignorance could be excluded as a cause of death, as far as was possible at that time. Could it not perhaps be that the comprehensive knowledge of popular medicine enabled the head of the family to prevent the worst in some cases? Among the many medicines in his album there were some prescriptions especially for children. It was also exceptional good luck that the marriage of Eva Maria Heyde lasted so long. The death of a partner ended marriages at least as often as happens today by divorce. This applies to both sexes, but it was normally much harder for the women because they lost not only their husband, but also the provider of the family. Often a new marriage was necessary for this reason and was promoted by the guild. Three young widows married into the Heyde family, and both daughters became widows at the ages of forty-one and forty-two respectively. Nothing is known about a remarriage of either of them. The young wife of the son of Johann Friedrich nearly met with the same fate. In 1771 when, in addition to other diseases, dysentery spread in Berlin, our chronicler was informed of the death of his son who had also been living in the house in Mittelstraße. The father made an entry about this in his album, but a little later the terrible news proved to be untrue. The son recovered, fathered another two sons, and the strange news was crossed out in the chronicle.

The relation of the chronicler to death seems unusual to us.[14] He recorded the death of adult relatives and other people in his surroundings in the chronicle but said nothing about his own little children. This confirms the prevailing attitude that people at that time regarded the death of infants and little children as unchangeable, natural, i.e., a God-given event.[15]

It was the only way to cope with the recurring blows of fate. It took much effort for Johann Friedrich Heyde to establish all his sons as masters and citizens in Berlin. The three of them were to become bakers according to his wish. They learned the baking trade and obtained the rights of citizens and members of the trade with their father's help after longer and shorter periods of travel. There were difficulties already with the oldest son. When he became a master baker in 1761, his father, who was fifty-eight years old, did not feel old enough to give up the bakery. Another bakery was not available, although the son married a baker's daughter. Therefore, the son Johann Friedrich, two years later, together with his brother-in-law, the young brewer Fiebelkorn, established a brewery and settled down in the vicinity of his father's house. Ten years later, when his son Gottfried became a master baker, Heyde still did not think of retirement. His energy did not decrease. The son worked for three years at his father's bakery as an assistant baker – as can be seen from the church register on the occasion of his marriage. In 1773 he married an orphaned relative, who had been living and working in the Heyde household since her childhood, and took over the bakery. At that time master baker Johann Friedrich Heyde was seventy years old, his son Gottfried thirty-

14. A.E. Imhof, *Die Lebenszeit. Vom aufgeschobenen Tod und von der Kunst des Lebens* (Munich, 1988).

15. J. Kuczynski, *Geschichte des Alltags des deutschen Volkes. Studien* (Berlin/ GDR 1980–81), vol. 2, *1650–1810*, pp. 189–191.

one. The youngest son, Heinrich Wilhelm, who made his master piece in 1772, married a baker's widow and settled down as a master in the quarter around Nicolai Church. The chronicler was very interested in giving his sons a respected and secure livelihood as guild members. He used his respected position in the guild and his good relations with the authorities to shield them from problems. This in his opinion also included military service. There is hardly another explanation why his oldest son Johann Friedrich served in the Seven Years' War as a royal baker for Prince Heinrich, the brother of the king, and why he returned home long before the war ended. His father surely brought to bear his full influence to free his youngest son Heinrich Wilhelm, who joined the army in 1776 "out of his own desire and longing" – i.e., against his father's will – after thirteen months of pleading for his discharge. Family life was, thus, not free of conflicts. There may have been worries about the son Gottfried who was drifting around the world for nine years and who at last returned from the West Indies via Holland in 1770. We wonder if he went there because of the military conflicts between England and France which are often referred to in the chronicle.

The daughters, who married early, at the ages of nineteen and twenty, into well-off bourgeois families, may have given him more pleasure. The younger one even married a merchant and "materialist," i.e., someone who dealt in different groceries, spices, and also medicines and who belonged to the lower mercantile guild. This marriage meant a step upward socially for the baker's daughter as well as did the marriage of her sister with Herr Büttner, obviously a preacher's son, who himself belonged to the civil service. The chronicler kept in close touch with the family of his older daughter. Her children and grandchildren are the only members of later generations who appear in his records.

Johann Friedrich Heyde could rise considerably within the framework of his family and of his guild. Let us first have a look at the material side. In 1731, he opened his bakery with nearly no money of his own. Within thirteen years, he succeeded in saving enough money to be able to buy his house in Dorotheenstadt, for which he had to raise two thousand *Taler*. He enlarged and reconstructed the house and modernized the baking room and the equipment for the brandy distillery. He evidently ran the distillery and the liqueur production as a profitable sideline because brandy replaced beer as the most favored drink with which the Berlin wage-earning workers and soldiers dispelled their cares. The main income, however, came from the bakery.

As elsewhere, the bakers in Berlin belonged to the most well-to-do craftsmen, and our chronicler was one of the most successful among them. Baking was, of course, a stable trade because there is always a need for bread. Even the poorest could not do without it, although they could deprive themselves of meat, beer, vegetables, new clothing, and a warm room. It was only after 1800 that potatoes to a large extent replaced bread as a basic food. The market for the bakers expanded permanently due to the rapid development of the city. The municipal bread tax left enough profits for the bakers, even if the king influenced the price of bread with the excise, the war peck, and other taxes. The city bread tax regulated the price of bread according to weight. The more expensive rye was on the market, the smaller the loaf was. The bakers sold it half raw and with inferior admixtures, as contemporaries often complained. It was only very rarely that the magistrate punished offenses against the tax. The chronicler reported only one such case. Speculations with rye up to eight years old that was used for baking opened additional sources for earning money.

We must, however, not impute such practices to the devout and upright thinking Master Heyde. Surely as head of the High Consistory and as senior chief of the trade he made every effort to observe the rules. But we should not be at all surprised if he succeeded in saving considerable sums of money, even in times of upheaval. Between 1761 and 1772 he not only paid the cost connected with his sons' master pieces and their attainment of the status of master and of citizenship, but also equipped each of them with 400 *Taler* of ready cash to establish their own firms. The dowry of the two daughters may have been as much as about a hundred *Taler* each. We can take it for granted that between 1754 and 1772 at least between 2,000 and 2,500 *Taler* were used for the marriage portion of the children. And this although Johann Friedrich Heyde lost nearly 1,400 *Taler* in 1763 because of the inflation of the war coins. Here we see the chronicler's business sense. It must appear somewhat odd to today's reader how carefully and precisely he added up the money he spent on his sons. But this way of calculating was an important part of the consciousness of this Berlin craftsman. It was the basis of his commercial rise, part of the bourgeois self-assurance, that considered striving for profits a virtue. In this respect one has to understand the precise calculations about the extension of the house as an appeal to the coming generations to preserve and to multiply the gains. In addition to success, there were official positions and honors. The chronicler became the senior chief of the bakers' guild – an appointment that could be made by the guild only when a member of the magistrate responsible for handicrafts confirmed and approved it. In this capacity, Heyde, first of all, carried out the decisions of the magistrate; only then was he allowed to represent the craftsmen before the magistrate.[16] Twice as head master, from 1760 to 1766 and from 1769 to 1776, he controlled the bakers' guild society and kept its accounts. This position was not too heavy a burden for him because the bakers' journeymen – in contrast to the companies of the shoemakers, the locksmiths, or the masons – did not oppose the masters and the authorities and did not go on strike. The majority were sons of well-to-do masters who could be sure ultimately to have workshops of their own. At the age of fifty-one, in 1754, Johann Friedrich Heyde began to hold an office that went beyond the framework of the guild. He was appointed head of the high consistory of the Dorotheenstadt Lutheran Church Community, to which, besides craftsmen and merchants, numerous academics and royal officials also belonged.

The Dorotheenstadt or Neustadt Church was used by a Lutheran and a Reformed community jointly. The Reformed community for the most part consisted of Huguenots. This church was, therefore, a crossroads of various social, religious, and cultural currents. To work as the head of this high consistory gave the chronicler numerous ideas and expanded his horizon. The appointment to this office was clearly a great honor. Johann Friedrich Heyde did not only meet the expectations placed in him because of his good reputation as a prosperous master baker, but also because of his extraordinary intelligence and education. Heyde was the only head of the high consistory in Berlin who came from the guilds; the others were merchants, academically trained people, or officials. This position also required the confidence of the state authorities. The police director and municipal president Karl David Kircheisen personally installed Heyde in this position. As we know from the Berlin address almanac, he held this office until shortly before his death. Master Johann Friedrich Heyde's elevation to this high office provided a basis for his self-assurance as a burgher. This can be seen clearly in the chronicle when he describes the parade of the burgher squadron at the queen's reception in Berlin in 1758. It is the pride of burghera that visibly runs through the whole description. But it is

16. E. Kolbe, *Geschichte der Bäcker-Innung zu Berlin* (Berlin, 1917), pp. 40–44.

embedded in the chronicler's strictly royalist, pro-government attitude, which one cannot simply pass off as blind conformity to the powers that be. His identification with the Prussia of Frederick was part of his conception of himself. His own rise was parallel to the rise of the Brandenburg-Prussian capital and to that of the late feudal state to a great European power. Large sections of the Berlin crafts were connected with the rise of the state. They had supplied the court and the army and thus had grown together with the city. Even the development of the manufacturers did not hinder this process. It was therefore plausible that he was proud of the state's power and of the victories on the battlefields. The inhabitants of the capital were impressed by the glamour of the foreign monarchs and embassies that came to Berlin, which brought diversity and color to the common man's life. The baker reports all this in his chronicle with visible pleasure. The life at court was obviously taken as a reflection of one's own bourgeois world, the "big world" as an expanded counterpart to one's own "little world." This can explain the sympathy with which the chronicler followed all events in the royal family and its collateral lines. Here, a citizen's pride and patriotism were not in conflict with each other, although the late absolutist character of the state actually contained sharp inner contradictions.[17] But the chronicler did not entirely agree with the social order and the policies of his king. He experienced strong jolts. The first was when Berlin was occupied by Russian and Austrian troops in October 1760. The reproach against the king who was not able to protect his capital and who came with his troops only when all was over can only be read between the lines. He expressed his anger against "our superior" who fled from the city and "about the hot air we were given to comfort us, which, when we looked at it was only hot air." There, the gap between the plain citizens on the one hand and the high officials and "court society" on the other was felt and expressed. Even more severely he criticized the royal economic and fiscal policy after the war, mainly the coin edict of 1763. The master baker explained in detail his financial losses in order to "give the future generations an understanding of the burdens of the war." He considered it a clear injustice that "the royal taxes, nevertheless, had to be paid with hard money," i.e., with old currency. The relation between the baker and the king changed. From the last years of the Seven Years' War, one no longer

17. I. Mittenzwei and E. Herzfeld, *Brandenburg-Preußen, 1648–1789. Das Zeitalter des Absolutismus in Wort und Bild* (Berlin/GDR, 1987).

senses any hero worship in the chronicle. This also confirms that the legend around Frederick II arose from a distance and was chiefly the work of Prussian historians.[18] The Brandenburg subjects were too much affected by his policies to be able to share the feelings of later Prussian-German historians for "great old Fritz."

The chronicler's relation to war is our testing stone for his character and humanity. Naturally, Johann Friedrich Heyde also was influenced by the Prussian propaganda in 1756 that tried to justify the invasion of Saxony as a preventive measure against the imminent Austrian and Saxon invasion. He also believed the reports that exaggerated Prussian victories and that presented even the battle at Kolin in 1759 as a "draw." It was obviously hard for any burgher not to be impressed by so many victories. One has to value the baker's judgment all the more highly as he then turned against the war, although none of his sons lost their lives on the battlefields. He came to doubt the sense of the war, although he and his family did not suffer horribly, but in wartime actually earned even higher profits from the bakery. He was still able to be interested in the price of veal and partridges when the majority of the Berliners were only interested in the price of bread and firewood. But he saw the misery resulting from the war not only in Berlin, but also recorded reports about shortages in Dresden, in Silesia, and in other areas that served as battlefields. These reports came to Berlin from the soldiers and from his own son. At last, to be sure, Heyde closed his door to the hungry people, to sell his bread through the window, but did not close his eyes and his heart.

At the end of the war, he was not interested in the articles of the peace treaties; he was indifferent to who was the winner. There is only the fervent prayer left: "God, our creator, let us never again experience such awful things and let peace be solid until the end of time and guide the hearts of the princes, so that peace and justice embrace each other and so that such a hard war will never again be experienced by the small children!" As a citizen of the Prussian capital, Johann Friedrich Heyde did not have a parochial horizon. He was a politically educated, interested and informed man. From where may he have had his information? Once Hamburg newspapers were mentioned as a source. Should we exclude the possibility that the baker read the press regularly? The news appears in very

18. I. Mittenzwei, *Friedrich II. von Preußen. Eine Biographie* (Berlin/GDR, 1979), pp. 209–11.

shortened form in his chronicle. Numbers, dates, and names are rather precise, although sometimes the localities and persons were written down by ear. The main sources are obviously conversations with the other guild members and, even more important, with the educated heads of the church and the preachers of Dorotheenstadt. Some years later, after the Seven Years' War, there again was an attitude prevalent in these circles that Goethe expressed in a play thus:

I know nothing better on Sundays or on holidays
Than to have a chat about war and warlike pother
When far away, in Turkey say,
The peoples are socking one another.
One stand's at the window, drinks one's half of mild,
And sees the painted ships glide down the waterways
Then in the evening one goes happily home
And blesses peace and peaceful days.[19]

The concern of the chronicler about world politics was shaped by the alliances and interests of Prussian policy. Because of Prussia's alliance with England, he followed the colonial war between France and England with great interest. The Seven Years' War was closely connected with this conflict. The history of the first division of Poland is reflected from the point of view of Prussian policy. In keeping with official propaganda, the power-oriented aims of Russia, Prussia, and Austria were not the focus of his attention, but rather the religious conflicts between the Polish nobility and dissident inhabitants. This was evidently not enough for the master baker to justify the annexation of Polish territories. He excused the occupation of the wooded island of Danzig in his own mind with the fine phrase, "because of circumstances." The occupation of West Prussia was not explained. The Russo-Turkish War is given relatively broad space in the late entries, and the events are reported from the point of view of Russia, which was allied with Prussia. The chronicler's view of world policy was quite one-sided. The North American War of Independence, which culminated in the founding of the U.S.A. as a bourgeois state, was no more in his field of vision than the sensational progress of the productive forces in England that marked the beginning of the Industrial Revolution.

19. J.W. v. Goethe, *Faust*, pts. 1 and 2, an abridged version trans. Louis MacNeice (New York, 1951), p. 34.

His perception of his own city's development was limited in a similar way, namely, to the guilds. Besides his own bourgeois and guild sphere, only the world of the court was worth noticing to him. The life of the manufacture workers and soldiers was outside and below his awareness. Although these poor and hard-working people increasingly marked the picture of Berlin, they were, for master Heyde, nothing but an anonymous mass, "the mob." The entire impressive development of the Brandenburg-Prussian capital into an industrial city is not reflected in his chronicle. It is surprising to what extent Johann Friedrich Heyde kept the picture of an "intact" traditional monarchist world, which, after all, went to pieces once the signs of a new bourgeois age could be seen on the horizon. His awareness of his time was certainly distorted in this respect. How large may the circle of Berlin citizens with similar attitudes have been? Such a limited consciousness of what was taking place in a period of violent change naturally created a favorable climate for the stabilizing, conservative, indeed reactionary policy of the ruling class. It constituted a dam against the ideas of the French Revolution, which in the last year of the master baker's life ushered in the victory of the bourgeoisie in world history. Actually, the guild and mercantile bourgeoisie in Berlin remained unaffected by the anti-feudal ideas of the Enlightenment. Revolutionary ideas reached above all the academically educated and the officials. Only the journeymen and the manufacture workers of Berlin were involved in social struggles as a result of the French Revolution. It was precisely the Berlin bourgeoisie that took part in the economic rise of Berlin and that was a stronghold of intellectual and political conservatism. This is hardly astonishing. Political conservatism was not a sign of economic weakness and dependence on the Prussian state, but rather went with economic stability.

The chronicle of the Berlin master baker hands down to us a long, upright, and diligent life in which bourgeois norms were not yet deformed into the "Prussian virtues" of working, praying, and obeying, in which a critical mind and public activity grew from bourgeois self-confidence and led to possibilities for the development of democratic attitudes. Such attitudes could only develop within narrow limits in feudal-absolutist Prussia. In the 1780s, Johann Friedrich Heyde's entries gradually became sparser. The last ones announced the death of Frederick II and the price of rye – once again marking the poles within which the chronicle was written. On November 5, 1790, the chronicler died. The church register stated:

"Johann Friedrich Heyde, citizen, baker, and confectioner, master baker and former head of the high consistory at this church, eighty-seven years and three months old, died of physical weakness in Mittelstraße at the Kirchgasse corner, in his own house. He left a widow and five adult children (three sons, two daughters). The preachers declined to accept their usual fees."

DIETRICH MÜHLBERG

The Leisure Time of the
Working Class Around 1900

Today we take for granted the multitude of leisure facilities available to the public.* However, they only began to develop as the proletariat emerged. Industrialism created a new social context and new forms of productive labor and of rest and recuperation from it.

In preindustrial times, most people worked as a family unit. The type and amount of labor and recuperation were fixed for all. Periods of work alternated with rest and meals. The intensity and pace of work depended largely on the capacity of the individual. There were therefore natural constraints on the exploitation of labor. How a worker spent his leisure time was also determined by the customary habits of the village or the guild.

All this changed with the transition to industrial work and capitalist exploitation. Employers sought remorselessly to squeeze as much surplus value as possible from their work forces, first by substantially lengthening the workday and then by intensifying labor. As industry progressed, mental activity became more important, and the working day contracted. Recuperation now became a private matter for the individual worker, who assumed responsibility for ensuring that his wages and leisure activities sufficed to reproduce the work force. In a world of rapid technical progress, he had to do much more than merely recover from his exhaustion if he hoped to maintain the value of his labor by constantly refreshing his skills, or to participate in the union and its struggle against the

*Taken from *Arbeiterleben um 1900* written by a collective under the leadership of Dietrich Mühlberg (Berlin/GDR, 1985), pp.123–163.

employers, or to represent the interests of his class in organized political life. Workers had complex new needs, far beyond the mere reproduction of the work force, and the smaller proletarian family was clearly incapable of meeting these needs all by itself.

In comparison with earlier periods, leisure time within the family contracted sharply in favor of more public pursuits (various clubs and associations and the entertainments of the leisure industry). Various family members often took an interest in differing activities. A sociological study of leisure time at the turn of the century determined "that the importance of family activities is steadily diminishing because even the younger members of the family are economically independent and free to go their own way as a result of recent developments. Leisure time is increasingly spent in public, and numerous leisure facilities have arisen alongside one another, attracting a great mixture of social classes. There are theaters, art galleries, concert halls, coffee houses, clubs, reading rooms, and finally the cinema, this most modern means of mass entertainment."[1]

In a striking new departure, children now became independent at an earlier stage. They usually had their own money by age thirteen and were considered "youths" in an age category of their own. These "youths" remained until marriage the most important participants in most leisure activities – though this phase did not necessarily last very long because factory workers tended to marry quite quickly (by approximately age twenty).

> The leading new leisure activities for men and women were aimed largely at younger people. These activities encouraged that aspect of the value system of the working class that prized youth and physical vigor. It was young men who played soccer, young women who went on picnics, and young couples who attended the music halls. Older, married workers were largely excluded from these activities, not only because of their declining physical strength, but also because of the financial drain.[2]

There were some differences in the favorite leisure activities of working-class boys and girls, but both sexes spent roughly equal amounts of time and money on leisure pursuits. This caused much moralistic gnashing of teeth among the middle classes, and many proletarian parents were convinced that their daughters spent far

1. Emilie Altenloh, *Zur Soziologie des Kinos*, (Jena, 1914) p. 97.
2. Peter N. Stearns, *Arbeiterleben, Industriearbeit und Alltag in Europa* (Frankfurt a.M., 1980), p. 292.

too much time amusing themselves and far too little preparing for the domestic concerns of a wife and mother.

In earlier times, proletarians had grown relatively quickly from childhood into the various duties of adulthood. Now, however, with slowly increasing amounts of leisure time, working-class children first became "youths." Youth was seen as a social problem, which bourgeois reformers were quick to address in the hope of preventing armies of rebellious young people from swelling the ranks of the Social Democrats. This concern became particularly acute after 1890. The proletariat responded by founding the Arbeiterjugendbewegung (Young Workers' Movement).[3]

The mounting equality of the sexes during this youthful phase did not carry over into family life. This was clearly evident in leisure behavior. Among married couples, only the men continued for the most part to participate in activities outside the family. These pursuits became highly organized, and as men grew older their leisure activities tended to become much more demanding than those of women. The most popular site was the pub of their favorite association or political party. Here married women scarcely ever ventured. When working-class women had any free time, the cinema became the only public venue they regularly visited. (It was not until the advent of television that this changed.) "All other interests remained relatively insignificant, and large numbers of women went only to the cinema, apart from occasional visits to the theater."[4]

If married people still regularly attend the cinema, it is mostly at the instigation of women. They want a little sensation in their lives, want to experience exciting events and noble spirits, in order to escape their narrow domesticity for a while. Their husbands are usually too numb and often too disdainful to take much pleasure in it. Men also have other interests they find more satisfying, namely, their political and union activities, which take up more and more of their time.[5]

Besides the cinema, proletarian women took part in the social life in their own immediate neighborhoods: in the tenement courtyards, the stores along the streets, and possibly the churches as well.

3. See Jürgen Reulecke, "'Veredlung der Volkserholung' und 'edle Geselligkeit.' Sozialreformerische Bestrebungen zur Gestaltung der arbeitsfreien Zeit im Kaiserreich," in Gerhard Huck, ed., *Sozialgeschichte der Freizeit* (Wuppertal, 1980), pp. 157–60.
4. Emilie Altenloh (above, n. 1), p. 79.
5. Ibid., p. 74.

Family get-togethers were confined to Sundays and usually took place in the outskirts of the city, in restaurants (though here too young, unmarried people were in the majority) or in the allotment gardens that the workers cultivated.

With the emergence of the big-city proletariat after 1860, a number of public leisure facilities arose. Some were modern versions of such traditional institutions as pubs, theaters, allotment gardens, clubs, and churches, while others were more recent innovations such as cinemas, sports, tourism, and leisure-time associations. This highly developed network of leisure activities catering to workers was a striking break with the past. Never before had there been such a varied assortment of leisure pursuits.

1. Pubs and Alcohol

Pubs and alcohol should enjoy pride of place in connection with the newfound leisure time of the working class. At first, beer and schnaps were its only indulgences beyond the mere essentials for survival. The pub became the workers' prime gathering place outside the factory gates. We shall therefore begin our survey of leisure institutions with drinking establishments. There were many types: at first simple bars, pubs, and beer cellars in working-class districts; eventually inexpensive restaurants, beer halls, pubs with polka dancing, and dance halls in the inner city; garden restaurants, club and association houses in the allotment gardens, rooms in breweries on the city outskirts, restaurants in railroad stations, and pubs opposite the factory gates.

In overcrowded Berlin there were about four pubs per hundred families in 1905. There was one restaurant for every 129 inhabitants of Berlin, for every 159 inhabitants of Hamburg, for every 232 inhabitants of Dresden, and for every 290 inhabitants of Leipzig.[6] The pub at this time was a virtual extension of the family home, like the tenement courtyard, the laundry rooms, and the root cellar.

Among the tens of thousands streaming into the big cities, the proportion of single young men was especially high. They lived largely as *Schlafburschen*, renting only a place to sleep. They accordingly spent most of their free time on the streets and in the pubs. The smaller proportion of girls and single women who moved

6. See *Kommunale Praxis* (Berlin, 1907), no. VI, p. 764.

into the big cities before the First World War worked largely as servants, living in their "master's" home until marriage. They usually passed their scanty sparetime in the dance halls. The pubs were therefore overwhelmingly a man's world. Here a man could slake his thirst after a hard day's work (for there were more and more prohibitions against drinking beer on the job as exacting machine work became increasingly common). Here workers could mingle with those from other factories and discuss their respective working conditions, opportunities for better pay, and political events. Here they ate the sandwiches they had brought along or bought sausages, hard-boiled eggs, Harz cheese, and meatballs. Here family events were duly celebrated: births, the end of one's apprenticeship years, or the receipt of burial payments. It was here that men could enjoy their hard-earned leisure time.

All this was generally reserved for the male sex alone. There was a long working-class tradition of excluding women from the conviviality of the pub; however the crucial factor was that married women, after working all day in the factories or, more usually, as washwomen, cleaning women, cottage workers, or knitting and sewing, bore the main responsibility for their own households and were less willing to spend money in the pubs because of their intimate awareness of the needs of the family. Women usually had little sympathy for spending hard-earned money on "luxuries" like beer. These factors were reinforced by the preindustrial mentality of many women, which required that one spend what little money was available on durable goods. The pubs tended therefore to be inimical to family life (apart from the restaurants on the city outskirts that were generally frequented on Sundays by entire families). The pubs became the haven where the family provider sought refuge in the evening from his tiny apartment, noisy children, steaming laundry buckets, *Schlafburschen*, and the complaints of his exhausted wife. One stalwart male explained it this way: "Honestly speaking, I find the pub a much more pleasant place than home. At home, your wife shrieks and takes away the last ounce of your courage. In the pub, you can drink the rotgut and drown all your sorrows."[7]

However, this retreat from home life brought its own fellowship and new social relationships beyond those established at school, in the military, and within the strict hierarchy of the factory. Here

7. Adolf Levenstein, *Die Arbeiterfrage* (Munich, 1912), p. 248.

there was no need to obey. It was a place where a man could form opinions in conversation with other workers, whether locals or outsiders. There was of course one authority, the bartender, who was charged with enforcing the pub rules. But beneath the benevolent gaze of the bartender, everyone could give vent to his own experiences and talents: whether relating the latest gossip and funny stories, telling jokes about the authorities, analyzing the social situation, politicking, singing, playing cards, and last but not least, drinking. Everyone played a more or less active role in this social intercourse, during which all questions of proletarian life and of the social life of the nation under the domination of the bourgeoisie were thoroughly discussed and interpreted from a proletarian perspective. Though they voiced only the everyday viewpoint of average workers, subject to a variety of external influences, big-city pubs were still by far the most important forum for the exchange of proletarian views and experiences. They were the "salons of the poor"[8] and therefore also the place where the organization of the working class began.

Village pubs never played an equivalent role in the life of rural laborers and never became a hotbed of political activity and organization. Fellowship, intoxication, and satisfaction through alcohol played a major part of course in lives that offered so few other pleasures, but this was all interwoven with work, especially during the exhausting harvest weeks, or took place in the laborers' own huts, in the harvesters' barracks, at the waterpump, or on a bench in front of a house. Rural laborers only frequented the village pub in order to refill their jugs, since the regular patrons were farmers who did not feel particularly hospitable toward fieldhands.

Big-city pubs were very different. Here many workers' associations took root, especially after 1890. These associations played a large part in the social identity of the workers and provided scope for them to develop their talents. The spectrum of leisure activities taking place in pubs ranged from cheap dancing and variety shows to singing, theatrical presentations, sporting clubs, educational presentations, and even political gatherings and meetings of the workers' executive. Until the erection of the first *Volkshäuser*, organized proletarian cultural life had no other home. Hence it was at the pub that important elements of proletarian culture developed, including the organized selection, criticism, and reworking of such non-

8. Ibid., p. 244.

proletarian cultural artifacts as newspapers, popular songs, announcements, commands, trashy literature, laws, and decrees. However, pubs also had many drawbacks, largely connected with the more or less heavy emphasis on alcohol consumption. The pub was a place where one's miserable life could be forgotten for a few hours in an alcoholic stupor. This dependence on the relief provided by alcohol was more widespread among the lower strata of the proletariat than among better-paid workers. The former felt driven to drink, even though fully aware of their difficult financial straits. Alcohol and alcoholism were the result of social deprivation and the inability to adjust to life in the capitalistic big city. The cultural history of the seventeenth and eighteenth centuries shows increasing alcohol consumption in all social classes in almost all the countries of Europe. This is usually interpreted as a consequence of insecurity during times of profound social change, of primary accumulation and impoverishment. In addition, emerging capitalism now made large quantities of alcohol available to all.

Alcohol consumption in Germany rose rapidly after 1850 (accurate data are available from this point on), reaching a peak in the mid-1870s. At this time, Germans drank an annual average of 93 liters of beer and 5.3 liters of brandy and devoted 14 percent of total individual expenditures to alcohol consumption. Thereafter, the statistics indicate a slow but steady decline in alcohol consumption, a trend that did not halt until the late 1950s. During the period under study, the proportion of individual expenditures devoted to alcoholic beverages sank from 11.6 percent in 1895–99 to 8.7 percent in 1910–13 to the benefit of all other needs. (At the same time, the price of beer and schnapps was rising.) Beer also surpassed schnapps as the beverage of choice: while average expenditures for these beverages were roughly equal in 1870–74, twice as much was spent on beer around the turn of the century. Beer consumption had risen substantially to an annual average of 125 liters per capita while schnapps consumption slumped by almost 20 percent to 4.3 liters. However, these are overall averages;[9] other statistics show more subtle shifts in the alcohol consumption patterns of the proletariat. While schnapps consumption among field workers on the East Elbian estates continued to rise, big-city workers were switching from cheap schnapps to relatively expensive but more socially

9. See Kurt Apel, *Die Konsumtion der wichtigsten Kulturländer in den letzten Jahrzehnten* (Berlin, 1899).

prestigious beer. This was considered more cultivated behavior and a protection against drunkenness.

These changes can be traced back to two fundamental causes. First, mounting numbers of workers performed relatively demanding tasks requiring quick reactions, continuous concentration, and high performance. These workers needed to recover completely during their leisure time. Secondly, primitive forms of pleasure and relaxation through drunkenness were gradually replaced by more sophisticated needs and opportunities.

Contemporary studies in other countries produced different statistical results, but confirmed the general tendency. Industrially developed countries generally experienced high alcohol consumption rates. The following table shows annual, per capita consumption of beer, wine, and brandy calculated in liters of pure alcohol:

Table 9.1 *Annual Per Capita Consumption of Beer, Wine and Brandy*

	Year	Beer Liters of Pure Alcohol	Wine Liters of Pure Alcohol	Brandy Liters of Pure Alcohol
USA	1900	2.74	0.20	2.74
Great Britain	1900	7.20	0.23	2.54
France	1900	1.26	15.39	4.60
Belgium	1900	9.86	0.53	4.80
Germany	1900	5.63	0.73	4.40
Russia	1898	0.18	0.43	2.44

In Germany therefore average, annual consumption of pure alcohol was 10.76 liters per capita around the turn of the century (France = 21.25; Belgium = 15.19; Great Britain = 9.97).[10] These figures do not seem unusually high by modern standards. For instance, per capita consumption in the GDR in 1980 was 9.6 liters of industrially produced wine and sparkling wine, 138.7 liters of beer and 12.3 liters of spirits for a total pure alcohol consumption of 10.1 liters.[11]

High rates of alcohol consumption soon gave rise to both bourgeois and proletarian temperance movements. Howeve., neither was able to stem the spectacular growth of the schnapps and beer

10. See Hugo Hoppe, *Die Tatsachen über den Alkohol* (Berlin, 1904), p. 478.
11. *Statistisches Taschenbuch der DDR* (Berlin/GDR, 1981), p. 114.

industry. The Junkers' schnapps distilleries flourished. In the large
cities, top-fermented light ales such as *Berliner Weiße* and Leipzig
Gose were supplanted by bottom-fermented beers in the Bohemian
or Bavarian styles because the latter were easier for pubs to handle.
Breweries became increasingly productive, and retailers dependent
on the beverage industry sought to lure customers with an ever-
more sophisticated array of taprooms, bars, restaurants, corner
pubs, beer cellars, beer halls, and beer palaces. Business was so
profitable and steady that beer and schnapps suppliers became the
first industrial producers able to completely satisfy a mass market of
working people. The concentration of capital progressed rapidly.
With the end of the light-ale era, most beer was sold in bottles or in
kegs by itinerant peddlers, and pubs quickly became the breweries'
best customers.[12] The largest breweries were able to tie local retailers to the sale of their brands through loans, rental agreements,
and the supply of equipment. Counters, tables, and chairs became
standard equipment supplied by breweries. The innkeeper was
expected to pay for them through high sales. If he failed, he too
faced the danger of proletarianization.

Not surprisingly, the labor movement soon took up arms against
the monopolies and dictates of the large breweries, which were
bringing more and more working-class pubs under their control.
The most outstanding example of this struggle was the Berlin beer
boycott of 1894 against the great brewery "ring" of Schultheiß,
Patzendorfer, Böhmisches Brauhaus, and Adler.[13] Workers were
the main consumers of beer, which after all did have some nutritive
value, and they repeatedly attempted to gain the allegiance of the
innkeepers by boycotting various breweries. However, the labor
movement experienced considerable difficulty in attempting to assert its interests in the face of the mounting power of the great
industrialists.

The needs of big-city workers and office employees were satisfied
in other ways as well. The Aschinger brothers created a type of
restaurant that attracted many office employees and students as well
as substantial numbers of workers and quickly spread throughout
the inner city. Through rationalized, industrial-style production,
the Aschingers were able to offer good but simple food and drinks

12. See Gustav Stresemann, "Die Entwicklung des Berliner Flaschenbier-
geschäfts" (Ph.D. diss., Leipzig, 1902), pp. 5, 11.
13. See Eduard Bernstein, *Die Geschichte der Berliner Arbeiter-Bewegung*, pt. 3
(Berlin, 1910), pp. 324–54.

at a low cost. They opened their first *Bierquelle* in the Spittelmarkt area of Berlin in 1882. Thirty years later Aschinger AG employed 3,500 people and operated fifty barrooms and restaurants. The Aschinger brothers made a fortune on peas with bacon, salted spareribs with peas, pancakes with apple sauce, and consommé with rolls. Rolls were free with all meals and the beer flowed freely. The restaurants came to be called *Bierglocken* or beer bells because a bell was rung every time a cask of beer was freshly tapped. These were not particularly proletarian establishments but tended to cater instead to the rapidly growing armies of low- and mid-level office employees after 1900.

The stand-up bars that arose in the 1880s were similar in many respects. They were also tailored to the mass market, providing fast food and a quick beer.

Genuine working-class pubs could be found above all in traditional proletarian areas, especially in the northern outskirts of Berlin, in the Spandau area between the Prenzlau and Oranienburg gates and then spreading over the Prenzlauer Berg and the Weinberg into Wedding. The brandy shops, small bars, cellar pubs, and corner restaurants in these districts did not rely on a quick turnover but rather on the "regulars" who lived or worked in the neighborhood and felt at home in the local pub.

The prominent role of pubs and alcohol in proletarian life caused considerable controversy in the labor movement.[14] Some purists made a political argument against alcohol consumption, pointing out again and again the demoralizing effect of drink. It made proletarians dependent, they said, reconciled them with the rule of capital, and sapped their ability to carry on the struggle. A pamphlet of the Workers' Abstinence Union stated in somewhat exaggerated terms: "Workers had to consume countless barrels of beer in exchange for gathering in the great beer halls of the brewery owners. Thus the workers became beer slaves. The great goals that the workers had pursued in their meetings and discussions, while learning or playing, were drowned in alcohol."[15]

The minority of abstainers in the German labor movement had many arguments in their favor. However, their sectarian views often seemed rather divorced from reality, as can be seen in the following newspaper advertisement:

14. See Benno Laquer, "Die Alkoholfrage. Bibliographische Übersicht," *Archiv für Sozialgeschichte und Sozialpolitik* 33 (Jena, 1906).
15. Heinrich Peus, *Das Volkshaus wie es sein sollte* (Berlin, 1913), p. 7.

Those who drink schnapps
pay voluntary tax,
fill the wallets of Junkers,
despoil their bodies,
destroy their families,
make idiots of their descendants
and help fill the insane asylums.[16]

Alcohol is condemned here as an instrument of bourgeois domination. The exaggerated radicalism of the teetotalers prevented them from advancing their views within the German labor movement and persuading the Social Democratic party to demand abstinence from its members and to urge it on all workers. However, any such attempt would surely have failed in any case, first because pubs were about the sole venue where workers could move in a socially just atmosphere and secondly because demands that the proletariat voluntarily renounce one of its few pleasures in life would have brought the party into conflict with the basic desires of the masses. Karl Kautsky commented on this in *Neue Zeit* as early as 1891:

> The consumption of alcoholic beverages has not always been the road to ruin. Formerly it was a source of cheerful companionship, a means of enhancing the pleasures of idleness. But capitalism is poisoning this source more and more. How then should we seek to combat this poisoning of mankind? By stopping up the source of delight, by depriving mankind of a pleasure it has enjoyed since times immemorial? Or by eliminating the poison, purifying the source, and allowing it to bubble away as refreshing and invigorating as ever?[17]

As was mentioned above, the pub should not be seen solely as a place of joyful companionship or of refuge for the underclass, as a den of drunkenness or iniquity. Since the very origins of the labor movement, it was the headquarters of the union and the party. This was where the workers held their meetings, where the movement distributed its newspapers and brochures, and where secret meetings could easily be disguised as drinking rounds. Whereas the coffee house had been an essential ingredient in the intellectual and political life of the rising bourgeoisie two or three generations earlier, the pub now played a pivotal role in many types of working-

16. *Coburger Volksblatt*, July 11, 1912.
17. Karl Kautsky, "Der Alkoholismus und seine Bekämpfung, III," *Die Neue Zeit* 28 (1890/91): 51.

class organization. Many innkeepers helped to advance the interests of their working-class clientele not only for business reasons but also because they operated "party pubs." As small business people they were social opponents of the big breweries on which they were economically dependent and therefore had reasons of their own to support the labor movement. Social Democrats in Berlin founded the newspaper *Der freie Gastwirt (The Free Innkeeper)* in 1901 in order to attempt to organize and unite innkeepers sympathetic to Social Democracy in the Union of Free Bartenders and Innkeepers. By 1913 *Der Freie Gastwirt* had a circulation of some eleven thousand.[18]

To a certain extent, the rising masses of workers in Berlin and the strengthening labor movement helped stimulate the growth of breweries and pubs. During the 1870s smaller pubs such as the old *Zur Linde* in Skalitzerstraße and *Zum Schweinekopf* in the Spandau area had been the norm, but now the workers needed larger rooms for their surreptitious political meetings. Thus the construction of huge beer halls was indirectly assisted by the anti-Socialist legislation in Prussia, which forbade large outdoor meetings within the city limits of Berlin.

As the Bohemian- and Bavarian-style beer usually drunk today gained in popularity, the breweries built huge halls or "beer palaces." In the early 1880s, the Munich breweries Pschorr, Sedlmayr and Münchener Hofbräu erected halls in Berlin. The Böhmische Brauhaus had already expanded its production facilities in the Friedrichshain area in 1872 and erected the great Friedrichshain beer hall between 1886 and 1888. In 1890 the Berliner Unions-Brauerei considerably expanded its hall in Hasenheide, and in 1891 the Schultheiß Brauerei built its hall on Schönhauser Allee. Berliners often called the new halls "beer cathedrals" because of their resemblance to the nave of a church and because of the overladen, "old-German" style of architecture with which the great breweries tried to outshine the simple, traditional pubs serving light ale (*Weißbier*). The "beer cathedrals" offered their own brand of "care for lost souls" and were backed by their own "beer snobs" – the brewery stockholders.

Some momentous occasions in the history of the German labor movement took place in these beer halls, for instance, in the Tivoli Brewery hall at Kreuzberg, renowned for its draught bock beer, or

18. See Dieter Fricke, *Die deutsche Arbeiterbewegung, 1869–1914*, (Berlin/GDR, 1976) p. 461.

in the Concordia halls in Andreasstraße, the Germania hall in Chausseestraße, and in the Prater in Kastanienallee. The latter is the only hall rich in this kind of proletarian tradition that remains standing.

2. Books and Newspapers – the Worker as Reader

Just as sociability and entertainment, political organization and worker education all played a part in working-class pubs, so too printed texts and pictures fulfilled many different functions. The history of the labor movement has thoroughly documented the important part played by newspapers and Marxist books in forging a link between workers and their class organization. Equally well known are the attempts of the liberal bourgeoisie to solve the "social question" by educating the workers, attempts in which books and libraries also played a key role. However, the bulk of the workers were primarily interested in quite different materials. Industrialization made the mass production of books and newspapers possible and stimulated a demand for news and printed entertainment. The range of printed texts and pictures that workers consumed stretched therefore from sensational newspaper stories and numerous kinds of amusement and entertainment to political information, advice about life, philosophic views and professional, political, scientific, and technical education.

When workers around 1900 specified reading as one of their favorite leisure activities, the emphasis on entertainment and news was far greater than on any of the other possibilities. Though reading ranked well below anything that smacked of nature, fresh air, sunshine, or sociability, printed texts and illustrations were in strong demand for the few hours of workday rest and relaxation, for times when there was insufficient money for other forms of entertainment, or when interesting reading promised to enliven time spent out-of-doors. However, reading materials for these purposes had to be easy as well as exciting or relaxing, they had to offer "quick and easy pleasure." Astute capitalist businessmen soon learned how to sate the need for primarily light entertainment with a vast array of choices. Among the most successful authors of the time were Zola, Gerstäcker, Verne, and Dumas alongside Eschtruth, Heimburg, Marlitt, and Frenssen.

The broad masses read serialized novels and light periodicals acquired from lending libraries or door-to-door salesmen. Those who read newspapers and magazines vastly outnumbered those who read books, both within the population at large and to an even greater extent within the working class. The workers acquired their literary tastes largely from what they read in newspapers and magazines. The key means of literary communication around 1900 was accordingly the popular press, which satisfied the interest in reading with an inexhaustible variety of materials ranging from news to serial novels.

Although the influence of revolutionary Social Democracy and its press on the working class steadily increased from year to year, the segment of the bourgeois press that aimed at light entertainment also succeeded after the mid-1870s in steadily expanding its market share, including among the proletariat. In so doing, it sought to tap the feelings of pride aroused in the working class by German unification thanks to a people's struggle for generations against national dismemberment and impotence. The "small German" solution to the national plight seemed to be validated by the integrative effects of rapid economic growth. The popular bourgeois press – the main mouthpiece of nationalist sentiments – was represented above all by the so-called family magazines such as *Daheim, Gartenlaube, Bibliothek der Unterhaltung und des Wissens, Buch für Alle*, and *Stein der Weisen*, which relied, besides on "uplifting entertainment," on the demand for general information, "useful instruction," "candid enlightenment," and "instruction in the national heritage" for readers "of all ages and social classes." It is instructive that little economic success was experienced by similar liberal-bourgeois publications such as *Vom Fels zum Meer*, which attempted to limit their readership to the middle classes by promising to combine "the glamor of exclusive revues with . . . warmth, friendliness, and a language that is readily understandable." They hoped to offer "piquant" selections, though without "pandering to the great masses."

By 1900, the family publication industry had accumulated some fifty years of experience in catering to the tastes and desires of working people and increasingly after the late 1860s to the industrial proletariat in the big cities. The industry knew its market very well, and a review of the topics it covered provides a fairly accurate survey of the subject matter, themes, and styles preferred by workers at the time. This assumption is corroborated by the fact that Social Democratic publications such as *Neue Welt* offered very similar headlines. A study of the volume of various kinds of articles in the family publications reveals the following points of emphasis: (1) novels and short stories; (2) miscellany, humor, mixed; (3) advice, home economics, health; (4) applied technology and natural science; (5) geography and ethnology; (6) biography and history. The themes that frequently recur within these genres are: love and marriage; crime, injustice, violence; home towns and native regions; news from the families of the kaiser, kings, or princes; the life and works of famous inventors, artists, politicians, military men; lifestyles within the upper bourgeoisie; upward mobility from the lower classes; petty bourgeois living under extreme circumstances; new inventions and their application; war and military service; puzzles and enigmas, mysticism, superstition; morals and mores of exotic peoples; the cities and countryside of Germany and Europe; unusual buildings; illnesses, their prevention and cure, taking care of one's body; production and use of luxury foods such as tea, coffee, tobacco, etc.; animal behavior. All of this conforms quite well to the topics with which the modern mass media attempt to entertain their audiences, with the exception of those materials aimed specifically at the desire of the lower middle class to model itself on the upper classes.

Reading played a prominent part in the life of the rapidly expanding mass of workers. In the 1890s, their reading habits and needs accordingly became a prime topic of public debate. Social Democratic party workers and union organizers, theoreticians, working-class educators, journalists, liberal pedagogues, social scientists, librarians, civil servants, ministers, and politicians in the areas of culture and education were all eager to make their opinions known. While some detected and offered evidence of "an enormous appetite for knowledge in the rising class," others saw "readers numbering in the millions" who wasted time, money, and energy on the surrogate pleasures of "the literary filth and trash industry." Though for opposing reasons, both the cultural planners of the labor movement and bourgeois educators were shocked by the way the workers devoured all the products of the capitalistic publishing industry.

Liberals and elements of the democratic bourgeoisie felt that the large numbers of literate proletarians confirmed their view that the friction between the working class and the bourgeoisie was due above all to differing educational opportunities as influenced by differences in wealth. "The ultimate root of all the social danger lies not in differences in wealth but in education. All attempts at social reform must begin here."[19] The proletarianized petty bourgeoisie was particularly convinced that knowledge was the key to power and social advancement. The best method of overcoming class hostility seemed therefore to be continuation of elementary school and acquisition of the common "intellectual foundation" by means of adult education during leisure time. Educated bourgeois considered it a particular duty of theirs to provide suitable knowledge and instruction to the proletarian "underclasses" and thus to secure the social peace.

Bourgeois educators saw themselves facing a double challenge. First, they hoped that the dissemination of "knowledge" would help to counter "the false doctrines of socialism." "It is a patriot's duty to save every German man from the clutches of Social Democracy."[20] Secondly, they hoped that more knowledge would help to bring the proletarian lifestyle more into line with the interests of capital. They hoped to encourage workers "to employ their spare time in a healthier and more valuable fashion, to lure them away from empty barroom conversations in dark, unhealthful atmospheres and to make them receptive to more noble and virtuous pleasures."[21] They considered it evident that "alcoholism and a desire for education are antithetical" and that "strengthening the one necessarily weakens the other."[22]

The social peace had another formidable enemy in the liberal view: "literature that poisons the people," such as trite novel series that glorified crime, violence, anarchistic self-reliance, and recalcitrant proletarians while disparaging the "genuine benefactors of mankind," "the rich, the prominent, and the educated."[23] Liberal, bourgeois educators were convinced that reading such materials would propel proletarian behavior in dangerously uncontrollable directions. The view that popular reading materials were dangerous "if they aroused sexual emotions or stimulated aggressive behaviors" was only corrected over an extended period of time. It was not realized until much later that these materials actually "encouraged

19. Constantin Nörrenberg, *Die Bücher- und Lesehalle: Eine Bildungsanstalt der Zukunft* (Cologne, 1896), p. 4.

20. Philipp Huppert, *Öffentliche Lesehallen, ihre Aufgabe, Geschichte und Einrichtung* (Cologne, 1899), p. 9.

21. Karl Hesse, "Kulturelle Wohlfahrtspflege in Oberschlesien," *Comenius-Blätter für Volkserziehung* 6 (Berlin, 1908): 41.

22. "Die Bedeutung öffentlicher Lesehallen im Kampfe gegen den Alkoholismus," ibid. 4 (1905): 115.

23. Kurt Apel, *Die Verbreitung guten Lesestoffs* (Berlin, 1896), pp. 1, 7.

and entrenched reactionary views and opinions . . . because instead of provoking thought they merely sowed political disinterest."[24]

The Social Democrats encouraged reading as a vehicle for disseminating the necessary knowledge to carry on the class struggle for political power, in accordance with the principle enunciated by Wilhelm Liebknecht, "Knowledge is power and power is knowledge." In contrast to the bourgeois ideal of "universal education," the Social Democrats propagated "the education of the workers for the class struggle."[25] However, this theoretical view did not prevent them from actually carrying out an education policy compatible with the existing order and from encouraging and striving to improve the public training and retraining of workers within the established capitalist economy.

The Social Democratic concept of education for proletarian readers was governed by an attempt to induce them to undertake a thorough study of socialist literature, thus enabling them to propagate a socialist world view among their fellow class members. The labor movement accordingly sought to extract from bourgeois culture all those elements that would further its revolutionary struggle for emancipation. These approved cultural elements certainly did not extend to the products of the "writers and publishers of people's literature" who sought to encourage a "muggy" Prusso-German patriotism consisting of deference to authority, nationalism, reactionary Romanticism, and antisocialist prejudices. The aversion of Social Democratic educators to all forms of trite, frivolous literature is understandable in the light of their ultimate goals. In their view, sentimental novels distracted attention from the class struggle and diminished the reading of "works about politics and the social sciences." However, the blanket condemnation of "light entertainment" frequently found among Social Democratic authors only demonstrates that they did not take sufficiently into consideration the genuine leisure needs of proletarian readers.

In accordance with their respective educational programs outlined above, bourgeois liberals and Social Democrats drew up reading lists for workers. They both decried trite mass literature, though again for differing reasons, and only tolerated the "educational entertainment" of light fiction as a kind of concession to tastes that were as yet not fully developed.

24. Rudolf Schenda, *Volk ohne Buch* (Munich, 1977), p. 493.
25. S. Koperbe, "Was muß eine Arbeiterbibliothik tun?" *Der Bibliothekar* 4 (1910): 31–32.

Both liberals and Social Democrats intensified their efforts to influence what proletarians read in order to propel the intellectual energy of the workers in the direction of the final outcomes that they respectively supported. Their main instrument in this struggle, alongside the popular press, was the lending library, which offered at no cost an array of books selected from all those available on the market according to the ideological and pedagogical viewpoints of the person in charge.

Both bourgeois educators of the "people" and socialist educators of the "workers" hoped that the development of an extensive system of lending libraries would have a profound impact on proletarian reading habits. This purported shift in tastes was idealized as progress from "passing the time by reading" to the intermediate stage of "educational entertainment" and finally to the ultimate stage of the conscious appropriation of cultural values.

3. The Cinema

None of the new leisure activities was embraced quite so readily and enthusiastically by big-city workers as the cinema. This was facilitated by the popular roots of cinema in technical entertainments at fairs and nineteenth-century panoramas. The cinema made its first appearance in local pubs, in the hope of attracting additional customers (similar to television a good half century later). Large crowds were indeed attracted by the technical triumph and aesthetic fascination of the cinema, and it soon moved out of pubs and into its own facilities, thereby becoming a chief competitor of the pubs. By the turn of the century, going to the cinema was the second most popular leisure activity of the working class. "Expenditures on the movies have become a standard item in the budgets of proletarian and middle-class households, encroaching on essential expenses. People have their local cinema, which changes its program twice a week, normally Wednesdays and Saturdays. . . . (The "movies" are usually filled to overflowing on the days of the switch.) The cheapest seats cost 30 pfennig (in the modern Union-Theater in Friedrichstraße in Berlin the prices vary between 95 pfennig and 4.50 marks). The prices are a little less by subscription."[26]

The labor movement looked askance at this new form of enter-

26. Victor Noack, *Der Kino. Etwas über sein Wesen und seine Bedeutung* (Gautzsch bei Leipzig, 1913), p. 9.

tainment (behind which a flourishing industry soon stood) and at first rejected cinema as a cheap distraction. It would certainly have been difficult to imagine the potential power of movies and film on the basis of the early examples. The functionaries in the trade unions and the Social Democratic party rejected cinema not only because of its banal content and because it obeyed the capitalist laws of profit making, but also because the workers thoroughly enjoyed it. It therefore, in their view, diverted attention from the main task of class organization, and indeed, attendance at party meetings did suffer from the popularity of movies.

As the popularity of cinema grew by leaps and bounds and as techniques improved, the labor movement gradually began to understand that movies could be used not only as light entertainment but also as an educational tool, as a picture newspaper and as a medium for the dissemination of theatrical productions.

4. Allotment Gardens on the Outskirts of Town

German industrial cities, with their masses of tenement buildings in the downtown area, were characteristically surrounded by miles of allotment gardens (*Laubenkolonien*). This was where workers frequently spent their leisure time, participating in numerous proletarian or petty-bourgeois clubs and associations. These gardens offered their particular brand of companionship and cooperation, of competitions, feasts, and celebrations. Workers tended to stick together in the allotment gardens, just as they did in the tenements of the city, and distinctive styles of public, proletarian life developed here.

It was the denizens of the "most frightful working-class areas"[27] of Berlin who began in the spring of 1862 to work the first parcels of land, each about 280 square meters in size. They often erected little shacks on their allotment, which they called their "dry bread." However, this first *Laubenkolonie* endured only five years before being reclaimed for a city hospital. Such a fleeting existence typified the allotment gardens around Berlin until the 1920s. It is well established that these gardens were rented primarily by workers.[28]

27. Ernst Hirschberg, *Die soziale Lage der arbeitenden Klassen in Berlin* (Berlin, 1897), p. 31.
28. See Friedrich Coenen, *Das Berliner Laubenkoloniewesen, seine Mängel und seine Reformen* (Göttingen, 1911).

Increasingly tight housing conditions in Berlin after the Franco-Prussian War prompted a rapid increase in the number of allotment gardens. Highly paid skilled workers were especially capable of renting a piece of land from one of the primary leaseholders, usually an innkeeper. These innkeepers also held the pub concession for their lands and contractually required their subtenants to consume large quantities of beer and schnapps in the local tavern or bar.[29] However, complaints about the encouragement of alcohol abuse stemmed more from middle-class reformers than from the workers themselves.

The chief concern from the workers' point of view was rising rents. Not only verbal protests ensued but also mass occupations of land, especially in times of acute housing shortages. Disregarding the established order, workers built their gardens and shacks on any available piece of city or church land or private property. This then served as emergency housing for homeless families. At times some 40,000 people lived in these unauthorized allotment gardens, which became one of the sources of summer cabins. Another source was the barracks for shelterless migrants erected by the civic authorities outside the gates to the city. When the housing crisis eased, some of these barracks were turned into further garden allotments.

Within each group of allotment gardens, the workers cooperated in order to master agricultural skills unfamiliar to industrial laborers, and they also organized many social clubs and events, such as summer and autumn festivals with exhibitions of their fruits, vegetables, flowers, chickens, doves, and rabbits. There were parties for children with lantern parades and outdoor dances in front of the garden pub. The allotment gardeners in each area usually formed an association. Their experience in labor unions and politics made them well aware of the power of organized coalitions, and they soon learned how to counter the attempts of the primary leaseholders to charge excessive rents. After the turn of the century, the Alliance of All Garden Associations in Berlin and the Surrounding Area sought general, secret and equal elections at the local level, thus championing one of the principal demands of Social Democracy on the local level.

All in all, the proletariat developed a complex network of leisure activities in the allotment gardens, directed primarily at satisfying the needs that arose from living and working in the big city.

29. See ibid., p. 21.

5. Hiking, Tourism, and Sports

It has become standard practice in the twentieth century for city dwellers to seek out nature and to hike and travel around in the countryside for pleasure and relaxation. A hundred years ago, this was still a privilege of the aristocracy and wealthy bourgeoisie, which developed an exclusive lifestyle of their own as they strolled and took pleasure trips in the country and relaxed over picnics and at spas. Eventually, the workers found means to participate in this sort of activity. In response to the exclusivity of the mountaineering and tourist associations of the ruling class, they founded their own associations (the proletarian hiking association Naturfreunde, or Friends of Nature, was founded in Vienna in 1895) and began to take advantage of every opportunity to relax in the countryside. River ships, horse-drawn carts, and quick, motorized transportation through the suburbs now brought working-class families into the countryside on Sunday outings. Young workers began going on hikes together, and no longer was the pub the sole venue where they could mingle. Farmers and small rural leaseholders offered refreshments; new facilities sprang up with signs announcing "families can make their own coffee here;" public bathing areas appeared along lakes and rivers; overnight huts were constructed beside hiking trails; and country paths were reinforced and marked. The extent of the demand for rest and relaxation in nature is evidenced by the mushrooming of touring organizations for hikers, bicyclists, rowers, anglers, and mountain climbers and by the construction of shelters for vacationing workers.

Sports were closely connected with hiking. Numerous sports facilities were constructed around the turn of the century for the use of the general public, including workers. Ice sports and gymnastics facilities had been available for many years, but now new roller-skating and bathing installations were constructed (both open-air and the first enclosed pools), as well as boat houses, gymnastics halls, meadows, and soccer fields. Billiard rooms and bowling alleys were installed in restaurants. Some of these facilities only became available to workers when they joined together in corresponding associations. Working-class sports became widespread in Germany somewhat later than in Britain, and the British model was popularized through middle-class sporting clubs. During the first few decades, sports and attendant clubs were almost exclusively the domain of highly qualified and better-paid workers. The English word *sport* did not become widespread until the 1920s, and at the turn of the century all these organizations continued to call themselves *Turnvereine* or gymnastics clubs. After the Socialist Laws were rescinded in 1890, working-class athletes were able to form independent organizations. Numerous proletarian gymnastics clubs arose in the industrial centers of Germany and united in Gera in May 1893 to form the Workers' Gymnastics Association. The new association numbered 9,096 members; twenty years later it numbered 186,958.

6. The Arts and Sensational Entertainments

All kinds of artistic presentation were becoming increasingly popular among the working class. This was true not only of gradually emerging artistic films but also of traditional popular art forms, which still played the primary role. As the ranks of the urban proletariat swelled, new life was breathed into garden theaters and itinerant troops, into people's theater (*Volkstheater*) and theaters in the suburbs. The Neue Welt, the Belle-Alliance theater garden, the garden stage of the Friedrich-Wilhelmstädtischen-Theater on Chausseestraße, Puhlmanns Garten on Schönhauser Allee, the Prater, and the Vorstädtische (Suburban) Theater on Weinbergsweg were only a few of them. The people's theater movement facilitated working-class access to bourgeois theaters, though these remained primarily interested in white-collar audiences. Artistic pleasures were also offered by street musicians, tenement courtyard singers, and organ-grinders. Actors and acrobats appeared alongside musicians in the summer gardens, at bandstands, and at the open-air concerts that military bands gave in city squares, often in the middle of working-class districts. It is difficult to draw a line between art and the new sorts of carnivals and mass entertainments that could be put on in amusement parks and fairgrounds, music halls and circuses. The first circus was constructed in Berlin in 1821, and Renz, Dejean, and Kroll initiated the transition from carnivalistic amusements to the modern circus. The curiosity of the crowds was satisfied less through gawking at human abnormalities, such as those of dwarfs, giants, or Siamese twins, and increasingly through sensational new entertainments such as high-wire acts, animal tamers, clowns, and horseback performers.

The desire for spectacle and sensation brought working-class crowds to new types of performances that gradually eclipsed the old carnival acts, street singers, jugglers, and medieval entertainers. The locations for the new forms of entertainment moved to large soccer fields, regatta courses, boxing halls, and wrestling tents. Modern zoological gardens replaced the itinerant animal shows. Racetracks were built for bicycles and automobiles, and airports were established. The Deutsche Flugplatz-Gesellschaft Berlin was founded for the purpose of providing spectacles for the public. However, horse racing in Karlshorst and Hoppegarten remained largely a preserve of the wealthy, even so far as the spectators were concerned. German workers took little interest in some spectacles that were popular in other countries such as rooster fights, cockroach racing, bull fights, and the dog racing so beloved by British workers. The Germans preferred their homing-pigeon competitions, which did not really suit very well the category of games and spectacles.

Finally, the big city itself contributed to the cornucopia of new leisure activities with its colorful street life and abundance of locales where people could congregate and communicate with one another. Crowds gathered in public baths, soup kitchens, shelters for the homeless, job procurement centers, markets, department stores, and in the waiting rooms and along the platforms of mass transportation. Most important of all though were the big train stations. They were the gateway to the city, indeed a veritable city within a city, with their array of cinemas, barber shops, toilets and washrooms, restaurants of all classes, post offices, bookstores, waiting rooms, and lodging offices. Tenement courtyards also vibrated with activity – the incessant chatter of neighbors, the cries of barkers and peddlers, the performances of organ-grinders, and the tumult of children. The streets too offered innumerable shops, advertising pillars, benches and water pumps, kiosks and newspaper vendors. Workers also frequented the grand boulevards and public squares where the ruling classes paraded and held their celebrations. Not to be forgotten as locations for leisure time are the quiet areas in the big city, the cemeteries and public parks. In 1840, the Berlin city authorities had decided to carve out a public park for the largely proletarian and petty-bourgeois inhabitants of the eastern and northern suburbs. Hence in the jubilee year of Frederick the Great, not only was Rauch's equestrian statue unveiled on Unter den Linden but also the creation of the Friedrichshain park was announced, to be completed in 1848.

SIGRID JACOBEIT

Clothing in Nazi Germany

Until the 1960s and 1970s, the history of clothing as dealt with in ethnography (*Volkskunde*) focused primarily on rural apparel, that is, on folk "costumes."[1] Very little attention was paid to such questions as the origins of these costumes, the reasons for their adoption, and the ebbs and flows in their popularity, in short, their socioeconomic basis. Now, after the early work of Paul Nedo and Martin Nowak-Neumann, the studies of Wolf-Dieter Könenkamp, Gitta Böth, Ingeborg Weber-Kellermann, Gaby Mentges, Dagmar Neuland, and others have brought about a change of focus in the history of clothing.[2]

1. See above all G. Böth, "Kleidungsforschung," in R.W. Brednich, ed., *Grundriß der Volkskunde* (West Berlin, 1988), pp. 153–69.
2. M. Nowak-Neumann and P. Nedo, *Die Tracht der Sorben um Schleife* (Bautzen, 1954); M. Nowak-Neumann, *Die Tracht der Niederlausitzer Sorben* (Bautzen, 1965); also L. Balke and A. Lange with the assistance of Frank Förster, *Sorbisches Trachtenbuch* (Bautzen, 1985); W.-D. Könenkamp, *Wirtschaft, Gesellschaft und Kleidungsstil in den Vierlanden während des 18. und 19. Jahrhunderts. Zur Situation einer Tracht*, vol. 9 of *Schriften zur niederdeutschen Volkskunde* (Göttingen, 1978); G. Böth, *Kleidungsverhalten in hessischen Trachtendörfern. Der Wechsel von der Frauentracht zur städtischen Kleidung 1969–1976 am Beispiel Mardorf. Zum Rückgang der Trachten in Hessen*, Europäische Hochschulschriften, ser. 19, vol. 18 (Frankfurt a.M., Bern, Cirencester, 1980); idem, *"Selbst gesponnen, selbst gemacht . . ." wer hat sich das nur ausgedacht? Trachtenforschung gestern – Kleiderforschung heute*, booklet accompanying an exhibition, ed. H. Oftenjam (Cloppenburg, 1986); I. Weber-Kellermann, *Der Kinder neue Kleider. Zweihundert Jahre deutsche Kindermoden in ihrer sozialen Zeichensetzung* (Frankfurt a.M., 1985); G. Mentges, "Erziehung, Dressur und Anstand in der Sprache der Kinderkleidung. Eine kulturgeschichtlich-empirische Untersuchung am Beispiel der Schwälmer Kindertracht" (Ph.D. diss., Marburg, 1985); D. Neuland, "Kleidung und Kleidungsverhalten werktätiger Klassen und Schichten in der Großstadt Berlin zwischen 1918 und 1932/33 – eine empirische Studie" (Ph.D. diss., Humboldt-Universität, Berlin, 1988); *Mode-Tracht-regionale Identität. Historische Kleidungsforschung heute*, papers given at the international symposium, ed. H. Ottenjann (Cloppenburg, 1985).

This new approach, with the raft of information it has uncovered, has helped to draw attention to more general, socially motivated aspects of clothing. Broader social strata have been included, styles have been reassessed, the influence of high fashion on everyday clothing has been examined, and much more. "Clothing has many levels," summarizes Gitta Böth. "Clothes are not only worn but also manufactured, sold, handed down, repaired, turned to uses not originally intended, and finally discarded."[3]

The following paper aims to continue this line of research by delving from the larger point of view into the history of clothing during the Nazi era, into the ability or inability to satisfy basic clothing needs, and into the effect of the clothing situation on everyday life in urban and rural areas.

The clothing situation was never so complicated in this century as during the era between 1933 and 1945. The Nazi takeover had very little immediate effect on the clothing worn by most of the population. Consequently, there was considerable continuity in the practical-elegant clothing that had become fashionable in all classes and strata among both men and women in the years following the First World War. However, uniforms were beginning to appear with increasing frequency on the streets of Germany. High fashion had been in crisis ever since the onset of the Great Depression. In 1929, when Franz Hessel was still strolling the streets of Berlin and delighting in the elegance of the fairer sex (the women of Berlin, he said, could bear comparison with the "most sophisticated women in Europe"), such prominent high fashion houses as Hermann Gerson and Valentin Manheimer were in the throes of financial disaster. Manheimer eventually went bankrupt and committed suicide. Berlin, as the fashion capital of Germany, was "well on the way to becoming an elegant city," with a "clothes sense" that had become "less dramatic, but more democratic and therefore more elegant."[4]

This elegance found expression after 1930 in clothes that clung ever more tightly to the body. The smooth "flapper-style" haircuts became slightly waved after permanents were invented in 1925, and in the years that followed, women sought ever more splendid hairdos. A thin figure was still de rigueur, but the waist was again emphasized and hemlines sank. Clothes patterns came to resemble

3. Böth, *Trachtenforschung gestern* (above, n. 2), p. 12.
4. F. Hessel, "Von der Mode," in *Ein Flaneur in Berlin* (Berlin/GDR, 1984), p. 37 (the first edition appeared in 1929 under the title *Spazieren in Berlin*).

the plans of an architect, making homemade fashions more difficult. Gone were the days when every women could stitch together her own frock. Men cruelly mocked this simple, practical style, as in the following song "The Newest Fashion":

> She stands in the window to be seen by all,
> a skinny thing, unmoving.
> Cloth for her costume apparently there was not –
> for what she shows on top is woeful.
> She cannot boast, she has no bust,
> a body packed into a tube.
> She has no hip – she has no zip
> This shadow of a woman!
> She raises her arms – she turns in circles.
> What is she? What does she want? What can she do? – Who knows!
> Who is this deprived stick?
> An emissary of death?
> Starvation personified? –
> Or just the latest fashion?[5]

However, it is simple, unobtrusive clothes and the art of wearing them that make a stylish woman into an elegant one. Gabrielle Chanel, the Parisian designer of this simple, contemporary wear, showed the way, commenting: "Clothes are less important than the art of wearing them." It was not a question of originality, she said, and elegance was not a matter of age: "You have to summon the courage to be your own age: for you can be delightful at twenty, charming at forty, and simply irresistible for the rest of your life. Fashions grow old much faster than women."[6] To be genuinely elegant, thought Coco Chanel, clothes had to allow "free-flowing movement." Only such clothes, appropriately designed for the various age groups, could become stylish. This was the reason why this elegant female fashion became widely popular in Germany. As the thirties progressed, Elsa Schiaparelli, Nina Ricci, etc., imparted new impulses from Paris, which remained the fashion capital. The increasingly elegant female fashions that they created after 1930 came to symbolize the new search for individual fulfillment in the years before 1933, an opportunity for women to lend visible

5. Cited in U. Westphal, *Berliner Konfektion und Mode. Die Zerstörung einer Tradition, 1836–1939* (West Berlin, 1986), p. 83.
6. Cited in R. König and P.W. Schupisser, *Die Mode in der menschlichen Gesellschaft* (Zürich, 1958), p. 339.

expression to their individual personalities. The new Nazi authorities, however, immediately denounced these Parisian styles and their disciples in all larger German cities. Fascist agitators decried the new styles, especially those of women, as exhibiting "base sensuality, shameless eroticism, and an animal maleness and femaleness." They continued:

> Now under the signs of the swastika, the *Wendekreuz* and the sun wheel, fashionable German "ladies" and "gentlemen" can no longer worship Paris and London. . . . It is time that the sense of German brotherhood within the new, all-encompassing state began to stir in the hearts of fashion-conscious German shoppers. Or else the all-embracing state will have to resort to force in the realm of taste as well. What we hope to achieve some day can only be described as German fashion.[7]

The argument focused on "dignified, German womanhood," while internationally renowned Jewish couturiers and fashion houses were denounced by racist agitators: "We know that Parisian whores set the tone for German women, that 'high' fashion is concocted by Jewish couturiers, in worthy alliance with the magnates of the spinning and weaving industries and with the able assistance of the sluts and trollops who parade their wares."[8]

The propaganda campaign against Jewish couturiers and department stores began long before 1933. Such anti-Semitic attacks can be traced back to the very origins of the Nazi party, simply in the columns of its official organ, *Der völkische Beobachter*. For instance, the edition of July 13, 1928, carried the following item about department stores: "The shoppers (they are all workers) stream into the store, only to be blinded by all the false glitter and swindled by Jews. Meanwhile, the good German merchant, whose long years of experience is the guarantee for the quality of his goods, slowly starves because he refuses to cheat anyone."

The importance of department stores in the economy as a whole was never discussed. According to Julius Hirsch,[9] shops and department stores[10] had a total sales volume in women's wear of 250

---

7. J. Wulf, *Die bildenden Künste im Dritten Reich. Eine Dokumentation* (Frankfurt a.M., Berlin, Vienna, 1983), p. 286.

8. Ibid.

9. J. Hirsch, "Die Bedeutung des Warenhauses in der Volkswirtschaft," in *Probleme des Warenhauses. Beiträge zur Geschichte und Erkenntnis der Entwicklung des Warenhauses in Deutschland* (Berlin, 1928), p. 62.

10. The boundary between department stores and shops was rather fluid. Shops

million marks in 1926, or one-third of all sales. Department stores held a 15 percent share of total textile sales for that year. Jews neither owned all department stores nor did they control the entire garment industry; however, fascist propagandists used their strong presence in the garment industry to fan the latent anti-Semitism that had existed long before 1933. All their talk of a "Jewish cartel" in the garment industry was entirely without foundation and served only to promote racial discrimination.

Let us remain, however, with "dignified German womanhood," which according to Nazi propaganda should dress in accordance with its "innermost nature," i.e., "nobly and purely" and in line with its "own German fashions." This viewpoint too was not without its antecedents, as can be seen for instance in the nationalist and chauvinistic propaganda directed against the "hereditary enemy" France before the First World War. A pamphlet about the clothing of the *Wandervogel* movement stated in 1913 that it should be "German" and totally immune to the styles of the "Parisian whores." Three years later, the same author defined how German clothing differed from French: it was not "as changeable as the seasons, as mercurial as a hydrometer, always searching for the kind of piquant surprise that only coquettes can find attractive."[11] Accordingly France, the land of coquettes, allowed individuality in clothing, while Germany was the land of solid, durable clothing for the "dignified" woman. This "concern for national values" and the attendant demands for "German fashions" continued after 1918, reaching their high-water mark after 1930. It was all grist for the mill of the Nazis.

Alongside the traditional schools of fashion design, the Deutsche Meisterschule für Mode was founded in Munich in 1930. Its director, Gertrud Kornhas-Brandt, left no doubt about the leading role of Parisian and international design. However, this institution too was to succumb to the service of "German fashion." Ellen Semmelroth, one of the most industrious female propagandists in Nazi Germany, formulated the new agenda in the "international,

---

were to be found especially in towns and villages, but "the greater the size and the greater the variety, the more they resembled department stores." Cf. L. Berekoven, *Geschichte des deutschen Einzelhandels* (Frankfurt a.M., 1987), p. 39.
11. Cited in M. Grob, *Das Kleidungsverhalten jugendlicher Protestgruppen in Deutschland im 20. Jahrhundert*, vol. 47 of *Beiträge zur Volkskultur in Nordwestdeutschland*, ed. Volkskultur Kommission Westfalen-Lippe (Münster, 1985), pp. 135 and 150.

Jewified world of fashion: elimination of foreign manufacturers and a clothing style that reflects the nature of German women and the German way of life."[12] However, "no one in Munich thought that these official guidelines were to be taken seriously. They continued to take their cues [even after January 30, 1933] from Paris, Vienna, and London, as well as Berlin to a limited extent."[13] Long before 1933, however, dirndl-like clothes had been produced in Munich and were presented with great success by the firm Julius Wallach and others at the Berlin Fashion Week of 1921. In contrast to the previously rather expensive peasant costumes, hunting outfits, and loden green jackets, Wallach was able to offer dirndls in all price ranges. What is more, they satisfied the mounting interest in good health. All this, together with the fact that these dirndls resembled most Alpine peasant costumes, explains their popularity in the Munich area.

There is much evidence that these dirndls came closest to fulfilling the aims of those who sought a style of German clothing independent of international fashions. They were always highly recommended for rural women alongside a so-called *Eigenkleid*. Farm women and their daughters were especially encouraged not to succumb to fashion and never to wear international styles. A *Primer for Girls in Agricultural Schools* warned them "always to be wary of so-called stylish materials,"[14] for the best materials were always rooted in the local soil. "Genuine country clothing" could only be made from materials that one had produced and fabricated oneself. This kind of clothing was encouraged in a pamphlet issued by the *Reichsnährstand* after 1936, which advised: "Old Germanic women's clothing is ideally suited as a pattern: the loose dress and close-fitting bodice, sleeveless or with sleeves in one piece, together with a blouse worn underneath." This was then completed by an apron, "jewelry based on the rich forms of prehistoric times," and so forth.[15] The result was a dirndl-like creation with old Germanic trimmings, far removed from the world of international high fashion

    12. E. Semmelroth, "Neue Wege zur deutschen Modegestaltung," *NS Frauenwarte* 9, no. 2 (1933): 260f.
    13. A. Ley, "Aufschwung erst nach Dreiunddreißig. Mode in München zwischen Erstem Weltkrieg und Drittem Reich," in *Die Zwanziger Jahre in München* (the catalogue of the exhibition of the same name in the Munich city museum), *Schriften des Münchener Stadtmuseums* 8 (Munich, 1979), p. 215.
    14. W. Wagner, ed., *Die Schule der Jungbäuerin* (Berlin, 1932), pp. 189ff.
    15. *Nationalsozialistische Landpost* 48 (1936) or *Die deutsche Landfrau* 29 (1936): 156ff.

and symbolizing, it was emphasized, the "National Socialist outlook of the wearer."[16]

However the "German style," as it was described in countless
advertisements for dirndls, for "farm clothing," or for similar
fashions utterly disassociated from international high fashion, remained largely a matter of propaganda and demagoguery. The
German style was an ideal of a few people, far removed from the
reality of daily life. Not even the women who moved in the highest
Nazi circles deigned to wear "racially appropriate" clothing. Quite
the contrary, whenever they appeared in public they wore high
fashions of French inspiration. It is therefore not surprising that the
Nazi leadership never took an official position on fashion. "Nazi
adjurations about clothes that expressed innermost Aryan nature
were never intended to describe a real trend in fashion but rather to
foment anti-Semitism and promote the expulsion of the Jews from
the garment industry."[17] "Racially appropriate German clothing"
was said to depend above all on "the elimination of Jewish influence
and Jewish taste from the garment industry," according to a moving
account of the extermination of this tradition in Berlin by Uwe
Westphal.[18]

Here in the fashion capital of Germany were concentrated 91
percent of all garment manufacturing for women and girls. Jews
controlled about 50 percent of this production, and it was one of
their great accomplishments that they made Berlin a leading center
in the world of international fashion. They were helped in this by
the knowledge they had accumulated over the years under often
difficult conditions, their judgment and understanding of textiles
and clothing. The Nazis used this involvement from the outset to justify
their impending attacks on the allegedly Jewified garment industry and
finally, far worse, for the expulsion and annihilation of Jews.

The ejection of Jews from the economic life of the nation began
with the Enabling Act of February 28, 1933, which in the name of
"protecting the people and the state" allowed "expropriation and
restrictions on property" among other things. In April 1933 there
followed boycotts of Jewish businesses, while "voluntary Aryani-

16. Cf. S. Jacobeit, "Vom 'bäuerlichen Kleid' zur Kleidung von Klein- und
Mittelbäuerinnen im faschistischen Deutschland, 1933 bis 1945," in *Kleidung zwischen Tracht und Mode*, ed. Staatliche Museen in Berlin/Museum für Volkskunde
(Berlin/GDR, 1989), pp. 145–51.
17. Westphal (above, n. 5), p. 102.
18. Ibid., p. 110.

zation" and emigration began. In May the fascist Syndicate of German-Aryan Garment Industry Manufacturers was founded in Berlin for the purpose of Aryanizing the apparel industry. Membership in this organization, which fell under the federal Ministry of the Economy, was conditional on cutting all business connections with Jews. However, since this would have amounted to self-imposed isolation from much of the garment industry, no one joined voluntarily until 1936. At the same time, the Guild of Tailors of Women's Apparel refused to admit any new Jewish members and in the spring of 1936 established a fashion center in Frankfurt am Main in order to help drive Jews out of the fashion industry, to promote "German fashions," etc. The Nazi press worked particularly diligently at fomenting enmity against Jewish couturiers, first and foremost the SS organ *Das schwarze Korps*. The "forced Aryanization" that was later achieved could be foreseen as early as August 1935 in an article entitled "Fashion – An Economic Weapon." The final steps in the "exclusion of Jews from the economic life of Germany" and the expropriation of their property were taken when Jews and Aryans were forbidden to work together (April 22, 1938), Jewish citizens were required to register their possessions and property (April 26, 1938), and finally when the *Kristallnacht* or state-organized destruction and plundering of Jewish businesses was perpetrated in November 1938.

One example among many could be the experience of the department store and fashion house Nathan Israel on Spandauer Straße at the corner of Königstraße, which was one of the oldest and most respected women's fashion stores in Berlin. This family business had been founded in 1815 and Wilfried Israel was its final proprietor. On January 30, 1933, the company employed two thousand people. Through his foreign contacts and offers of financial support, Wilfried Israel was able to help thousands of young German Jews to emigrate. He himself was arrested repeatedly by the Nazis. By 1938 the Nathan Israel company still employed some one thousand people. Physical attacks on the company began on the afternoon of November 10, 1938:

> With cries of "Jews out," the Jewish employees were herded together and arrested. Young men armed with sticks and steel rods demolished displays, windows, and equipment. . . . Wilfried Israel managed to secure the release of those arrested and arranged for the emigration of the remaining two hundred employees. On February 6, 1939, . . . W. Israel

took leave of his colleagues and the employees of his company in a letter of thanks. Just five days later, the advertising pillars in Berlin announced that the business was henceforth in Aryan hands under a new name: The Downtown Store.[19]

Wilfried Israel himself emigrated to London. Thus by the end of 1938, the Nazis had made the Berlin clothing and fashion industry almost entirely "free of Jews," and "Aryan trustees" had been appointed to handle all "affairs and legal matters inside and outside the courts." The Syndicate of German-Aryan Garment Industry Manufacturers proved particularly "helpful" in these respects. On June 1, 1938, it introduced its own label, which guaranteed "goods from Aryan hands." With over seven hundred members by this time, its influence extended throughout "the entire garment industry in Germany."[20] With the help of the syndicate, the highly fertile cooperation of Jewish and non-Jewish companies in the garment industry was obliterated. Meanwhile, the syndicate's own dreams of booming production and vibrant German exports faded. Plummeting exports and reduced total sales were the immediate results as the diversity and quality of German clothing declined. However, this leveling and flattening of the clothing industry only made the switch to uniform production all the easier and therefore probably served the wishes of the Nazi hierarchy much more than an elegant fashion industry for the German people, who, in any case, were obliged to adapt to mounting war production with the adoption of the four-year plan of 1936. What little fashionable clothing was still manufactured was intended largely for export. As the production of uniforms soared, it could only have been "neurotic anti-Semitism" that prompted the author of a 1935 brochure on men's clothing to laud the "discarding of fashion trends hostile to the German people" and the "return to healthy clothes production for the sake of the people."[21]

The destruction of Jewish influence in the garment industry itself was accompanied by the Aryanization of the fashion press. For instance, *Der Konfektionär*, the most important source of information about the fashion industry alongside *Textilzeitung*, was already Aryanized in 1933 by Nazi editors who gave it the subtitle:

---

19. See ibid., p. 183, where Westphal expressly mentions the "W. Israel" book by Naomi Shepherd.
20. Ibid., p. 113.
21. H. Riecken, *Die Männertracht im neuen Deutschland* (Kassel, 1935), pp. 7f.

German Textile Culture in Clothing and Homes. The former editor in chief, Erich Greiffenhagen, left Germany. In 1936 the *Textilzeitung* was renamed the *Neue Textilzeitung.*

Die Dame, one of the oldest and most elegant German fashion magazines with an international reputation, was published by Ullstein, later renamed Deutscher Verlag. In spite of Aryanization, the splendidly arranged magazine managed to retain a few Jewish contributors, for instance, Alice Newman and Helen Hessel who wrote regular fashion reports from Paris. This irked the Nazi press and prompted another nasty, anti-Semitic outburst from *Das schwarze Korps:* "We at *Das schwarze Korps* have already taken many a stand and exposed the deceit behind many claims of loyalty. We shall also vigorously expose this salute to romanticism and charm, so that the front of international fashion fools is unmasked for what it really is: alien to the ways of our race in spite of all Aryanization!"[22] Clothes that emphasized the charm of the wearer, that had a "libertarian life of their own," did not suit the uniformed scribes of the SS and were decried as "alien to our race." There was no place in the Third Reich for "alien," "non-Aryan" clothes. Not only clothes were destroyed but a whole tradition was annihilated before the war even began – the result of being liquidated or Aryanized. Jews were expelled, deported, and killed in numbers that can no longer be accurately determined. Uwe Westphal looked into 176 Jewish companies in the women's fashion industry in Berlin alone around 1933; by 1940 there were none left. What tragic biographies lie behind many of these names. In some cases, even their old addresses have been lost. We would like to name a few in memory of all: Altschul & Sinzheimer in Friedrichstraße; Martin Burger; Herman Gerson; I. Herz on Markgrafenstraße; Hesse & Heyl on Krausenstraße; Kersten & Tuteur on Leipziger Straße; Küchler & Punkus on Jägerstraße; Löb & Levy on Krausenstraße; Michel & Koppel; Schwarz, Sachs & Wolfsohn on Mohrenstraße; Semmel & Friedlaender; and H. Taus on Kronenstraße. Many more from regions far beyond Berlin could be included; the number is endless. A long list can be found in the "Deutschland= Information" put out by the Central Committee of the German Communist Party in 1938.[23]

22. Cited in Westphal (above, n. 5), p. 131.
23. See H. Eschwege, ed., *Kennzeichen J, Bilder, Dokumente, Berichte zur Geschichte der Verbrechen des Hitlerfaschismus an den deutschen Juden, 1933–1945* (Berlin/GDR, 1981), pp. 136ff.

Henceforth, the urge to press the German population into uniform knew no bounds. The increasing militarization of everyday life helped drive elegant fashions from the streets, while "racially pure" couturiers drew their inspiration from the military. Standardized clothing lacking all individuality became ever more widespread throughout all age groups (after all, it was good for discipline). The wearing of standardized, staple clothing became a badge of support for the regime or at least evidence of one's willingness to go along with it.

Many manufacturers, merchants, and even fashion magazines adopted the sartorial views of the Nazis, and soon, with their help, street clothing was characterized by swarms of uniforms. Thus *Vobachs Familienhilfe*, a hitherto highly respectable "practical family and fashion magazine, " recommended as early as its 1933 edition a pattern for a sports shirt for eight- to sixteen-year-olds as well as a so-called SA shirt in neck sizes 36 to 46 centimeters, which "sports-loving gentlemen will welcome with special joy" and which women, of course, were supposed to make.[24]

Clothing with a Nazi stamp filled the local press already in 1933, as can be seen, for instance, in an example from the Bavarian town of Dingolfing. Here the *Dingolfinger Anzeiger* dedicated a whole page at the end of April 1933 to the uniforms and insignia of Nazi organizations under the heading, "The Brown Battalions." Business reacted immediately: "Special Sale" announced the M. Kammerer department store on May 9 in the Dingolfing daily: "Thanks to a large contract with our producers, we are able to offer substantial savings in the purchase of SA uniforms. Compare prices and quality! You will be convinced and head right on down. Good corduroy SA trousers, excellent needlework, gentlemen's sizes, only 6.50, boys' sizes correspondingly less. Good twilled brown shirts, 4.50." The edition of May 20 offered "brown-shirts made of good cotton" and "SS trousers of good wool gabardine" for 6 marks and further recommended the White Cross drugstore for "Hitler-brown for the dying of shirts, cloth, etc." A Christmas insert of several pages in the local paper in 1933 suggested above all "practical presents," including, according to an advertisement for M. Meindl Söhne, a "specialty shop for gentlemen's and boys' clothing," various peasant costume outfits for big and small as well as a *Jungvolk* uniform to fulfill "his Christmas wish with shirt,

24. *Vobachs Familienhilfe* 7 (1933): 19.

trousers, cap, belt, shoulder strap, scarf, and a leather knot."[25] Children and young people were to be diverted at an early age from the individuality of the family and streamed into authoritarian state organizations. The attempt to assimilate the youth after 1933 found symbolic expression in standardized clothing and the identification it expressed with the ruling Nazi ideology. "Especially among the youth, clothing must become an integral part of training," Hitler had written in *Mein Kampf*. This "training," which was to be "physically, mentally, and morally in the spirit of National Socialism and service to the people and our national community," was the keystone of the Hitler Youth. In accordance with the Nazi maxim, "You are nothing, the people are everything," even ten-year-olds were habituated to unquestioning conformity and subordination. "This tallied with the German tradition of submission and obedience toward authority, except that the guiding values of family and kin were replaced by the anonymous 'people.' Devotion to the 'people' prepared the youth blindly to obey and to carry out orders of a kind as yet unsuspected."[26] The external and visible sign of this willingness was the uniform, which for the first time in the history of children's clothing was distinguished from the uniforms of those over eighteen. After abolishing all previous youth organizations, the Nazis incorporated certain popular fashion features, taken especially from hiking organizations, in the uniforms of the Hitler Youth. Typical of the didactic intent behind this clothing were strict rules about when it should and should not be worn. Curious anomalies emerged however, for instance, the recommendation that the Hitler Youth uniform be worn to confirmation, as explained by a former candidate for confirmation in the Swabian town of Bodelshausen: "We were confirmed on March 18, 1934. We were told in school, 'You can't go to confirmation in traditional garb any longer' (at the time, it was customary to purchase a first confirmation suit and to wear a top hat for the first time). We could, however, wear the brown uniform and approach the altar to be confirmed in this way."

The boys therefore went in this dress and sometimes even went so far as to set up their Hitler Youth pennant in church.[27]

25. F. Markmiller, "Fest- und Feiergestaltung während der NS-Zeit. Im Spiegel der Lokalpresse Dingolfing, 1933–1937," *Der Storchenturm. Geschichtsblätter für die Landkreise um Dingolfing, Landau und Vilsbiburg* 21 and 22 (1986–87), vol. 42/43, pp. 255ff.

26. Weber-Kellermann (above, n. 2), p. 198.

27. Cited in *Nationalsozialismus im Landkreis Tübingen. Eine Heimatkunde*, ed.

No less strict were the rules governing sex roles, and various other roles, and prohibitions against anything that might have diminished the standardized look. Girls, for instance, were not allowed to wear any jewelry with their Bund deutscher Mädel uniforms, and their hair had to be styled in the "German" pigtail. An ever increasing number of ten- to eighteen-year-olds accepted these prescribed uniforms: though only 2,300,000 young people out of a total of 7,529,000 were members of the Hitler Youth in 1933, these numbers rose by 1939 to 8,700,000 in a total youth population of 8,870,000.[28] (Beginning in 1939, refusal to join was punishable after passage of the implementation order of the Hitler Youth Act.) Very few boys and girls managed to remain outside this compulsory organization. Most were fascinated by uniforms and compulsory group behaviors, which provided an illusion of egalitarianism. Any boy or girl could aspire – so long as he or she exhibited the appropriate Nazi mindset – to a leadership role in the Hitler Youth or the Bund deutscher Mädel and to wear a multitude of various braids and cords or decorated shoulder straps as visible signs of his or her distinguished position. Hundreds of thousands exercised power here for the first time – with little thought for the mounting perversion of the youth. Most did not even notice the state of subordination and submissiveness into which they had been "led" when they later slipped off their Hitler Youth uniform in exchange for a *Wehrmacht* uniform.

The onset of the Second World War brought a radical change in the clothing situation. As with foodstuffs, the switch from a rearmament economy to a war economy brought immediate rationing of all essential clothing commodities. The rationing system and the controlled economy that accompanied it had been prepared for years, though they were not formally introduced until Sunday, August 27, 1939, when rationing was announced on the radio without any forewarning. Henceforth rationing cards were required for the purchase of textiles, shoes, and shoe leather.

On November 1, 1939, the first National Clothing Card came into effect, valid until October 31, 1940. In order to cover clothing needs as determined by the state, one hundred "points" were awarded to be spent on clothing, underwear, and sewing and

---

Ludwig-Uhland-Institut of the University of Tübingen under U. Jeggle (Tübingen, 1988), p. 144.
   28. See A. Klönne, *Jugend im Dritten Reich* (Cologne, 1982), p. 34.

knitting yarn, subdivided into points for men, women, boys and girls (from three to fifteen years of age), and infants. The first two clothing coupons were valid for one year and the third for sixteen months, while the fourth was supposed to last from January 1, 1943, until June 30, 1944.

Though abundant clothing reserves were said to be available, they did not suffice in reality to cover even the first coupon. After a few weeks, an appreciable shortfall in certain clothing items was reported everywhere. Supplies were particularly tight in three critical areas: children's clothing, shoes, and work or professional clothing. Primarily responsible for this situation were mounting difficulties in obtaining raw materials and a steep increase in orders from the *Wehrmacht*. The shortage of all types of clothing, from shoes to every kind of cloth, grew worse as the war progressed.

The Nazi policy of economic autarky included the textile industry, of course, and led to a shift in the raw materials and the yarns and fabrics utilized.[29] While cotton and wool had previously been the most popular materials, they were now increasingly displaced by rayon and spun rayon.

Jews suffered especially under rationing. "No clothing coupons," noted Victor Klemperer in his diary on the evening of June 2, 1942, as he turned up a total of thirty-one different ordinances governing Jewish life in Nazi Germany.[30] "A lesser race requires less room, fewer clothes, less to eat, and less culture than a superior one," Reich labor leader Robert Ley had announced in the January 30, 1940 edition of the anti-Semitic hate sheet *Angriff*. Degraded to noncitizens, Jews could hardly continue to receive clothing coupons and rationing cards, and these were eliminated for Jews on November 14, 1939. However, the Jewish Winter Assistance Works had already organized various forms of self-help; emigrants, for instance donated clothing for those who remained behind in Germany.

After September 1, 1941, Jews were required to wear a "yellow patch." The Police Ordinance on the Identification of Jews forbade "Jews of seven years of age or more to appear in public without a Star of David plainly visible."[31] After years of isolation and degradation, a cloth mark was the first step on the road to ghettoization

29. According to *Forces of Production in Germany, 1917–18 to 1945*, edited by a collective (Berlin/GDR, 1988), p. 134.
30. *Nach Sonntag. Kulturpolitische Wochenzeitung* 46 (1988), ed. Cultural Union of the GDR, p. 5.
31. Eschwege (above, n. 23), p. 177.

and annihilation. The first mass deportations began in October 1941.

Section 1, paragraph 2 of the ordinance proclaimed: "The Star of David shall consist of a six-pointed star, the size of the palm of the hand, drawn in black on yellow cloth, with the inscription 'Jew.' It shall be firmly attached and visible on the left breast of the clothing." The new ordinance took effect on September 19, 1941. Among the German population, yellow had actually lost its meaning as the color of contempt many centuries earlier. However, the Fourth Lateran Council had decreed in 1215 that "nonbelievers, especially Jews, should wear clothing that distinguished them from Christians. In order to identify them, most European countries introduced a 'yellow patch' made of cloth that had to be worn in a visible location on the chest." In 1530 Jews were again ordered to wear a yellow patch.[32]

In Hitler Germany, however, Jews had been branded long before the introduction of the star. No individual identity was left to them. The "J" stamp in their passports, the given names Sarah or Israel, and now the Star of David became "signs that deprived Jews of all human dignity and symbols to all except those who were meant. Thus the bestarred 'Jew Israel' and 'Jewess Sarah' were first deprived of everything that did not suit the 'Aryan superman' and then 'exterminated'."[33] Erich Fried had written in his remembrances of "These the Dead": "Cease making them a sign of all that is alien!"

In the year of the third clothing card (1941–42), the consumer goods industry experienced its greatest production decline, beneath the low attained when the Great Depression bottomed out in Germany in 1932. The population began to experience genuine privation in respect to clothing. The Fourth Reich Clothing Card was announced in November 1942. After the turning point of Stalingrad, the resort to total war caused such cutbacks in civilian clothing that not even 1 percent of total demand for some products could be met.[34] In the district of Meissen, for instance, only five

32. H. Nixdorf and H. Müller, *Weiße Westen – Rote Roben. Von den Farbordnungen des Mittelalters zum individuellen Farbgeschmack*, catalogue of the exhibition of the same name (West Berlin, 1983), pp. 103ff.

33. H. Rosenstrauch, ed., *Aus Nachbarn wurden Juden. Ausgrenzung und Selbstbehauptung, 1933–1942* (West Berlin, 1988), pp. 80f.

34. Cf. D. Eichholtz, *Geschichte der deutschen Kriegswirtschaft, 1939–1945* (Berlin/GDR, 1985), vol. 2, *1941–1943*, pp. 385f.

men's suits and two boys' outfits were available to meet the demand generated by 25,000 men's clothing coupons and 6,000 boys' coupons. The cutbacks, according to a report, went "far beyond acceptable limits."[35] The situation deteriorated so badly that only one article of underwear and outer clothing was produced per child of all age categories. Only five diapers were available.[36] Public outrage over the clothing penury was greatest in areas such as Leipzig, which saw the Bund deutscher Mädel receive "thousands of meters of material for dance costumes" at the same time that there was a "severe shortage of diapers" and the "collection of old clothes and cloths" was encouraged.[37]

Actions such as the Reich cloth collection, the clothing collections of the NSV, and continual collections in the schools were intended to improve the situation. Sought after were "pieces of cloth that are no longer required,"[38] i.e., rags. Collections of articles of clothing that were no longer worn were carried out time and time again to the accompaniment of loud propaganda campaigns. At the same time, there were also campaigns to "make new from old" and "make one from two." Eventually, the willingness of the population to continue contributing went into steep decline and discontent spread. Sicherheitsdienst reporters passed along the information in June 1943 that "housewives say that they have no intention of contributing outmoded or partially worn-out articles of clothing. Textiles that can no longer be worn are used as dusting and cleaning rags because the latter have not been available for a long time."[39]

"Make new from old" had been a standard principle of thrifty German women for many generations. Now, however, the Nazis turned their powerful propaganda machinery to elevating the old cliché to a national mission and to suggesting that in so doing one could "take pleasure in creative activity." Instructions and recommendations were available in countless books and brochures about the education and training of women, in calendars and almanacs, in fashion magazines, and in many other publications. Almut Junker and Eva Stille came across a striking example in the

35. H. Boberach, ed., *Meldungen aus dem Reich. Die geheimen Lageberichte des Sicherheitsdienstes der SS, 1938–1945* (Herrsching, 1984), 12:4780.
36. See R. Wagenführ, *Die deutsche Industrie im Kriege, 1939–1945* (Berlin, 1963), pp. 174ff., table 5.
37. Staatsarchiv Leipzig, "SD-Inlandslagebericht" of June 24, 1942.
38. Since collections of this type were carried out during the First World War under the name "rag collections," the Nazis did not use this term.
39. *Meldungen* Boberach (above, n. 35), 14:5351.

magazine *Mode und Wäsche*, which informed its readers how to
make a single pair of men's trousers into: one brassiere, two sanitary
napkins, two dust cloths or one dish cloth, one washcloth and two
reinforcements for stocking toes. All that remained was a stitched
piece of cloth – just perfect for polishing silver. The instructions (all
in verse in German) ended:

> Do not think me insignificant,
> For my sense of economics is just magnificent,
> Cotton costs a lot of dough,
> So make it stretch, and don't be slow,
> Everything – whether shirt or pants or coat
> Ends up far too soon in the rag heap!
> So turn your heart and your hand,
> To the service of our dear fatherland![40]

This sort of alleged service to the fatherland was drummed into little
boys and girls in their first readers and into young women who
were expected to collect all manner of patches and pieces of cloth in
their trousseaus in order one day to turn to making "new from
old."[41]

Tailors too were required to make an extra effort in this direction,
using and reusing worn materials. As early as 1940 their professional association, the Reich Guild Union, had initiated an action
"tatters into treasures in the clothes closet." Tailors, however,
showed little enthusiasm for all this. They were increasingly occupied producing uniforms and were burdened with requests from the
civilian population to make garments using cloth that had been
hoarded or stolen.[42] The *Report from the Reich* announced that
tailors were then swamped with work in 1943 when they were
forbidden to produce new outer clothing and were confined to
repair jobs. The definition of repairs resulted in some difficulty,
because they included alterations and redesigning as well as
mending.[43] Offers to repair outer clothing, underwear, and shoes
came not only from Nazi women's organizations, but also from

40. Cited in A. Junker and E. Stille, *Die Zweite Haut. Zur Geschichte der
Unterwäsche, 1700–1960* (Frankfurt a.M., 1988), vol. 39 of *Kleine Schriften des
Historischen Museums Frankfurt*, pp. 329ff; see as well *Flick-Werk. Reparieren und
Neunutzen in der Alltagskultur*, catalogue of the exhibition of the same name in the
State Museum of Württemberg (Stuttgart, 1983).
41. *Taschenbuch für Haushalts- und Berufsschulen* (Dresden, 1940), p. 45.
42. pp. 1874f. Boberach (above, n. 35), vol. 6.
43. Ibid. 13: 5251f.

department stores and factories. In the Berlin light-bulb works OSRAM, "the girls in the factory pool" called in 1940 for worn-out textiles, and in October 1944 a drop-off area was established on the premises for "heels and stitching repairs, stockings that need soles or footlets," etc. In the same year, the C & A department store operated by the Dutch firm Brenninkmeyer near OSRAM offered to repair gentlemen's, ladies', and children's clothing.[44]

In spite of all the hardships, contemporaries report that the clothing situation was still generally tolerable until German cities came under heavy bombardment. Clothes after all are one of those durable consumer items whose use can be prolonged, if necessary, for a very long time before all possibility of mending disappears. However, intensified bombing toward the end of 1943 resulted in total or partial destruction of more than 6 percent of all housing in Germany,[45] including of course private clothes closets. After August 1943, the third and fourth clothing cards were virtually useless because so many supplies were diverted to help those who had lost their clothes in the bombing. The dimensions of the problem are evident in the Nazis' own estimate that clothing production lay "about one-third beneath the minimum necessary wartime level."[46] Reports to this effect flowed in from Breslau, Danzig, Kiel, Königsberg, Stettin, and Weimar. In Berlin it was reported in December 1943 that "there are almost no supplies of cloth at the present time."[47]

As more and more housing and factories were bombed and textiles were destroyed, the clothing crisis intensified. Particularly hard hit were forced laborers who had been deported to farms in Germany and were supposed to be clothed by the local population and prisoners who worked on war production in lice-infested work camps, where clothing hardly deserved the name and sanitation was very poor. By the autumn and winter of 1944–45, "what we prisoners wore could hardly be called clothing," reports Ruth Elias, who survived Auschwitz and worked in the camp of Taucha near Leipzig. "We had no underclothing at all, only the striped overalls – no socks or stockings, only wooden clogs on our feet."[48]

44. Stadtarchiv Berlin, OSRAM records 0.431/311; 0.414; 0.665/146.
45. According to Eichholtz (above, n. 34), 2: 387.
46. Ibid.
47. Boberach (above, n. 35), 15: 5790f., 6159–65.
48. R. Elias, *Die Hoffnung erhielt mich am Leben. Mein Weg von Theresienstadt und Auschwitz nach Israel* (Munich, 1988), p. 213.

Wooden shoes and clogs were produced by the millions in Hitler Germany, apparently 2.6 million pairs in 1943 alone, though never enough for the millions of needy feet. The clatter of wooden shoes and clogs could be heard far and near when the columns of closely guarded men and women set out to work each morning in their peculiar striped uniforms and returned each evening to camp, whether in Mauthausen or Oranienburg, in Ravensbrück or Regensburg. The sound continued to echo long after they had passed – an unforgettable experience that many still remember to this day as a symbol of Nazi barbarity.[49]

49. Representative of the many sources is the impressive work of Peter Brendel's class: "Das Lager Collosseum in Regensburg," in D. Balinski and W. Schmidt, *Die Kriegsjahre in Deutschland, 1939 bis 1945* (Hamburg, 1985), pp. 251ff. (a result of the high-school student competition in German history for the prize given by the president of the Federal Republic of Germany).

HARTMUT ZWAHR

Young Academics and Their Concerns

Notes on Social History Taken from the Letters of Carl Friedrich Gauß (1802–1812) and Moritz Wilhelm Drobisch (1827–1837)

This selection focuses on academic conditions in the early nineteenth century as perceived by young academics, touching on questions of career (though only tangentially), communications, the place of women, the family, and economic conditions at the time.* The views of the young academics necessarily reflect the bourgeois lifestyle to which they were accustomed and which must be taken into account as we sort and evaluate the results of our research. Seen in this way, our research is comprised within the larger topic of the bourgeoisie, bourgeois society, and civil consciousness. It would be tempting but rather misleading to compare the situation a century ago with conditions today, though our modern imaginations and experiences will inevitably be involved as we read or listen to this text. Academic discourse does not after all require intensive communication. The academic conditions enumerated above are illuminated through the biographies of two men: the mathematicians Gauß and Drobisch, as well as some of their correspondents. The lack of significant personal contact between these two men facilitates our endeavor: the typical views of their generations thereby stand out all the more clearly. Since the basic situa-

---

* Taken from *Wissenschafts- und Universitätsgeschichte in Sachsen im 18. und 19. Jahrhundert. Beiträge des internationalen Kolloquiums zum 575. Jahr der Universitätsgründung am 26. und 27. November 1984 in Leipzig* (Berlin/GDR, 1987), pp. 207–16. Academics is used here as the best but not fully adequate translation of *Gelehrte*.

tions in which young academics found themselves were so similar, the number of cases under study was not extended any further. Several additional academic careers are mentioned in passing, though more for the sake of contrast. It is general academic conditions in the early nineteenth century, as revealed in our basic types, that makes up the significance of the topic, rather than all the possible individual variations in them. First we wish to look at the two young academics themselves. Do they deserve to be called academics at all? Gauß in Braunschweig and Göttingen after 1802, carrying on an exchange of letters with the physician and astronomer Heinrich Wilhelm Olbers;[1] Drobisch in Leipzig after 1827, exchanging letters with Johann Friedrich Herbart.[2] It seems to me that they certainly do deserve to be considered academics. Both were twenty-five years old at the time their correspondance began and held doctorates. Drobisch had married young and was a professor in his second year; Gauß, still single, was already famous,[3] and his *Disquisitiones arithmeticae* form the foundations of modern number theory. Much older men showed genuine respect for the young Gauß, who hoped not to waste the "precious time" allotted to him on "bootless tasks."[4] The mere thought of intruding on the time of this genius dismayed many people, who excused themselves in advance. Drobisch did not enjoy such fame, either as a mathematician or as a philosopher under the influence of Herbart after 1842. However, his eminent *Neue Darstellung der Logik nach ihren einfachsten Verhältnissen* (Leipzig, 1835) and his many contributions toward the founding of the Saxon Academy of Sciences in Leipzig link his name as well with modern scientific developments and make it an integral part of the scientific life of the GDR.

Both were certainly *young* academics, at an age when modern male students at the University of Leipzig are just finishing their

1. See *Carl Friedrich Gauß – Heinrich Wilhelm Matthias Olbers, Briefwechsel*, vol. 1 (Berlin, 1900; repr., Hildesheim and New York, 1976). The first letter from Gauß to Olbers is dated January 18, 1802.
2. See Joh. Fr. Herbarts collected works, edited in chronological order by Karl Fehrbach and Otto Flügel, 17 vols. Revised by Theodor Fritzsch: *Briefe von und an J. F. Herbart*, vol. 2, *1808–1832* (Langensalza, 1912); vol. 3, *1833–1838* (Langensalza, 1912). The correspondence began in November and December 1827: Herbart to Drobisch (Königsberg, November 22, 1827), Drobisch to Herbart (Leipzig, December 23, 1827). See *Briefe*, 2:161f.
3. The pertinent biographical material can be found in the *Allgemeine Deutsche Biographie* (Berlin), 8: 430ff.; 48:80ff.
4. To Olbers, October 26, 1802, *Briefwechsel*, p. 106.

studies while female students are preparing to defend their A thesis. The process for selecting promising pupils soon picked out both Gauß and Drobisch, sending the former to the Rechenschule in Braunschweig and the latter to the Nikolaischule in Leipzig. Although of simple origins (Gauß's father was an artisan and Drobisch's father was a town clerk), they were not stymied by the educational system, which only later began to discriminate systematically against children of non-middle-class backgrounds. They also enjoyed the support of benefactors, in Gauß's case Duke Carl Wilhelm von Braunschweig himself.

The registration records of the University of Leipzig provide an insight into the social origins of the student body, though not before 1832 when Drobisch was already a professor. Among 1,000 registered students in the years 1832 to 1834, 172 were still sons of the working class. By 1846–49, this number had dropped to 113 per thousand. Rather striking in these statistics is the elimination of artisans' and farmers' sons, who were replaced by the sons of lower-level city and state employees and soon afterwards of office workers as well. The pivotal educational decisions were made lower down the ladder, in the high schools (*Gymnasien*), where scholarships established in the estates of wealthy citizens were no longer awarded to the progeny of farmers and guild masters as frequently as had been the case.

It was at this time that the university took on its middle-class hue, both in the social composition of the student body and in the combination of teaching and research, which established the reputation of Leipzig and several other German universities as working universities (*Arbeits-Universitäten*). Rhetoric alone no longer sufficed. Now the trend was toward hard work in laboratories and institutes, with the source material and with the material world in general. Germany's substantial underdevelopment in the natural sciences was becoming apparent. This drove young men such as Gustav Theodor Fechner, a pastor's son from Lausitz and a private lecturer in physics after 1823, to spend long hours trying to close the knowledge gap in the damp chambers of the old Pauliner cloister, which had housed the University of Leipzig for centuries. He held lectures in his own tiny apartment, carried out experiments using the unsuitable facilities of the Physikalischer Apparat, and then spent his evenings translating English and French texts. The result of the enormous output was physical collapse, temporary blindness, deep depression, and writing by means of dictation.

Many other young academics shared this sort of fate.

We do not wish to tarry, however, with these exhausting struggles to overcome what appeared to be Germany's hopeless backwardness in science. Our view of the times would be distorted if we failed to examine the careers of other academics as well, with particular attention to the specific concerns of young scholars. It will suffice simply to outline the careers of a few Leipzig professors, for instance, that of the founder of Semitic paleography, Eduard Friedrich Ferdinand Beer (1805–1841). The son of a master tailor from Bautzen, Beer supported himself through his studies by working on the side, starving his way to his doctorate and first academic position in 1833. As a private lecturer, he wrung scientific achievements of enduring value from his weakened body and was rewarded in 1838 by being appointed an associate professor without salary. He died in 1841 at the age of thirty-six, already assured of lasting fame and an annual pension of one hundred *Taler*. The latter came too late, for Beer had already expended the "last breath of his life on his *Explanation of Sinaitic Inscriptions*,"[5] which appeared in 1840.

Contrasting experiences are offered by Eduard Brockhaus (1806–1877), the jurists and legal historians Gustav Friedrich Hänel (1792–1878) and Gustav Ernst Heimbach (1810–1851), and Eduard Friedrich Pöppig (1798–1868), the research explorer who undertook a journey down the Amazon River in the early 1820s.[6] The scions of entrepreneurs, they lived off the wealth accumulated by their parents and grandparents and devoted themselves entirely to their academic studies. Working at self-selected tasks, they finally forced open the gates of academe by virtue of their undeniable accomplishments.

Neither Gauß nor Drobisch followed these alternative paths to scientific success. Outside assistance in addition to their accomplishments enabled them to become recognized academics while still young. Their problems were neither material, as in Beer's case, nor the lack of scientific recognition and long years in the wilderness before achieving academic success, as in the case of Brockhaus, who delved deeper and deeper into Sanskrit and Persian between 1825 and 1835 before finally attracting attention with his first successful translations from the old Indian folk tales of Somadeva. Brockhaus received a university appointment at the age of thirty-two, became an assistant professor of Oriental languages in Jena in

5. See the *Allgemeine Deutsche Biographie*, 2:247.
6. See ibid., 47:263ff.; 26:421ff., 49:751ff.; 11:326f.

1839 and in Leipzig in 1841, and later, in 1848, became a full professor of East Asian languages.

The concerns of Gauß and Drobisch were more mundane and therefore, perhaps, more representative of their entire generations because they touched most academics working under similar conditions. These concerns tended to be broader and more existential in nature and underlay the specific social and career concerns of particular academic groups.

1. Communication Problems

Overland distances could be covered in the early nineteenth century only on foot or by postal carriage. The first railroad connections in Germany were not established between Leipzig and Dresden until 1836 to 1839 and the second between Leipzig and Magdeburg until 1838 to 1840. Good communications, however, are the lifeblood of science, and so scientists living in different, though not so very distant communities, carried on lifelong correspondences. Olbers wrote to Gantz in 1802: "I thank you from the bottom of my heart for the friendly communication of your outstanding methodology."[7] He regretted that "it has been a long time since I last had the pleasure of corresponding with you."[8] Drobisch, back in Leipzig, advised Herbart in Königsberg that it was a great delight "to leap by pen over the one hundred miles that separate us and to carry on at least a one-sided conversation with you."[9] The rapidity with which a response could be received depended on horses, whose endurance also determined the stages, i.e., the points at which fresh horses were substituted. Olbers, for instance, wished to provide Gauß "as quickly as possible by this galloping post with the news of a comet,"[10] The departure time of the post often determined the end of letters (written of course with a goose quill): "The last quarter hour before the departure of the post has arrived."[11] Correspondences such as those carried on by Gauß and Olbers or by Drobisch and Herbart until 1837 belonged to the final days of the horse-powered mail delivery. The letters constituted the conver-

7. To Gauß, August 18, 1802, *Briefwechsel*, p. 67.
8. To Gauß, October 28, 1803, *Briefwechsel*, p. 164.
9. To Herbart, June 17, 1831. *Briefe*, 2:241.
10. To Gauß, March 14, 1804, *Briefwechsel*, p. 182.
11. To Olbers, February 1, 1802, ibid., p. 10.

sation. Gauß in Braunschweig anticipated the arrival of a particular piece of information *"posttäglich,"*[12] i.e., on those days when the post returned. The correspondents counted in "postal days." Herbart wrote to Drobisch: "I cannot possibly let this postal day pass without expressing to you my boundless gratitude."[13]
Actual meetings were infrequent and carefully prepared. They were seen as important occasions bringing hours of delightful conversation with long-lasting consequences, fruitful exchanges, productive disagreements, or happy accord, sometimes bitter disappointments. Gauß visited the aging Olbers in Bremen in 1803. First, a flurry of letters were exchanged by jolting postal carriage, expressing a curious array of needs and concerns. Travel was looked upon as a great adventure, and every attempt was made to minimize the risks (Kant, it is well known, never brought himself to leave Königsberg). Olbers began on April 2, 1803: "I would like very much to meet you in person. The eighteen miles from Braunschweig to here are easily traversed. You would feel entirely at home in my house, could live quite as you please, and could use my books and telescopes." Gauß responded six days later: "Your friendly invitation matches my desires exactly, and I hope at least by the end of this summer to have the joy of embracing you in Bremen. I look forward to it already and expect that I will be able to learn a great deal from you." One month later, Olbers wrote to Gauß (May 5, 1803): "May it be God's will that you do not meet with any unexpected obstacles; then I shall be able to rely on your word." Gauß replied on May 30: "I hope that the gathering storm clouds in this region will not pose any serious hindrances to my dearest desire." Olbers responded on June 8 that Gauß should not let himself be "dissuaded by any military clashes" from granting Olbers "the great pleasure" of a visit and an opportunity to meet personally. "Here in our neutral imperial city all is peaceful, and the French make every effort not to intrude on our territory. Your room, dear Gauß, is always ready, and my arms are always open to receive you."

Gauß finally set off for Bremen on June 22, 1803, arriving on the following Friday. The visit ended with a declaration of lasting friendship.[14] Gauß expressed his gratitude in a letter of June 19,

12. To Olbers, December 21, 1802, ibid., p. 118.
13. To Drobisch, November 26, 1828, *Briefe*, 2:181.
14. For the various texts see: *Briefwechsel*, pp. 144f., 150ff. Equally informative is

"with the sweet memory of our wonderful days together" still fresh in his mind. "I returned from my trip in a wonderful frame of mind," he added.[15] Drobisch visited Herbart in Berlin on Good Friday, 1830, and the latter visited the young professor in Leipzig in May. The desire to meet had first arisen in July 1828.[16] Drobisch asked his correspondent whether he "considered that a particular purpose could be served beyond the general usefulness of a personal meeting and the rapid exchange of ideas which it would afford" and whether Herbart hoped for instance to achieve "an oral settlement of our opinions, or an agreement to further our studies or any joint undertakings."[17] Herbart had been in Berlin in April 1829, "eighty miles closer" to Drobisch than previously, as he pointed out. Drobisch, however, still failed to appear, despite the shortened distance.[18] Herbart decided in January 1830 that something must be holding Drobisch back, and so he resolved to take "the express postal carriage from Berlin to Leipzig."[19]

Though academics were eager to meet, conditions were very difficult, and travel in a postal carriage could easily become a ghastly experience. Communications had not improved appreciably since the Gauß-Olbers exchange at the beginning of the century. Advanced applied research produced specialists who were keen to meet their colleagues, if only in order to converse about their common field of study. But communications still posed an immense obstacle. The manifold barriers and impediments to meeting colleagues and exchanging views with them in person made letter writing a cornerstone of academic communication in the late eighteenth and early nineteenth centuries. It was still highly unusual to attend congresses on specialized topics, with the exception of the fairs in Leipzig or Frankfurt am Main, for example. Associations and learned societies communicated with one another by letter or by exchanges of papers and newsletters. Lecture tours were rare and only became more frequent with the development of railroads. These created new supraregional and even national forms of communication that al-

a comment from Olbers in 1815: "Easter is finally in view. . . . If the weather stays good, the roads will be in excellent condition." Ibid., p. 582.

15. To Olbers, July 19, 1803, ibid., p. 115.
16. To Drobisch, July 24, 1828, Berlin, April 8, 1829; *Briefe*, 2:172, 188.
17. Ibid., p. 189, Drobisch to Herbart, April 10, 1829.
18. Ibid., p. 188, Herbart in Berlin to Drobisch, April 8, 1829.
19. Ibid., p. 206, Herbart in königsberg to Drobisch, January 31, 1830.

lowed oral conversation to begin to replace written correspondence. The art form of letter writing was slowly overshadowed by other forms of communication. Finally the telegraph and telephone delivered the coup de grace to written correspondence. Who indeed is more aware of this than the historian who, amid the sudden lack of written records, notes that academics began speaking with one another rather than corresponding at a certain time and place.

Herbart and Drobisch agreed – by letter, of course – on the slightest details of their meeting. Herbart proposed the hotel Zum Großfürsten Alexander near the "new" Friedrichstraße where it goes down to the Spree and cuts across Burgstraße. This hotel was not exactly magnificent, "but also not bad, and I shall take up quarters there with my wife if at all possible. It would be most helpful if you could take a room there or very close by, in the König von Portugal, for instance, if you want to live in grander surroundings. Our best hope, I believe, is the morning hours, because hosts of visitors are inevitable. If we fail to take up lodgings near one another, the big city will prove very distracting."[20] Here a new impediment is added to the original difficulties of communication: the affability and friendliness of the local society, which was difficult to escape even if one so desired. Visitors and appointments could not be avoided. Herbart's warning seems to imply that one is constrained to make an appearance in the salons, one must take part, even though all this can only detract from scientific discussions.

When Herbart moved to Göttingen from Königsberg in East Prussia, his communication problem was somewhat reduced. He and Drobisch found easier halfway points at which to meet: in 1834 in Weimar at Easter (with leave-taking on the Wartburg)[21] and in 1835 in Nordhausen on Maundy Thursday. All eventualities were cleared up in advance by letter. Herbart preferred to stay at the Römische Kaiser in Nordhausen and Drobisch in the Berliner Hof, which was frequented by merchants and managed by a native Leipziger.[22] But, they both worried, did their colleague really wish to go to Nordhausen? "If you decide instead on any other locality on the road between Halle and Göttingen, I would hope to take the express carriage there, the Kassel-Cologne express, which is doubtless joined at some point by an express from Göttingen, if you wish

20. Ibid., p. 211, March 1, 1830.
21. Ibid., 3:56, March 19, 1834.
22. Ibid., pp. 145, 147, to Herbart, April 5, 1835; to Drobisch, April 16, 1835.

to use it in a different manner. The latter departs Leipzig on Mondays and Thursdays at seven o'clock in the morning, arriving in Sangerhausen late in the evening and then in Nordhausen between two and three the next morning."[23]

Such visits remained the exception, however, and so to the wish for intensive correspondence with one's colleague was added the desire for his picture, in order to carry on quiet dialogues. The letter writing was therefore augmented by an exchange of portraits. Gauß wrote to Olbers in 1803 that he soon hoped to decorate his observation room with the likeness of his friend, a wish that was fulfilled in May 1805.[24] No longer were portraits primarily intended for a place in the ancestral gallery but rather became a form of social communication and intimacy, a pledge of enduring friendship. Portraits also became a symbol of support and admiration and, later, a political statement in the revolution of 1848 as well as in 1830. For example, there was the print of Robert Blum in the days of mass mourning following his summary execution in Vienna, which swelled the new cult of bourgeois-democratic martyrs. Later one can think of portraits of Lassalle, Bebel, or Marx, or of the likeness of Napoleon found in a cobbler's shop in a small German town that was reproduced in volume two of the Jacobeit's *Illustrierte Alltagsgeschichte*. Drobisch wrote to Herbart in 1836: "Even Rocco, the art dealer in Göttingen, assumes the ascendancy here of the Herbart philosophy, for he has publicly announced that your portrait is available in his shop."[25] The emergence of a mounting tribe of self-proclaimed acolytes was under way. This soon became a mass phenomenon and thereby a sign and symbol of mounting civil consciousness. It was part of the century-long trend toward the creation of associations and political parties and was an expression of the political struggles, which can be demonstrated in detail using the example of Herbart's philosophy and pedagogy, even going so far as the battle to win over individual reviewers on the learned journals of the day. Concerns about prestige and influence, about the acceptance of scientific views and strategies, were spared only a few giants of the scientific world such as Gauß.

Small groups of students sought out Herbart in Göttingen, coming from Leipzig on foot or using the postal carriage. The desire to

23. Ibid., pp. 145f.
24. *Briefwechsel*, pp. 167, 258.
25. *Briefe*, 3:206, to Herbart, May 20, 1836.

preserve one's experience of him in a lecture hall or in his home or to satisfy one's curiosity about him with a picture probably inspired this public demand for portraits, just as Gauß wished to have a portrait of his friend Olbers. It is easy to see how these early beginnings of cheap black-and-white prints later evolved: the flood of pictures and posters of one's heroes with whom one, like Gauß, hopes to carry on a quiet dialogue over vast distances of space and time.

The stunning progress in communications, which opened up broad new vistas of scientific communication and indeed of communication in general in emerging bourgeois society, seemed in August 1837 rather to annoy Drobisch. He was an eyewitness to the new breakthrough, standing at the train station watching travelers arrive on foot or in carriages in order to be whisked away on the railroad, and he noted that it distracted students and professors alike away from their work in that summer of fledgling steam service on the first German railroad from Leipzig to Dresden. "This is the general complaint: one cannot remember a time when the students were so inattentive, slovenly, etc. The reasons? The railway, the long winter, the beautiful summer, the sojourns of many professors at spas, mounting industrial activity, declining studiousness, the dwindling prestige of the educated class and of the universities in particular, etc."[26] Was the thought of mounting a train and vastly increasing the pace of scientific exchange so alien to a practical man like Drobisch? Or was a far-flung German railroad system still unimaginable at this time? Science had been an international endeavor ever since books were loaded into broad-throated barrels and unloaded here and there along with other fair guests. However, the scientific debate did not become truly international until the advent of the steam engine and the railroad.

2. Women in Young Academic Circles

The women in the lives of Gauß, Drobisch, and Olbers clearly played no part in the scientific discussion. They were mentioned in the letters: healthy, sick, or extending their greetings. They were a source of joy as well as of sadness, but their only place in academic life was on the periphery, responsible for children, the

---

26. Ibid., 3:281, to Herbart, August 23, 1837.

home, friends, guests, and servants. There were no academic marriages and therefore none of the highly personal concerns that can tear them apart. Occasional female contemporaries of Gauß and Drobisch sought to become the intellectual equals of men, but most such attempts floundered, like that of Günderode. This half-forgotten destiny of a woman, whom Christa Wolf rescued from obscurity,[27] reflects the impulse in the direction of the liberation of women emitted by the French Revolution. Thus Gauß and Olbers encountered for the first time in 1807 (though through their publications and not in person) a woman in science: a French woman named Sophie Germain. She had published, under the pseudonym of Le Blanc, expert reviews of some of Gauß's mathematical works. When the pseudonym was exposed, Gauß commented: "I am as startled as I am sure you are to discover that Le Blanc is the fictitious name of a young woman, Sophie Germain."[28] The pseudonyms under which women wrote in order to avoid recognition or, as perhaps was more frequently the case, in order to be taken for men would comprise an entire topic in themselves. Marlitt selected such a pseudonym, and Bertha von Suttner published her first novels under the pseudonym of Odilot, until finally Countess Kinsky signed her famous novel *Die Waffen Nieder!* with her actual bourgeois surname, Suttner, out of a newfound sense of female emancipation.

3. Paternal Concerns

Science, at this time, was a masculine endeavor. Fathers hoped that their sons would continue their work, and all such hopes faded when their male heirs died. Gauß remarked in 1809 about his second-born son: " . . . but Louis (if he lives to support his father) looks to me to have the makings of a solid mathematician."[29] The scientist's dual concern in noteworthy here. Gauß's wife, whom he had just married in 1805, died in 1809 after three quick pregnancies, and he noted how "very much" his son missed "maternal nurturing and care." He added that his son "seems this time to have escaped

27. See Karoline von Günderrode, *Der Schatten eines Traumes. Gedichte, Prosa, Briefe, Zeugnisse von Zeitgenossen.* Edited and with an essay by Christa Wolf (Berlin/GDR, 1979).
28. To Olbers, March 24, 1807, *Briefwechsel,* p. 331.
29. To Olbers, December 14, 1809, *Briefwechsel,* p. 443.

the rather deadly epidemic of measles here, something which I had scarcely dared to hope."[30] Olbers, the physician, answered: "I am very pleased to hear that your children have survived an illness against which no vaccine has yet been invented."[31] But in April 1810, Gauß informed his friend that the winter had been "the unhappiest" of his entire life: his three children had been the cause of "deepest concern." Little Louis had been the worst: "after eight hours of convulsions, which suddenly destroyed many of his teeth," he had passed away. Gauß concluded with a bitter farewell to his dreams of "passing along to him his father's love of the serious sciences. Foolish plans, soon turned to dust."[32] Drobisch, for his part, had placed his hopes in Emil, an "intelligent, very promising" child.[33] Despite his love for his daughters, Drobisch found such words of remembrance only for this son who indeed died in 1836.

Death intruded for the first time into the correspondence between Gauß and Olbers in 1803: a colleague had lost his wife and daughter.[34] Thereafter bereavement seemed always to lurk along the edges of their learned correspondence, if not in every letter. It was no empty phrase when Olbers concluded a letter with the comment, "My wife and children are well,"[35] or when Drobisch informed Herbart: "My wife and child, thank God, are well this winter," or "My wife and children are well."[36] Death was all-pervasive at this time, even in comfortable young families.

As in the preceding centuries, death was faced everywhere with grim fatalism – until finally progress in modern medicine at the rising, bourgeois *Arbeitsuniversitäten* largely overcame death among the young, robust age-groups, first among the wealthy and then increasingly among broader strata of the population, though tens of thousands of young proletarians continued to die. However at the time we are discussing, tuberculosis still posed a lethal threat to Olbers when he fell ill at the age of forty-eight. He wrote to Gauß that he was deathly ill, and though "I don't wish to die, I can face it with equanimity." His wife and children were unaware of the danger. "Perhaps all will still turn out for the best," he wrote, "if

30. Ibid., p. 444.
31. To Gauss, January 17, 1810, ibid., p. 444.
32. To Olbers, early April 1810, ibid., p. 448.
33. *Briefe*, 3:226, to Herbart, August 12, 1836.
34. To Olbers, December 18, 1803, *Briefwechsel*, p. 168.
35. To Gauss, October 18, 1803, ibid., p. 165.
36. *Briefe*, 3:55, to Herbart, February 28, 1834; 3:113, to Herbart, November 6, 1834.

the fates so ordain."[37] Gauß answered, "Dear heavens, leave us our Olbers for a little while yet! . . . So precious a life must not end so soon."[38] Given the state of medical knowledge and hygiene at the time, everyone was exposed to death, regardless of age. Death through disease was apparently of far greater concern than war, especially as relatively few civilians died as a result of military campaigns. Passing troops disturbed Gauß's work, but he showed little sign of any fear for his life.

The correspondence between Herbart and Drobisch began to falter in 1830. The latter explained his silence with administrative duties and "many worries and upsets at home – e. ecially a potentially fatal bout of diphtheria that threatened our little Eugenie and that was supposed to be cured by leeches, that almost resulted in her bleeding to death."[39] The twenty-nine-year-old Drobisch reported again in June 1831: "Sickness has descended on our household." The so-called Berlin influenza struck first Drobisch's wife, then him, and then their two servant girls. "The first of our servant girls had just recovered from her fever when the other fell ill, and indeed so seriously and chronically that I was forced to dismiss her."[40] Drobisch apparently thought nothing of warding off infection and sickness from his family by taking this sort of action, which was the common practice. Everyone was aware of the factory ordinances of the time which allowed employees who had contracted infectious and repugnant diseases to be summarily dismissed.

The fear of epidemics and wholesale death weighed heavily on the people of the time, especially in the cities. When a cholera panic hit Leipzig in the summer of 1831, the Drobisch family abandoned the inner city for the surrounding area. And yet outbreaks of the disease were still distant: the press began reporting the first cases from Danzig and Königsberg, where Herbart was still holding his lectures. Drobisch wrote that the cases "there are beginning to frighten me and we are already taking the most energetic countermeasures." All lightness of spirit was gone, he reported.[41] Herbart replied that "when cholera appeared in Danzig, I set down my last will."[42] Drobisch had in his possession two letters from Königsberg, one

37. To Gauss, January 21–29, 1806, *Briefwechsel*, p. 282.
38. To Olbers, February 3, 1806, *Briefwechsel*, p. 287.
39. *Briefe*, 2:230, to Herbart, February 11, 1831.
40. Ibid., p. 242, to Herbart, June 17, 1831.
41. Ibid., p. 242.
42. Ibid., p. 245, to Drobisch, July 16, 1831.

"with a slight smell of cholera," which "thank heavens have not yet been opened and smoked through."[43]

The traveling fairs brought the greatest danger. The plague spread by way of Posen and Frankfurt an der Oder toward the great commercial cities of central Germany. Informed contemporaries had noted the empirical connection between poverty and the danger of infection, and they strove to avoid poor areas. "Leipzig is heavily populated," reported Drobisch. "It has many narrow streets and lanes, cellarlike dwellings, and in the suburbs, especially, many poor people. The land is somewhat swampy and the danger therefore is not to be lightly dismissed. I myself live on the third story, though not in the highest part of the city, and the extensive buildings behind the house in which I dwell house many poor families. In addition, many Jews move up and down our street during fairs. These are worrisome conditions, and my abdomen in any case is not the strongest part of my anatomy."[44] Herbart's responses relayed the mounting terror. "The Furies continue to run amuck. In just four weeks, 1 percent of our population have been swept to their graves."[45] In Berlin, Hegel fell victim to cholera, prompting Drobisch to review his relations with the great thinker: "I do not count myself among those who consider Hegel an out-and-out madman and who now would like to strike up a song of triumph, whether openly or quietly, because this prince of darkness is dead. I have never really studied Hegel but have noted that you always treat him as an independent philosopher."[46] This judgment reveals something of the vacuity of the philosophy department at the University of Leipzig, which had not been able to achieve greater effulgence during the middle-class upheaval. Philosophy here aimed primarily to annul the splendid beginnings of classical German bourgeois philosophy, either by following Kant before ultimately rejecting him or in opposition to Hegel. Some feared that systematic rationalism of these thinkers spelled the end of theology, while others rejected the Hegelian system as speculative and therefore inimical to the scientific method.

In the summer of 1833, Drobisch's children died. The now thirty-one-year-old academic lamented that he seemed to have been

43. Ibid., p. 247, to Herbart, July 29, 1831.
44. Ibid., p. 247.
45. Ibid., p. 250, to Drobisch, August 26, 1831.
46. Ibid., p. 271, to Herbart, November 30, 1831.

"hunted down and tortured by misfortune in an almost demonic way." "How can my science flourish, when it lacks the sustenance of a soul at rest with itself? And yet I have never entirely forgotten it, for it has been a source of great comfort." Drobisch's wife, however, was entirely bound up with domestic issues, the absence of the children was all-pervasive, and Drobisch expressed, though unwittingly perhaps, the plight of academic wives when he wrote: "I only wish I had such a distracting balm for my good wife."[47] The couple again attempted to defy death and had two more children, but the youngest died two years later in 1835. "What an enormous amount of my time has been consumed by paternal concerns," Drobisch lamented, "but no earthly power could help me get over them."[48] This admission evinces the value placed in the bourgeois family, but also the kind of concerns that burdened academic life and society in general at the time.

4. Contemporary Economic Conditions for Academics

Gauß believed that he would derive the greatest possible satisfaction from his scientific studies if he could just pursue his thirst for knowledge free from all restrictions and disturbances. "I would gladly assume a nonacademic job that required nothing more than diligence, exactitude, dedication, etc., and that did not demand any particularly specialized knowledge or confer much prestige or influence, if it only afforded a comfortable life and sufficient spare time to serve my personal gods."[49] Devotion to one's personal god of scientific discovery was a fundamental characteristic of all these young academics. It certainly characterized Drobisch and, though perhaps to a lesser extent, many others as well who cannot all be named here.

Gauß was very aware of the passage of time and wrote to Olbers late one night: "But the time admonishes me to end my long epistle."[50] He considered it irresponsible and an affront to science "unnecessarily to rob" his friend of even a minute of "his precious

47. Ibid., 3:32f., to Herbart, June 9, 1833.
48. Ibid., p. 147, to Herbart, April 24, 1835.
49. To Olbers, October 26, 1802, *Briefwechsel*, p. 106.
50. To Olbers, September 21, 1802, *Briefwechsel*, p. 96.

time."[51] However, standardized time of the kind that industrial capitalism was beginning to introduce, first in Great Britain, with fixed time intervals and the disciplining effect of machine work, was still quite alien to scientific work. Academics as yet did not feel the tension between "work" and "leisure time" characteristic of alienated industrial labor, the longing for free time, for "something else," which permeated the lives of generations of factory workers, office employees, and other wage earners as a result of their often unbearable working conditions.

Only slowly did the concept of standard work periods make its way into academic life. Traditionally, the work periods of artisans, farmers, or academics arose from the task itself. One worked as long as the sun shone and one's physical strength allowed. It is easy to imagine how people managed their work. Natural cycles such as the seasons largely determined individual work periods. Periods of intense effort were followed by rest. Journeymen kept Saint Monday, which was only eradicated from the lives of small producers by the industrial conception of time after much stubborn resistance and over a lengthy period. Academics followed wherever their curiosity and thirst for knowledge led them. Leisure activities, in the modern sense of the word, rarely concerned them. All available time, understood as "free" time, was devoted to the topic at hand. Science at this time had goals, but no strict schedules like those that were developed to govern every aspect of industrial production. Science was much more to these people than a mere livelihood. Only when it was largely reduced to a livelihood could it become a task performed in accordance with prescribed working hours. Gauß wished only to serve his gods in peace. He devoted every spare minute to theoretical and practical work and accordingly much regretted spending New Year's Eve 1805 with company, when he would have preferred to be at his telescope. "I was unfortunately compelled to spend the lovely night of January 1 at the card table and saw nothing of the northern lights."[52] Marriage too signified an interruption in otherwise unrelenting work. This "important change" threw the young Gauß off the accustomed track for a few days. "I am now gradually getting back into my work," wrote Gauß to Olbers twenty days after the ceremony.[53]

51. To Olbers, January 29, 1802, *Briefwechsel*, p. 7.
52. To Olbers, January 25, 1805, *Briefwechsel*, p. 249.
53. To Olbers, October 29, 1805, *Briefwechsel*, p. 274.

No discipline, academic review, and painful calculation of productivity was necessary, precisely because work and leisure had not yet diverged. Being left in peace and quiet by those whose job it was to manage time not belonging to them placed these young academics in a situation in which their efforts were limited only by their own physical and mental capacity and in which dry spells were the rare exception.

Postscript: Two young academics met in the elevator of the University of Leipzig tower, both in their mid-twenties and concerned with the final hurdles before obtaining their doctorates. "We certainly do have our problems," said X to Y, thinking by no means primarily of academic concerns. Z in the front of the elevator turned away, though still listening and thinking. And thus the seed of this essay was planted.

Notes on Contributors

Hartmut Harnisch, Institute for Economic History of the former Academy of Sciences of the GDR, Berlin

Sigrid Jacobeit, Member of the former History Section, Humboldt University, Berlin

Wolfgang Jacobeit, Emeritus Professor, former History Section, Humboldt University, Berlin

Jürgen Kuczynski, Emeritus Professor, Institute for Economic History of the former Academy of Sciences of the GDR, Berlin

Dietrich Mühlberg, Professor of Cultural History, Humboldt University, Berlin

Hans-Heinrich Müller, Institute for Economic History of the former Academy of Sciences of the GDR, Berlin

Jan Peters, Institute for Economic History of the former Academy of Sciences of the GDR, Berlin

Susanne Schötz, Department of History, University of Leipzig

Helga Schultz, Institute for German History of the former Academy of the Sciences of the GDR, Berlin

Hartmut Zwahr, History Section, University of Leipzig